www.cclive.co.uk No Exchange No Refund

ODEON HAMMERSMITH Tel. 01-748-4081
Manager: Philip Leivers
ADVANCE BOOKING TICKET
CONCERT As advised at the time
DATE } of purchase. (See re-
TIME } verse). Please see full
PRICE seating plan on display
CIRCLE
BLOCK
1 | 071
NO TICKET EXCHANGED NOR MONEY REFUNDED
This portion to be retained No re-admission

T0153250

JOAN BAEZ
IN CONCERT
PLUS SUPPORT
Tuesday 24th October 1995
Showtime 7:30pm
Tickets £16.50 in advance - Doors 7:00pm
ROW : C SEAT : 24
LEVEL 1
RESERVED SEATING
NO SMOKING
00066

28587847

Mark Time Music presents
Joan Baez
Fare Thee Well Tour
No Support & No Interval
Mon, 28 May 2018
At 7:30 PM
Doors open at 6:45 PM

Issued by
Mark Time Music

Royal Albert Hall
Door 9

Mark Howes
present
An Evening with Joan Baez
No support
Sun, 4 Mar 2007 8:00 PM
Flat Floor
D 17
Account:10130043 FULL £29.50
BOX OFFICE 01223 357851 ONLINE: WWW.ARTSANDENTERTAINMENTS.COM

CAMBRIDGE
CITY COUNCIL
ARTS &
ENTERTAINMENTS

Fairfield
Concert Hall
JOAN BAEZ
WITH SINEAD LOHAN
Mon 24 Jun 1996 07:30PM
0.00 COMP V 31 Pat No. 401093
Front Stalls
BOX OFFICE 0181 688 9291

27.50
3.25
30.75

JOAN BAEZ
PLUS SPECIAL GUESTS
CARLING APOLLO HAMM
QUEEN CAROLINE
SUN 01-F

www...co.uk No Exchange

colston hall

Wed 23/05/1
Enter on Level 1. Door A
Rear Stalls
T 20
£0.00 / Guest
Artist Guests (10578623)

ODEON HAMMERSMITH Tel. 01-748-4081
Manager: Philip Leivers
Harvey Goldsmith presents
JOAN BAEZ in Concert plus support
Funds from this concert will be donated to the
OPERATION NAMIBIA and CAAT
EVENING 8-0 p.m.
Monday, Dec. 19th, 1977
STALLS
£3·75
BLOCK SEAT
23 A23
NO TICKET EXCHANGED NOR MONEY REFUNDED
NO RE-ADMISSION TO BE RETAINED

ODEON HAMMERSMITH Te
Manager: Philip Leiv
ADVANCE BOOKING TICK
CONCERT As advised at th
DATE } of purchase. (S
TIME } verse). Please see full
PRICE seating plan on display
STALLS
BLOCK
24 | K23
TICKET EXCHANGED NOR MONEY REFUNDED
portion to be retained No re-admission

STALLS
£3·75
BLOCK SEAT
25 H 4
NO TICKET EXCHANGED NOR MONEY R
NO RE-ADMISSION

Philharmonic Hall Liverpool
JOAN BAEZ IN CONCERT
Thu, 26 Oct 1995 7:30 PM (X)
COMP £ 0.00
BALCONY Row J Seat 035

JOAN BAEZ
fare thee well... TOUR 2018
RAH AFTERSHOW

JOAN BAEZ

I fight off the snow
I fight off the hail
Nothing makes me go
I'm like some vestigial tail
I'll be here through eternity
If you want to know how long
If they cut down this tree
I'll show up in a song
I'm the last leaf on the tree

From "The Last Leaf" by Tom Waits & Kathleen Brennan

JOAN BAEZ

THE LAST LEAF

ELIZABETH THOMSON

PALAZZO

To Maureen, who bought me my very first guitar and in whose record collection I came upon *Joan Baez Vol. 2* in summer 1969. And to the memory of my parents who, on 18 December 1971, took me to my first Joan Baez concert, at London's Rainbow Theatre. With love always.

PALAZZO

First published in 2020 by
Palazzo Editions Ltd
15 Church Road
London, SW13 9HE
www.palazzoeditions.com

Text © 2020 Elizabeth Thomson
Design and layout copyright © 2020 Palazzo Editions Ltd

All rights reserved. No part of this publication may be reproduced in any form or by any means — electronic, mechanical, photocopying, recording, or otherwise — or stored in any retrieval system of any nature without prior written permission from the copyright holders. Elizabeth Thomson has asserted her moral right to be identified as the author of this work in accordance with the Copyright, Designs and Patents Act of 1988.
Every effort has been made to trace and acknowledge the copyright holders. If any unintentional omission has occurred, we would be pleased to add an appropriate acknowledgment in any future edition of the book.

A CIP catalogue record for this book is available from the British Library.

Hardback ISBN 978-1-78675-096-9

eBook ISBN 978-1-78675-110-2

10 9 8 7 6 5 4 3

Designed by Becky Clarke for
Palazzo Editions

PAGE 2: Very early Joan: Baez performing in 1960 (Charles Frizzell)

CONTENTS

AUTHOR'S NOTE

This book was finished and ready to go to press in March 2020, just as much of the world went into lockdown. Like every other aspect of life, book publishing has been affected by the Covid-19 crisis and will be for a long time to come.

Joan Baez: The Last Leaf was commissioned as a large-format, fully illustrated book. However, it was agreed that the best way to proceed, given global publishing restrictions and the need to have books on sale in good time for Joan Baez's eightieth birthday in January 2021, was to publish it as a straight biography with a plate section, and a detailed Discography, Filmography and Bibliography. I hope this will enable what is essentially a serious study to find a readership beyond those who have followed Baez's long career – an international readership among university students studying music, American social-political history, including Vietnam and the anti-war movement, human rights, women's studies and much besides for whom Baez's life and work are vibrant threads in a larger tapestry.

In April 2020, she was elected to The American Academy of Arts & Sciences, founded in 1780 by John Adams, John Hancock and "sixty other scholar-patriots who understood that a new republic would require institutions able to gather knowledge and advance learning in service to the public good." Its mission is "to cultivate every art and science which may tend to advance the interest, honor, dignity, and happiness of a free, independent, and virtuous people." Baez is in good company, for its membership roll includes Renée Fleming, Jimmy Carter, Toni Morrison, Martin Luther King Jr., and Henry David Thoreau.

During the worst weeks of the Covid-19 tragedy, Baez sang to the world from her kitchen: songs in Italian, French, Spanish, German and, of course, English, each of which had millions of views. On Memorial Day, she sang in support and honor of "my sisters and brothers" in the American Indian community. "Forever Young" was dedicated to "the heroes of our time": the healthcare providers, farmworkers, truckers, pickers, and growers; the store clerks, the janitors, and the morticians – "to the people working on the front lines so that I can stay at home." To the governors and mayors, battling to keep people safe in the face of "the indifference, the callousness, the cruelty of the non-leadership of the federal government." And to Navy Captain Brett Crozier for "exhibiting extreme courage in the face of this new war". At the close of the song she smiled and saluted.

The paint splatters visible on her fingers and jeans showed Baez had not been idle, and a painting, "Viva Italia!", depicting the Italians, in their darkest hour, singing from their balconies, was printed and sold in a signed limited edition, all proceeds going to Foundation Specchio Dei Tempi, the Italian relief agency. "Hello in There," a portrait of Covid victim John Prine, benefited the Pandemic Resource & Response Initiative, a nonprofit directed by Dr Irwin Redlener, a pediatrician and public health activist at New York's Columbia University.

As America burned and Trump fanned the flames, Baez sang "Let Us Break Bread Together," a spiritual from the Underground Railroad which the great Marian Anderson had sung so often. She prefaced it with an appeal for "a nonviolent show of moral force against the ugliness, the treachery, and the seemingly endless stupidity which has run through our society and which led to the death of Gorge Floyd and hundreds of others who suffered fates like his."

"Forever Young" is Bob Dylan's most universal of prayers:

May your hands always be busy
May your feet always be swift
May you have a strong foundation
When the winds of changes shift
May your heart always be joyful
And may your song always be sung
May you stay forever young

Of one thing we can be sure: Joan's song will *always* be sung.

Elizabeth Thomson
London, June 2020

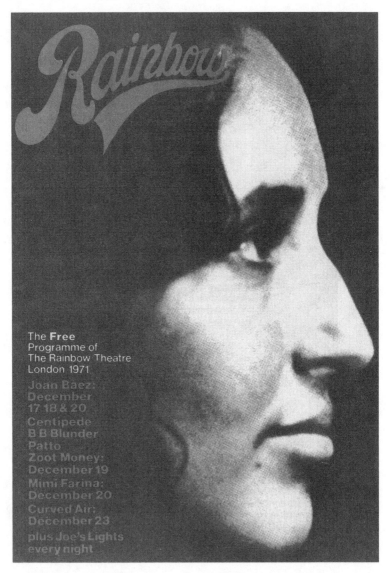

The **Free**
Programme of
The Rainbow Theatre
London 1971

Joan Baez:
December
17 18 & 20
Centipede
B B Blunder
Patto
Zoot Money:
December 19
Mimi Farina:
December 20
Curved Air:
December 23
plus Joe's Lights
every night

Program from Joan Baez's Rainbow Theatre season in December 1971. Sister Mimi Fariña joined her for one night

PRELUDE

Madrid, July 28, 2019. Almost exactly fifty years to the day since I first knowingly heard the voice of Joan Baez, I've come to hear her final concert, which will bring down the curtain on a career launched almost exactly sixty years ago with a now-legendary unannounced performance at the Newport Folk Festival. I have invited my sister, who lives near Malaga, for it was Maureen who inadvertently launched me on this journey, buying me my first guitar—half-size, brought back from her first Spanish holiday, when she fell in love with the country. A few years later, Emilio, the cigar-smoking, whisky-drinking Spaniard whom Franco had imprisoned during the country's brutal civil war and for whom she was then working in Spain, came to spend an English Christmas. Shortly after he'd returned, a package arrived from El Corte Inglés, Barcelona. It contained a proper Spanish guitar, blonde and beautiful. Now I had to learn to play it.

I tried a few books from the library, but they weren't what I was looking for. (I'd been studying the piano for a few years so I knew how music worked.) Then a neighbor showed me some chords and I was launched. The first songs through which I fumbled my way were the sort of numbers familiar from *Singing Together*, the BBC program listened to one morning a week by primary schoolchildren across Britain. But what next? Rummaging through Maureen's modest record collection in the summer between primary and secondary school, I came upon *Joan Baez, Vol.2*. I had no idea as to its contents, but the back cover showed a young woman playing a Spanish guitar. Curious, I slipped the disc from its thick cardboard sleeve. It was a heavy old Vanguard pressing, and I placed it on the turntable.

Oh, hard is the fortune of all womankind
She's always controlled, she's always confined
Controlled by her parents, until she's a wife
A slave to her husband the rest of her life.

"Wagoner's Lad" was disappointingly unaccompanied, but it gave way to "The Trees They Grow High," which seemed vaguely familiar, if a little complicated—too many chords, some requiring a barre. "Barbara Allen" was much more straightforward, and then there was "Banks of the Ohio" and "Plaisir d'Amour." By the time the new term rolled around I had a modest repertoire. I soon discovered that the school library contained two Joan Baez records, her 1960 debut and *Joan Baez/5* which featured an extraordinary semi-operatic track, "Bachianas Brasileiras." At that point my twelve-year-old ears registered that this woman, whoever she was, had a truly magnificent voice.

Over the next couple of years, for Christmas and birthdays, I began to acquire a library of my own, the songs and the sleeve notes leading me in various directions, not least to Bob Dylan—and at a time when my classmates were screaming for David Cassidy and The Osmonds. And as I listened and read, I realized that Joan Baez had somehow played a role in many of the significant events of the 1960s, events that went beyond music and which were then very recent history. Baez's life and work became a sort of Venn diagram through which to explore a vast swathe of music and American social history—not as easy in the pre-wired world as it is today, of course. Anthony Scaduto's biography *Bob Dylan*, which included a lengthy interview with Baez, was published in 1972, opening up new paths to follow—one of which led to Dobell's Folk Record Shop on London's Charing Cross Road. There, in a basement recording studio in 1963, Dylan, under the pseudonym Blind Boy Grunt, recorded with Eric Von Schmidt and Richard Fariña, Baez's late brother-in-law. The store, sadly long gone, was an Aladdin's cave of music by people whose names were becoming familiar, much of it imported from the United States. Eventually, I was there at the right time to count out a good deal of pocket money for the coveted LP that featured the celebrated Baez/Dylan duets from Newport 1963. And it was there a few years later that my great friend David bought me a copy of the Folkways recording of the March on Washington, when 250,000 souls listened to Dr Martin Luther King dream his dream and to Baez singing "All My Trials" and "We Shall Overcome." It still makes me cry.

I first heard Joan Baez in concert on December 18, 1971, the second of three dates at London's Rainbow Theatre, a spectacular old cinema which John Morris, head of production at Woodstock and at the legendary Fillmore East in New York City, had recently opened as a rock venue – kind of Fillmore Far East! I was fourteen and my parents insisted I could not go alone, so we all went. My mother yelled out a request for "Lily of the West." Afterwards they waited in the drizzle so I could get an autograph, and Baez eventually came out with her parents who were then living in Hampstead—her father had recently been appointed the Open University's first Visiting Professor of Physics. A week later, *Blessed Are . . .*, Baez's latest album, was under the Christmas tree. I thought that would be the only time I'd see her play live and certainly never dreamed that I would hear her innumerable times in three countries and would interview her on more than a half-dozen occasions. I was thrilled to be flown to New York City in April 1995 for the live sessions that became *Ring Them Bells*, the album that began her musical renaissance.

The late Jacqueline du Pré recalled how, aged four and perched precariously atop her mother's ironing board, she heard this *sound* on the radio and was transfixed. It was a cello and at her insistence her parents bought her a quarter-sized instrument which she began learning to play. I was, I suppose, similarly transfixed by Baez's music, hooked initially on what Adorno called "the grain of the voice" and shortly thereafter by her political and social activism. Sadly, I had none of her natural gifts but I did learn to sing and play the guitar from her records and, because she was so extravagantly talented and such a natural, I learned well, subliminally absorbing lessons about phrasing, breath control, and diction, and imitating, where I could, her skilled and often innovative guitar style, which has gone mostly unremarked.

It's strange to acknowledge, but without Joan Baez my life would have taken a more conventional turn—probably teaching music, in which I took a very conventional degree. I should have tried for a postgrad on an American campus where I could have researched and written about the folk revival and its symbiotic relationship with 1960s social activism and the civil rights and anti-war movements. But one thing led to another. In 1979, with the ink on my degree certificate scarcely dry, I took my first tentative steps in journalism, writing about music whenever I could. I published several books, and I always hoped that one day I could write at length about Joan Baez, putting her life and career in context.

In 1978, I saw Bob Dylan live for the first time, at Earls Court and then Blackbushe, his first British concerts since the Isle of Wight in 1969. I was blown away (listen to the live *Budokan* album to get the idea) and the experience led me to Dylan Revisited '79, in reality a fairly desultory conference attended mostly by male Dylan obsessives. Robert Shelton, *The New York Times* critic who wrote the review many credit with launching Dylan's career, was guest of honor. We talked, became friends (he had been living in Britain for a decade) and suddenly the whole 1960s New York music scene came alive before my eyes. I helped with the final push on his Bob Dylan biography, which was eventually published in 1986, "abridged over troubled waters" as he liked to put it, and which he would have revisited had he not died prematurely. (I prepared an author's cut using his original manuscript in 2011.)

Almost fifty years after that first fateful Baez encounter, I founded a festival celebrating the history and heritage of Greenwich Village, which I'd come to know well. It was made possible by the support and partnership of my friends the Paul family, owners of the Washington Square Hotel with which Baez and Dylan were very familiar, back in the day. It was the Hotel Earle, that once "crummy hotel over Washington Square." When Baez and I met again in Bristol, England in May 2018, her Fare Thee Well tour underway, I told her about The Village Trip, as the festival was called, that it was all her fault that I'd embarked on such an expensive project. She laughed, her brown eyes crinkling behind rimless specs, and wished me luck, pleased to know she'd inspired a fifty-year journey.

So here I was in Madrid, with Maureen, about to witness a performance that for singer and audience would be freighted with emotion. The venue was the Teatro Real, the historic opera house where the great Montserrat Caballé had so often sung—in a spoken tribute from the stage on the day of her death, Baez had praised "the glory and mystery, the sheer unfettered beauty" of her voice and the woman who "may be the greatest soprano who ever walked this earth." For *La Vanguardia*, reviewing the concert, Baez's was "one of the most influential voices of the twentieth century" and the woman herself "a singer who transcended the world of music and was a symbol of political activism." *"Adiós, amigos, adiós"* Baez sang in "Dink's Song," her final encore. When the applause had finally died down, the house lights come up, Maureen and I drifted out into the warm late-night air to raise a glass or two of Verdejo on the terrace of the old Café de Oriente. *"Gracias* a *la vida!"*

Joan Baez is a singular figure, more influential than anyone coming to her music in her wilderness years of the 1980s and 1990s could ever appreciate. And she was always *so* much more than just a singer, putting her glorious voice at the service of causes in which she believed. Many times she also put herself in danger—in the South in the 1960s, when that part of the United States was, as her friend Dr King put it, "sweltering with the heat of injustice and oppression"; in Hanoi during Nixon's Christmas 1972 bombardment; in Sarajevo during the siege.

The souvenir program for the final Joan Baez tour

Her life and career have attracted surprisingly little in-depth scrutiny and far too many people see her merely as a walk-on in some long-gone scene. "Joan *who?*" has been a frequent question, sometimes from individuals who really should know better. She will one day bring her own remarkable story up-to-date, but *Joan Baez: The Last Leaf* endeavors to show how central a figure she is in post-war socio-cultural history and how she used her gift to bring solace and hope to people who had little of either. Hers is a life that demonstrates the transformative power of music. As she wrote all those years ago in *Daybreak*: "To sing is to love and to affirm, to fly and soar, to coast into the hearts of the people who listen, to tell them that life is to live, that love is there, that nothing is a promise, but that beauty exists, and must be hunted for and found."

Elizabeth Thomson
London, December 2019

DEDICAMOS
ESTE APOSENTO ALTO
A LA MEMORIA DE

THALIA V. BAEZ

COMO MANIFESTACIÓN DE NUESTRO
AMOR Y EN RECONOCIMIENTO DE SU
NOBLE LABOR EN ESTA IGLESIA
ELLA DIO SU TALENTO, HABILIDADES
Y TIEMPO, INCONDICIONALMENTE
DESDE 1918 HASTA QUE DIOS
LA LLEVÓ A DESCANSAR, FEB. 2, 1951

SUS HIJOS: ALBERTO VINICIO
THALIA MIMI Y PEDRO HECTOR,
SU ESPOSO: REV. ALBERTO B. BAEZ

PRIMERA IGLESIA METODISTA
DE BROOKLYN N.Y.
FEB. 2. 1953

Joan Baez's grandmother, Thalia Flores Valderrama de Baez, known
as Mother B, commemorated at Immanuel—First Spanish United
Methodist Church in Dean Street, Brooklyn

1

THE YOUNG GYPSY

There's an old saying that charity begins at home. In 1980, asked by a journalist perplexed at her energetic fundraising for the Vietnamese Boat People, what she understood by "the old adage," Joan Baez responded: "I've always assumed that means what your parents teach you."

If that is indeed the case, Baez was well taught. The second of three daughters born to immigrant parents, she grew up peripatetic in a family that made up intellectually for whatever it lacked materially. Her Scottish-English mother, Joan Chandos Bridge, was born in Edinburgh and arrived in New York as a toddler. Her father, Albert Vinicio Baez, was born in Puebla, Mexico. He too arrived in New York as a small child. Both were the children of ministers, Episcopalian on her mother's side, a Catholic convert to Methodism on her father's.

It was a household filled with conversation, books, and classical music, but lacking for many years a television—with the result that when Mitch Miller, singer, conductor, and A&R man, attempted to lure the young Baez to a lucrative contract at Columbia Records she had no idea who he was, noting only that he resembled Colonel Sanders. Her father was working his way through college undergraduate and postgraduate degrees in maths followed by a PhD in physics, in which he would distinguish himself. The blandishments of the Cold War military-industrial complex were eschewed in favor of teaching and research, though the lucrative offers were at first tempting. It was his wife, known as Joan Senior or Big Joan, who suggested they went to Quaker Meeting. Amid the silence, Albert made peace with his conscience.

Years later, recalling the Baez clan lunching *en famille* at the Viking Hotel during a Newport Folk Festival, singer Judy Collins suggested they "looked like a scene out of Henry James," all elegance and a certain formality. According to *The Scotsman*'s obituary of Joan Senior, who died a few days after her centennial, the family is descended on the maternal side "from the English Dukes of Chandos, the Brydges family, originally from Gloucestershire." The Dukes of Chandos were patrons of the arts and most famously of George Frideric Handel, whose *Chandos Anthems* were composed for the first Duke, James Brydges, MP for Hereford from 1698 to 1714. A direct line is difficult to discern but, in life as in folk song, such figures often shared their lordly gifts with abandon.

Joanie, as the family called her, was a troubled child who was unhappy at school, and a good deal of her time seems to have been spent at home with her mother. She has talked and written frequently about their relationship: "Mother and Me," she wrote in *Daybreak*, her first brief, episodic memoir. "Tea and Vivaldi and Mozart, and Jussi Björling singing Puccini . . . comfort at home from the misery at school." Four of the records she chose for the BBC Radio program *Desert Island Discs* in June 1993 were classical—Björling singing Gounod's "Salut Demeure Chaste et Pure," Glenn Gould playing Bach's *Goldberg Variations*, Kathleen Ferrier singing an aria from Handel's *Messiah*, and Jascha Heifetz ("to me, the ultimate violinist") playing Bruch's *Scottish Fantasy*. Björling was the record she would choose above all others. As she talked about her choices, the performers at least as important as the music itself, she recalled how her mother would stop whatever she was doing, throw back her head, and listen, almost in ecstasy. From the earliest age, little Joanie learned to sing along.

★★★

Official records show that Joan Chandos Bridge was born in the early hours of April 11, 1913 at 19 Manor Road in the West End district of Edinburgh, not far from St John's Episcopal church on Princes Street, where her father, William Henry Bridge—listed on the birth certificate as a Clerk in Holy Orders—was a curate. He had married Florence Annie Bridge at St Ethelburga's in London's Bishopsgate on December 28, 1908. The couple were living at 57 Nile Grove, Morningside. Their marriage would be brief, for Florence died in January 1916 leaving William alone with two little girls, Joan and her elder sister, Pauline. The family had sailed to Halifax, Nova Scotia in October 1913, aboard the *Hesperian*, settling with William's mother in Cranbrook, British Columbia, where Florence passed away.

He married Mabel Amelia Roberts on June 13, 1917 in Cranbrook, and the family, without his mother, headed for Moscow, Idaho. William returned to Britain alone in 1919, sailing back to America a few months later. In the 1920 United States Census, he is by now an Episcopalian rector, in Latah County, Idaho, and the two girls have a stepbrother, one-year-old Robert Andrew Chandos Bridge, who would grow up to be a doctor. William's September 1918 draft registration lists him as a Canadian subject, though it's not clear if he ever served, but it appears that in 1920 he accepted a teaching post at Grinnell College in Lincoln County, Iowa. Established in 1843 by a group of Congregationalist ministers, it was progressive in terms of both its course offerings and its approach to women's education. William combined his religious duties with a post in the English department. By 1926, he was divorced and married for a third time, to Myrtle. Diana was born the same year. Records now put the family in Morristown, New Jersey. At his death in 1951, *The New York Times* reported that he had been a professor of English and drama at Hunter College in Manhattan, and in 1933 established a fellowship center in Mount Kisco, New York State, "an educational project for the promotion of peace."

In both of Joan Baez's memoirs, 1968's impressionistic *Daybreak* and the later and more substantial *And a Voice to Sing With* in 1987, a picture emerges of her mother's childhood of neglect and emotional cruelty at the hands of her stepmothers.

Her mother's sister Pauline married young to escape, while Joan Senior found love and security with a series of foster mothers. Then, in her early twenties, at a dance at nearby Drew University, she spotted the handsome young man who would become her husband.

Albert Baez had arrived in America aged two with his parents, Alberto Baldomero Baez Fonseca and Thalia Flores Valderrama de Baez, and two siblings. The family entered the United States via Laredo, Texas, and lived for a while in Corpus Christi, coming to New York City in 1917 and settling in Brooklyn. There was then no organized church for Spanish speakers and the Reverend Baez—brought up in a devout Roman Catholic family and a convert to Methodism—was invited to preach to a group of Latin Americans at Sands Street Memorial Church. He served as a volunteer preacher until 1920 when he was received as a member of the New York East Conference and appointed pastor at First Methodist Episcopal Church, the first Spanish-speaking Protestant church in the borough of Brooklyn, which, by the mid-1920s, was home to around half of New York City's Hispanic population. He quickly built up a substantial congregation—some three thousand souls by 1928 according to archives, despite several relocations. At nineteen, young Albert preached there too, but he would decide that his vocation lay elsewhere.

In 1939, the Baez family settled in the Carroll Gardens neighborhood, at 238 President Street, "an Anglo-Italianate-style building" dating from around 1853, according to the Designation Report of the New York City Landmarks Preservation Commission. Ten years later, First Spanish Methodist moved in next door, 236 President Street, which had originally housed the Hans S. Christian Memorial Kindergarten and in which a small sanctuary had been carved out. (In 2018, Joan Baez lent her support to the campaign to preserve the properties from developers. "In addition to their architectural beauty, these two buildings are of unique social and historical significance, and they should be protected and celebrated," she wrote. "Brooklyn's past was illuminated by the waves of immigrants who came to America seeking a better life and that legacy is alive in the structures representing those who lived and worked there . . . 238, as I remember it, was magisterial, with marble fireplaces and mahogany bannisters . . . In every way, these buildings are historic landmarks and will hopefully be treated as such." Both were given Landmark status, the designation citing their centrality to the neighborhood's history and identity.)

An early advocate of the Hispanic community's entitlement as citizens, the Reverend Baez took a holistic view of the church's role in society. In 1935, he wrote to President Roosevelt outlining the challenges faced by Puerto Ricans: "If anything is ever going to be done for the Puerto Ricans in Brooklyn and I can be of any help, I will be more than happy to do all in my power to help better their condition in general." His wife, who in 1925 was working for the YWCA's International Institute and was Secretary of its Hispanic Department, was out among Brooklyn's Spanish-speaking community, directing drama, dance, music, and children's events that showcased Hispanic culture and helped foster community relations. In 1934, as events in Europe darkened, she produced a pageant, *The Way of Peace*.

Both she and her husband, Mother B and Father B as they were known, are remembered to this day. Retired teacher Regalada Costello, aged ninety-one and still a parishioner at what is now Immanuel-First Spanish United Methodist Church, recalled them both vividly. "All members of the church were Father B's family," she told me after Sunday service. "He was a father to *everybody*." Mother B was "very, very dynamic, helping everyone in the area and working with young people. She played the piano and took the choir and organized the Women's Society."

The couple also ran a summer camp for Hispanic city kids who would never otherwise have had a holiday. The Baezes bought Villa Hermosa at Pine Bush, in the Walker Valley, in the 1930s and raised money to cover costs of the annual holidays. Regalada went as both camper and counsellor, and recalls taking part in music, arts and crafts, and games. "We would go on hikes and there would be trips into town so we could buy candy." Mother B insisted everyone swim in the brook, so they could bathe and wash their hair, and the day ended with the singing of "Now Is the Hour." Father B continued to run the camp even after his wife's sudden death in 1951, opening it for the last time in summer 1963, three years after his retirement from the church and shortly before his own death in Paris, where he was visiting Albert and his family. Both are buried in New Prospect Reformed Church Cemetery, near Pine Bush.

Young Albert, meanwhile, had opted to study mathematics and graduated from Drew University in 1933 and from Syracuse two years later with a master's degree. In 1936, he married Joan Chandos Bridge. Their first daughter, Pauline Thalia, was born on October 4, 1939, in Orange, New Jersey, and their third, Margarita Mimi, on April 30, 1945, in Stanford, California. In the middle came Joan Chandos Baez, born on January 9, 1941, in Staten Island, where she spent her earliest years. The family lived in Westerleigh, a residential neighborhood in the northwestern part of the borough. Her father was now a professor at nearby Wagner College.

In 1944, the family moved cross-country to Stanford, where Professor Baez was hired to teach mathematics and physics to undergraduates while working on a PhD with Professor Paul Kirkpatrick. His thesis was on *Principles of X-ray Optics and the Development of a Single Stage X-ray Microscope* and he graduated in 1950. Kirkpatrick and Baez invented the x-ray reflecting microscope, which opened up the field of x-ray optics. The crossed-mirror geometry is known as the Kirkpatrick-Baez Configuration.

Joanie has recalled this period as a happy time—"springtime in my chest, and a lucky star on my forehead," she has written, of what seems to have been a typically outdoorsy California childhood. With Mimi's arrival, the family needed more space, so Big Joan and Albert became house parents at the Peninsula School, a progressive establishment founded by Josephine and Frank Duveneck that emphasized social justice and "the whole child," though judging by her own account, Joanie seems not to have enjoyed kindergarten there. Next stop was a large house in Menlo Park—Stanford Village, as it was known in those days long before the tech boom—where the Baezes set up home with Joan Senior's sister Pauline and her two children. It was run as a boarding house, and the handful of lodgers would gather around the table on Sundays for dinner with the extended Baez clan. It was, Joanie recalled, "a chaotic two years" and once her father had gained his doctorate, there was a job offer back east.

Home this time was Clarence Center, Buffalo, a small town where for the first time Joanie, the most Mexican-looking of the girls, was made aware of being "different." Nevertheless, she recalls the "glorious calm" of the family stay, which was happy enough for her, decades later, to accept an invitation from a local historian and the town supervisor to visit. For the *Clarence Bee*, she recalled climbing trees with friends in order to peer into the house across the street to look at their television, and hanging on to cars before letting go and sliding down the street in the snow. She and Pauline took piano lessons and also learned to twirl a baton. And Joanie met Lily, about whom she has written, in print and in song—"my last really, really best friend when we were both eight."

Her father's latest job, at the Cornell Aeronautical Laboratory, proved a turning point in his own life and therefore that of his family. He had been hired as a physicist but soon found himself assigned to an operations research group working on a classified project. Already uncomfortable, he agreed to join the aircraft carrier *Coral Sea* to discover more about it. Also aboard was the admiral of Operation Portrex, the code name for Puerto Rico Exercise, the objective of which was to discover how America's combined forces would fare as "liberators" of an enemy territory. Although not yet a pacifist, Albert felt conflicted, concerned in the new atomic age at the application of science for deadly purposes—could such force really achieve peace?

Back home, his wife saw his anxiety and suggested they seek guidance from the Quaker community. They went as a family, the girls staying for twenty minutes before being dispatched next door with all the other kids to Quaker Sunday school. Not surprisingly, Joanie found it tiresome, as would any child forced to sit in silence, but the Baezes attended regularly from then on. Joanie has never entirely left the ritual of Quaker Meeting behind and it's clear from her own lifelong commitment to pacifism and nonviolence that, young as she was, the experience was a formative one. As for her father, he came to his own conclusions, writing years later that, while his embrace of pacifism took several years, it was "probably born on the aircraft carrier *Coral Sea* and in the silence of the Buffalo Meeting of the Religious Society of Friends."

The family was soon headed to Southern California, where Dr Baez would resume his research into x-ray optics at the University of Redlands. "In my dreams," Joanie has written, "our tiny one-story white house in Redlands is the one I return to most often." However, their stay in the San Bernardino Valley town was brief for, one evening in spring 1951, Dr Baez arrived home from work to find a letter from UNESCO in Paris, inviting him to serve as a visiting professor on the science faculty at the University of Baghdad. While in Buffalo, he'd read about UNESCO, a new UN initiative designed to promote peace through education, science, and culture, and he'd written a speculative letter. He'd also written to Redlands, whose job offer came first. That suited the Baez women who were all longing to return west, but now his wife was intrigued by the possibility of a year-long sojourn in "the

One Thousand and One Nights Baghdad." Joanie's only concern was the separation from her beloved collie, Mr Woolie.

The Baez family's Baghdad adventure was recalled many years later in *A Year in Baghdad*, written jointly by Albert and Joan, its pages adorned with line drawings penned by ten-year-old Joanie, who spent much of the year at home sick with hepatitis and its aftermath. They can have had little sense of what life in the faraway city would be like and their shock on arriving is palpable. The noise, the smells, the heat. And the idea of a country where women didn't much venture out and, when they did, were swathed in black abayas, was not something Westerners were yet familiar with. There was also the abject poverty and the casual everyday cruelty to animals—both of which troubled little Joanie. Not only did Professor Baez have to create courses in physics, chemistry, and biology at University College, Baghdad, but he had to oversee the building of labs, which required cutting through the country's vast bureaucracy, and the setting up of the family home. They lived in the Al-Wazireya district of old Baghdad, in a house shared with a Palestinian doctor and his British wife and children.

"It wasn't a happy time. I was introduced to poverty that I'd never have seen otherwise. I was ill with hepatitis, and my mother took me out of the local hospital because it was dirty," Baez recalled for *The Independent* in January 2004, the Iraq War a few months old. "Across the fence from our house, there were people living in mud huts, and I built little copies of them. And I watched ants forming colonies. I was fascinated. It was one of the best years of education I had. And the skies were orange and pink and red at night, with flocks of birds flying across them." Watching the news, her child's-eye recollections of the city "added a little extra to the horror of the whole insane enterprise" that was Operation Shock and Awe.

There's a bitter irony in Albert Baez's advocacy of science education, his concern that science be used for the good of mankind, and Iraq's 1960s and 1970s development of offensive weapons,

The plaque honoring Rev Alberto Baldomero Baez, founder of Immanuel-First Spanish Methodist Church, "with love and gratitude" from the community he served for 44 years

an irony he surely reflected on down the years. But for the Baez family, the hardships and material deprivations of that year would have a profound effect: Joan Senior would, in later life, travel on behalf of the Emergency Relief Fund International, while Mimi founded Bread and Roses, an organization devoted to bringing music to those confined in hospitals and homes for the disabled and the elderly, and those in juvenile detention and in prison. Joanie would establish the Institute for the Study of Nonviolence and Humanitas International and would over the years raise her voice in support of the voiceless all around the world. Of that year in Baghdad she wrote in her memoir: "Perhaps that was where my passion for social justice was born."

The family returned to Redlands, Southern California and Joanie, somewhat unhappily, to junior high school. The area had a significant Mexican population, then as now illegal aliens and fruit pickers who were useful to the white population but not much liked. Joanie, her looks enhanced by Iraqi sunshine, encountered prejudice. Her feeling of being "other" led her to join the school choir, her voice then "a plain, little girl's voice, sweet and true, but stringy as cheap cotton thread." She envied the "mature" vibratos of a pair of twins and, as she has recounted many times, set about developing her own vibrato, first of all manipulating her Adam's apple in front of the mirror and practicing in the shower. In no time at all, the vibrato that would come to characterize the Baez voice was nicely developed.

Meanwhile, Paul Kirkpatrick, the Stanford professor who had supervised her father's PhD, had given Joanie a ukulele and was helping her learn to play it. As with the guitar, four chords go a long way and soon she was learning songs from the radio, working her way through the charts, then filled with country and rhythm and blues numbers. When she gained sufficient confidence, she took the uke to school, entertaining her classmates at lunchtime. Their response made her feel less of an outsider, as did her facility with pencil and sketch pad.

After five years, the family moved again, back to the Bay Area: Her father was returning to Stanford as a visiting professor and Joanie joined Palo Alto High School in the eleventh grade. Her accounts suggest a happier time than at her many previous schools, music providing both solace and friendship. She had progressed from the ukulele to her first guitar, bought from a Sears catalog. And in February 1958, she committed her first act of civil disobedience, telling staff that as a conscientious objector she was refusing to leave school during an air raid drill. She had checked her father's textbooks and understood that a missile could reach California from Moscow in just thirty minutes, making nonsense of the two-hour warning system, as she explained to the *Palo Alto Times*. Many of her fellow students, she added, didn't really understand the drill or saw it as an opportunity to get out of school early and hold a bomb party. "I was invited to one myself," she said. Though her father had discouraged the action, he applauded her stand, but many fellow students and their parents were now wary of her. It was the height of the Cold War—fear of communists was palpable everywhere.

The protest cemented her friendship with Ira Sandperl, a self-taught Gandhian scholar and advocate of nonviolent social change whom she'd met at the Quaker Meeting her father insisted "the girls" continue to attend. By day he worked at Kepler's, the radical and intellectual bookshop that was to Menlo Park what Cody's was to Berkeley, and City Lights to San Francisco. A Stanford dropout, he was often on campus, talking about peace and disarmament, and Joanie found in him a mentor and friend. In 1965, they would co-found the Institute for the Study of Nonviolence.

She'd found friendship among the American Friends Service Committee, the Quaker social action wing, and in 1958 attended Freedom in Our Time: A High School Conference on Civil Liberties, at the Asilomar Retreat on the Monterey Peninsula. There were some three hundred student delegates, the main attraction an up-and-coming young preacher named Martin Luther King Jr. Joanie was "galvanized," intensely moved by King's talk about injustice and suffering, about the strength to love, and about the bus boycott in Montgomery which had led to mass civil disobedience. He gave "a shape and a name to my passionate but ill-articulated beliefs," she reflected years later. The long years of Quaker Meeting, the discussions around the family dinner table, the stay in Baghdad, and doubtless the influence of her grandparents—all had been a formative influence on Joanie Baez, who was now seventeen.

Belvie Rooks, writer, educator, and co-founder of Growing a Global Heart, was just fifteen when she attended the conference. One of very few African-American women in attendance, she too was excited about seeing King and took the coach from San Francisco to Asilomar. The first stop was Palo Alto, where a young girl with a guitar clambered aboard, joining her at the back of the bus. "I liked her immediately," she wrote in a blog, Peace Works: Century of Action.

Joan was an instant hit, not just because she could play the guitar and sing, but because as far as we could tell she was the only Quaker among us.

The high point of the weekend at Asilomar was of course Martin Luther King Jr.'s speech. However, before he spoke, those of us on the San Francisco/Palo Alto bus got the shock of our lives as the girl Joan from the back of the bus with us was introduced and walked slowly to the center of the stage. You could hear a pin drop as she sang Johnny Mathis's "Until the Twelfth of Never (sic)."

Only later would we learn that we were witnessing history, since this was the very first time that Joan Baez and Dr King appeared onstage together. She would later march with him in Grenada, Mississippi in support of school integration, and perform with him and at his request throughout the South. The historical high point, of course, was being asked by him to sing "We Shall Overcome" to over 250,000 people at the March on Washington! However, that day in Asilomar, Joan sang so beautifully and was well received, and we were *so* proud.

Rooks recalled how King's youth (he was just twenty-nine) made both him and his message seem very accessible.

We listened intently as he talked about the incredible courage of young people our age in the South, the risks they were taking and the dangers they faced willingly to make the world a better place. He talked about Gandhi and the creative power of nonviolence; he talked about the redemptive power of love, and how Truth, Goodness, Righteousness, and Love would always win out in the end; he talked about personal responsibility and the power that we each have to make a difference. I remember vividly how at the end of his speech he not only got a standing ovation, but we were on our feet yelling and screaming and holding each other and crying!

He spoke to our hearts! He spoke to our unformed visions of hope and possibility for the world. He appealed to our sense of fairness and justice, and to the fact that we were "special," but not in an elitist way. He made us feel special because he could trust us to "keep the faith" and honor the sacred call of *loving* a better world into existence!

Moist-eyed as she recalled the event in 2017 for the documentary *King in the Wilderness*, Baez said: "I just stood there and wept for the entire speech, because this man was doing what I had read about, you know, and studied about." Ten years after that Monterey meeting, King would be dead, American cities aflame. For five of those years, Baez would be with him at many of the key points of civil rights history.

Social justice and music were the north and south of Joan Baez's young life, and her performance at Asilomar gained her several bookings. Her repertoire was still drawn from the commercial songs she heard on the radio, much to her parents' dismay, so when Pete Seeger came to town, a family outing was organized in the hope that Joanie could be "weaned off" R&B. As she told Amy Goodman of *Democracy Now!* in an interview backstage at Seeger's ninetieth birthday concert:

They spirited me away with my auntie to a Pete Seeger show, and it was like a vaccine, it was either going to take or not. And it took, and I loved the music and I discovered that this man did what my family, in a sense, had done for many years which was, having become Quakers, fused everything with their politics. This was music and politics in a way I'd never known it but it was so natural to me, his music and what he did with his life, and I understood that very quickly. There was Harry Belafonte, Odetta and Pete. I listened to Pete's music endlessly and heard the stories about him, and learned the songs, and followed him.

Joanie's high school days were drawing to a close and her father had a new portmanteau position back east. He would work at Harvard and MIT; at the Physical Science Study Committee, which was seeking to develop a new science curriculum and new ways of teaching science in the post-Sputnik era; with Encyclopædia Britannica Films; and with the Smithsonian Astrophysical Observatory, where he would begin work on the optics for an x-ray telescope. Once again, Albert and Joan and the girls packed up the house, loaded the car, and headed cross-country, this time to Boston. It was the summer of 1958. As they drove, the preppy acoustic sounds of The Kingston Trio, formed in the Bay Area, filled the airwaves.

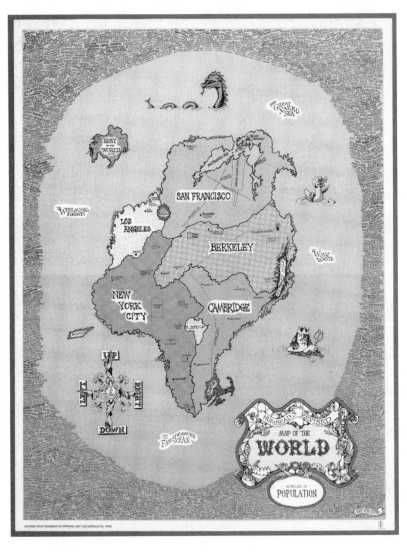

1969 Humbead's Revised Map of the World, depicting a world reimagined from the perspective of the West Coast folk scene and hippie counterculture. A "mattering map", it prefigures Saul Steinberg's celebrated *New Yorker* map of the world

2

PLEASE COME
TO BOSTON

Quite how the Baez women felt about upping and moving yet again is unknown. The lifestyle probably took its toll on Albert and Joan's marriage, for by the end of the 1970s they were living apart and would divorce, though they remade their vows some thirty years later because Albert wanted to die a married man. Free-spirited and creative, Joanie might have been less anxious and insecure if she'd been able to settle in one place and make lasting friends, but she has said she was eventually *afraid* to make friends because she knew they'd be lost in the next move. She appears to have had no idea why she was enrolled at Boston University's School of Fine and Applied Arts, only that no other school would take her.

Proud as he would become of Joanie and her sisters, it's easy to imagine Albert feeling disappointed that none inclined toward academia. No doubt he was keen for them to benefit from the education he'd struggled so hard to attain. As she wrote in *Daybreak*, she and her sisters always wished that "Popsy" had "one child to show some interest when he does physics experiments at the dinner table"—a role that would later be filled by Albert's nephew John, now a distinguished mathematical physicist in his own right: "When I was eight he gave me his college physics textbook, *The New College Physics: A Spiral Approach*. I remember staring fascinated at the hand-drawn pictures. Later that's where my interest in particle physics started."

Perhaps BU was Joanie's way of pleasing her father, perhaps just something to do. In any event it put her in the right place at the right time. The family was living in Belmont, a western suburb of Boston, a short drive from the intellectual hub of Cambridge, home to Harvard, Radcliffe (as it then was), and MIT. They'd not long been settled when her father suggested a family outing to one of the coffeehouses that were springing up in university towns. He chose the recently opened Tulla's Coffee Grinder, which the *Harvard Crimson* had said "smacks not one twit of the desperate degeneracy one sometimes associates with such places on this street." Perhaps Professor Baez had noticed its theatrical connections, for it was run by Harl Cook, whose father had founded the Provincetown Playhouse, where Eugene O'Neill got his start. Tulla's was named after Cook's partner, "a handsome Nordic blonde," and "pseudo Bohemians" were not welcome. "My father saw young minds interlocked in Socratic dialogues, expanding their horizons of knowledge and understanding, or simply reading books and playing chess," Baez recalled in *And a Voice to Sing With*. "I saw the guy under the tiny orange lamp, leaning over his classical guitar . . . playing 'Plaisir d'Amour.' I was entranced." The player was Dick Zaffron, a medical student whose performances were a regular feature of the Harvard scene and whom Joanie would shortly get to know. "I begged and borrowed everything I could off his guitar playing and repertoire."

BU was about going through the motions, and on freshman induction day Joanie fell in with Betsy Siggins, Jim Kweskin, Margie Gibbons, and Debbie Green, all of them refusing to wear their beanies at the freshman picnic. "It was totally serendipitous and from that moment on we all bonded around that little rebellion," Siggins told me. "Little did we know how much of a rebellion we'd all be involved with for the rest of our lives." Debbie was already a skilled guitarist—she'd hung out in Greenwich Village with Dave Van Ronk, learning at his feet—and she was soon coaching the newbie picker, introducing her to a folk song repertoire that included "All My Trials," which would become a Baez signature. The trio sought out live music, flirted outrageously with all the Harvard boys, and generally hung out, often at Margie's apartment. Any drama was strictly personal, and pretty soon Joanie had flunked college. It was said that while she could quickly master twenty-five verses of an English ballad, she could never memorize a single line of Shakespeare.

"Joanie would tell her parents she was in school and she was in my apartment," Siggins continued. "We would do a bit of fibbing. She reminded me of our trying to memorize a scene from a play. We would break out in giggles because it seemed so silly. We really weren't interested in being actresses." Sometimes the two students would meet at the Baez home. "We'd make believe we were learning lines but basically she was playing her guitar and goofing off, and having fun. We were busy doing other things. Life. I found the world at Club 47 was all-encompassing for all of us in that community. We're still friends. It's like going back to a college reunion."

Club 47, the coffeehouse with which Baez is forever associated, had opened its doors in January 1958, founded by Brandeis graduates Paula Kelly and Joyce Kalina and built from scratch, their aim to replicate a Paris café "where people would go listen to jazz, smoke cigarettes and talk a mile a minute," explained Siggins. Its menu featured a line drawing of a drum set and proclaimed it a *jazz* coffeehouse, though it quickly branched out into film and poetry. Yet even with their non-profit educational charter, Kelly and Kalina had trouble making ends meet and so were persuaded to try folk music. The first show featured Bill Wood, a folk-singing Harvard senior with a local radio show, and Joan Baez. A modest group of family and friends turned out, their number increased for the second set. Joanie was a success, hired for $10 a night. It didn't take her long to acquire a following.

What's remarkable is just how fully formed the teenage Joan Baez was as a talent. Film footage discovered in a fridge during the making of the PBS documentary *How Sweet the Sound* captures a Club 47 performance from 1958. She is perched on a stool, ramrod-straight, half in shadow, her hair long and wavy, wearing a patterned dress and playing a mahogany Martin. She is singing the English ballad "Barbara Allen" *exactly* as it would appear on her second album three years later. The voice is pure and secure, *pianissimo* on the most poignant verses, the diction clear. The guitar playing is simple but assured, the thumb emphasizing the tonic and dominant of each chord, and occasionally producing a tidy scalic run. The performance betrays none of the nerves she surely felt.

Joanie had been in Boston for only a few months, arriving with limited experience as a performer. Her parents encouraged her to entertain at home, but it's evident that around Harvard, she was a quick study. As with Bob Dylan, there are those who claim that she "stole" songs and made them her own to such an extent that it sounded as though other people were copying her. Such is the folk process, everyone learning from everyone else, yet there are some who claim that Baez stole not only Debbie Green's songs but her identity. Green herself has firmly refuted this. In response to a blog post entitled "Whatever happened to Debbie Green?," she wrote:

> I had asthma when I was an infant and I smoked in late teens. The reason I stopped singing and didn't make an album was scarring of the lungs. I didn't have enough breath to hold pitch. That was it. I had plenty of inspiration from music itself and wouldn't have been fazed by the Baez thing. I have said this many times in interviews but people seem drawn to the idea that someone stole my soul because I was passive. It was a matter of breath. Sometimes the lungs would clear and I could sing again.

Siggins acknowledges that there was "some tension between the two of them. Debbie would be in the audience and Joan would be on stage and there'd be some banter back and forth, but not much."

Green was for a time Siggins's room-mate though she contracted mononucleosis and returned home to her parents, her place taken by Pauline Baez who neither sang nor acted. Siggins believes Green was "a complicated woman and she never forgave me for being part of that inner circle with Joan and keeping her out, and I apologized to Debbie several times on camera before she died."

Baez herself has always credited Debbie Green: "'Fair and Tender Maidens,' that whole ilk of songs I got just from her, hanging out with her, and her teaching me. That's how a lot of us functioned," she recalled for the radio program *Off Ramp* in 2014. "I didn't read much. And I got practically *nothing* out of songbooks. I started collecting things like the Carter Family and learning from that. And some more esoteric stuff. I don't know, someone would give me a record."

Club 47 was "pretty typical of the clubs," Baez continued. "They served coffee, no drinks, and students came in and wanted to read or hang out or talk. And I was just *impossible*—if anyone said anything I would stop singing and make an issue out of it. I was pretty awful!" Indeed, both Paula Kelley and Joyce Kalina have recalled Joanie as being difficult to befriend, someone who could be "arrogant, rude, hysterical—she had stage fright half the time." It would be decades before she attained a sense of inner peace, the result of "serious work," and only in the second half of her career did she become truly comfortable onstage. She has long acknowledged that the angst-ridden "Queen Joan" did not always behave well.

Soon she was playing at the Ballad Room, Café Yana, and the Golden Vanity, which were across the Charles in Boston, making her one of only a handful of folk singers to play both sides of the river. Her reputation was building, a record inevitable.

Folksingers 'Round Harvard Square featured Baez with Bill Wood and Ted Alevizos, both of whom she has also cited as major influences. It was made in May 1959 at Fassett Recordings, located in a Beacon Hill brownstone. Joanie had the lion's share of the album with six songs, some of which she would revisit on her

The Veritas promotional poster for *Folksingers 'Round Harvard Square*, 1960, proclaiming the "FINEST AND MOST TALKED ABOUT FOLKSONG HI-FI LP FEATURING AMERICA'S TOP NEW OUTSTANDING FOLKSINGERS"

early Vanguard releases, and there were two Baez/Wood duets and one trio, which closed the album. The standout is "Oh, What a Beautiful City," which demonstrates the thrill and range of her young, untrained soprano—the recording had to be compressed in order that radio stations could handle the levels. At about the same time, posters appeared around Harvard Square featuring Eric Von Schmidt's artful drawing of Baez playing her guitar. (His drawing was taken from a photograph by Rick Stafford and would later feature on her 1960 Vanguard debut.) The calligraphy announced Club 47's summer program: Joan Baez on Tuesday evenings, progressive jazz Thursday to Saturday. There were lines around the block—not yet of folk music aficionados, just people who wanted to hear this young woman with an extraordinary voice. Before long she would be playing Fridays as well, but for now she needed to earn money elsewhere and worked for the Boston Vespa Company, teaching people to ride scooters.

Albert Grossman, owner of the famed Gate of Horn club in Chicago, was in Boston checking out the scene. He heard Joanie and invited her to the Windy City for a two-week residency, reportedly offering her $200 a week. Money was the least of her concerns— being alone in an unfamiliar city and playing a nightclub frightened her. She went anyway, staying at the city's YWCA. Bob Gibson, who played twelve-string guitar and banjo, was the MC, introducing new acts. Baez's arrival in June 1959 was no less thrilling for Gibson than it was for Joanie, who had the added excitement of meeting her idol Odetta ("the first real folksinger in my life") who dropped by the bar. She was "baffled, flattered and terrified" at the sense of being on the cusp of success, recognizing at the same time that "the cocktail crowd" was not for her. The *Chicago Tribune* wrote of "a Mexican songstress with sad eyes, long tresses and a steady guitar."

Gibson thought her "very very exciting" and invited her to join him at the inaugural Newport Folk Festival the following month—George Wein, founder and co-producer, had told him the bill was full but Gibson knew he could get away with bringing her onstage once he'd done a few songs. Odetta and her husband Danny Gordon would accompany Baez to Rhode Island—the moment recalled years later by the two women in "Blues Improv," performed at the New York concert to mark twenty-five years of Gerde's Folk City. It rained every day at Newport, but Joanie's enthusiasm remained undampened and she was thrilled to find herself rubbing shoulders with some of the great names of folk and blues. Among the stars that year were Earl Scruggs, Sonny Terry and Brownie McGhee, The New Lost City Ramblers, The Kingston Trio, John Jacob Niles, and Pete Seeger, as well as Odetta.

There was an audience of some thirteen thousand in Freebody Park when Bob Gibson closed the show on Saturday, July 11. Joanie stood at the side of the stage in her Jesus sandals, "petrified" as she awaited his introduction. They sang two songs, the slow, almost languorous "Virgin Mary Had One Son," which showcased Baez's voice to perfection as it soared, almost ethereal, in harmony with Gibson's. Then came the up-tempo and rhythmic "We Are Crossing Jordan River," the singers working a sort of call and response, Joanie adding a hint of scat, as the song builds to its climax. It's not quite note-perfect, but it *is* thrilling and you can feel the excitement in the audience long before they break into applause and cheers. She told Gibson: "I love the rhythm of these songs so much that I can hardly stand it."

Joanie descended the stage to "an exorbitant amount of fuss." Wein thought her gift "immediately apparent. She was an exceedingly talented vocalist, the Sarah Vaughan of folk-singing," he wrote in his memoir *Myself Among Others*. "Instantly she became not only the great discovery, but also the living symbol, of the first Newport Folk Festival." Among the critics present was Robert Shelton, the *New York Times* journalist who would chronicle the burgeoning Greenwich Village folk scene. He lauded her "achingly pure soprano," a quote which would forever follow her.

As Baez headed home to Boston, the singer reflected on her moment. "I realised in the back of my mind and the center of my heart that in my book of destiny the first page had been turned," she wrote a quarter-century later. Back at Club 47 the next week, lines snaked "right down the block and around two corners."

Grossman returned. He was just getting into artist management and he saw folk music as the next big thing, telling Shelton that "the American public is like Sleeping Beauty, waiting to be kissed awake by the prince of folk music," a metaphor that Baez, whom Gibson thought "puritanical," might not have appreciated. But a new folk revival *was* taking root among the college generation and it would shortly sweep the nation, with Boston/Cambridge and New York City the East Coast hubs. Martin guitars, once available cheap in yard sales, were now much sought-after. Grossman would become very successful very quickly but Joanie wasn't enamored, though she agreed to go with him to New York City to meet John Hammond, president of Columbia Records, who had signed Billie Holiday and created the all-star From Spirituals to Swing concert at Carnegie Hall. She was put off by all the "shine and glitter" and the pressure there and then to sign a lengthy contract. She wanted to see Maynard Solomon of Vanguard Records who had already reached out to her.

Vanguard had been founded in 1950 by Maynard and his brother Seymour Solomon, left-wing Jewish intellectuals, with a loan of $10,000 from their father. They were both classical musicians and the first Vanguard release was *Ich hatte viel Bekümmernis*, Bach's twenty-first cantata. In the mid-fifties, with McCarthyism at its height, they signed Paul Robeson and The Weavers. All of that surely endeared Vanguard to Baez, but there was the additional attraction that Odetta was with the label.

Despite pressure, Baez told Grossman she needed a couple of days to think it over though in reality her mind was made up. She was comfortable with Vanguard, who as it happened had the rights to record the Newport Folk Festival from its inception in 1959. Helped in large part by the success of Joan Baez, who at one point had three albums in the Top 10, the label would become pre-eminent in the field of what's now called Americana.

Her decision made, Joanie returned home to Belmont, singing Tuesdays and Fridays at Club 47 for $25 a night, a princely sum in those days. By day she worked as a housemother in the kindergarten at Perkins School for the Blind, where Amelia Earhart had been a volunteer reader and Helen Keller a student.

Grossman was "mortified," Siggins remembered, and having dispatched him, Baez began working with Manny Greenhill, a Boston-based impresario and "left-wing mensch" (as Siggins puts it) who came to folk music through his work as a union activist. He had founded Folklore Productions in 1957, presenting concerts by such figures as Josh White, Mahalia Jackson, and Pete Seeger, who he took on when he was blacklisted, both of them recognizing the pressures they would endure. Greenhill also looked after some of the great bluesmen now being discovered by a new generation, and he had a partnership with George Wein to turn the Mahogany Hall bar at Boston's Copley Square Hotel into a folk café. Joan Baez was his first managerial client, though for most of their ten years together there was no written contract, merely an annual handshake. At the outset, he secured her jobs opening the second half of concerts with established artists, notably Pete Seeger—*Very Early Joan* captures them together.

Manny's son Mitch Greenhill recalls that his father "had a sense of public service as well as a progressive political point of view. He once remarked at the number of blind artists he represented—felt he was being helpful. And Joan Baez certainly aligned with his politics, particularly in the struggles for civil rights and against the war in Vietnam . . . Joan was a pacifist, Manny was not. I think they agreed on the goals, a more just society, but not necessarily the means." Manny Greenhill and the young woman who would become his premier client first met at a rally. "Al Baez was speaking as a scientist concerned about nuclear bombs. When Al introduced Joan to sing a few songs, Manny's ears perked up. When Al moved on to a teaching gig in a different town, he asked Manny to look after his teenage daughter. Suddenly Folklore Productions had a new mission, artist representation," recalled Mitch.

Folksingers 'Round Harvard Square was released in January 1960 on Veritas Records. A mimeographed advance notice in purple type sent to Shelton at the *Times* describes Baez as "An 18 year old blend of Spanish, Mexican, and American beauty" who "pursues her hobby of folksinging by appearing for her legion of admirers at the Club 47 Coffee House in Cambridge on Tuesday evenings. Last summer she made her first professional engagement at the Gate of Horn in Chicago, the mecca of folksingers." The suggestion that she is a hobbyist is striking, since she was by this time busy with paid engagements, as is its assertion that she was "called from the audience" at Newport. The album received a respectable amount of coverage and Veritas put out a poster with a headline claiming it to be 1960's "FINEST AND MOST TALKED ABOUT FOLKSONG HI-FI LP FEATURING AMERICA'S TOP NEW OUTSTANDING FOLKSINGERS," below which were eight reviews, local and national. The Boston *Sunday Globe* referred to Baez as "a minstrel maid from Boston University," from which she had of course departed, while *Variety* saw her as a "young thrush . . . a standout talent in her genre." In the *Times*, Shelton waxed lyrical: "A star was born at the first Newport Folk Festival in the person of Joan Baez, a young soprano with a thrilling, lush vibrato and fervid and well-controlled projection."

Summer 1960 rolled around, and Joanie headed to Newport, appearing this year in her own right. Then it was time to go to New York City, where she would record her first album for Vanguard. Her parents would shortly be on the move again. Having worked with the Smithsonian Astrophysical Observatory in Cambridge on the development of optics for an x-ray telescope, Albert had now accepted a faculty position at Harvey Mudd College in Claremont, Southern California, putting a continent between them, a prospect that disturbed Joanie's always fragile equilibrium. "For the first time in my life my mother would not be waiting by the fire with a cup of tea for me and some violin or cello or piano on the phonograph."

Joan Baez shared the bill with Earl Scruggs, Lester Flatt and The Foggy Mountain Boys at New York's Fashion Institute of Technology in January 1961. There would be other performances with the bluegrass legend

3

THE EDGE OF GLORY

Vanguard Records had begun life in a one-room office at 80 East 11th Street, on the corner of Broadway just into the East Village. It soon expanded, relocating to 154 West 14th Street, the northern boundary of Greenwich Village but still only a five-minute walk from Washington Square, which had been the center of many things and would shortly be ground zero of the New York folk revival. By the end of 1966, the Vanguard Recording Society as it was formally known was able to announce swish new Chelsea offices at 71 West 23rd Street, with studios down the road at number 214. A *Billboard* feature in November 1966 proclaimed that these were suitable for folk, jazz, pop, and classical music, and could accommodate a fifty-piece orchestra. Vanguard boasted a distinguished catalog from across the musical spectrum, and in terms of folk music in its broadest sense it could be said to have laid the foundations of the 1960s urban revival, licensing Pete Seeger from Moe Asch's hallowed Folkways catalog for example—and at a time when Seeger was still blacklisted by TV networks. Vanguard had signed The Weavers in 1955, at the height of the red scare, and its recording of the group's Carnegie Hall reunion concert was both a musical milestone and a blue-chip calling card for many of the folk boomers who emerged as the dull gray of the Eisenhower years turned to Kennedy Technicolor. For the record-buying public, the Vanguard imprimatur—"Vanguard Recordings for the Connoisseur"—was a guarantee of quality. Joan Baez would be a key driver of the Seymour brothers' success.

When Baez arrived in the summer of 1960, most of Vanguard's recordings were made in the ballroom of the Manhattan Towers Hotel, situated on "a dingy block of Broadway" between 76th and 77th Streets, and immortalized by bandleader Gordon Jenkins on a 1946 two-disc 78 rpm set. Ian Tyson, of Canadian folk duo Ian and Sylvia, loved the acoustics of the place: "That room had the magic, a completely natural quality of reverb." Joanie stood barefoot "on the dirtiest rug in New York City, dwarfed by this huge musty room and sang into three microphones, two on the outside for stereo, and one in the center for monaural." There was a fourth mic for a second guitar, which Solomon had to persuade her to incorporate, though she worried it was "commercial"; it was played by Fred Hellerman of The Weavers. The nineteen songs were laid down over three days, with "Mary Hamilton," the long Scottish Child Ballad—from the nineteenth-century anthology of English and Scottish ballads identified by Francis James Child, a Boston-born polymath who became Harvard's first Professor of English—that would become a staple of her repertoire, captured in one take. The engineer was Swiss-born Marc Aubort, another classically trained musician who was Vanguard's chief engineer from 1958 to 1965. He handled all Baez's records during that period, trailing around Southern campuses to capture material for her two *In Concert* albums. He also presided over Vanguard's Newport records.

Asked about his recollections of working with Baez, Aubort acknowledged that some were "a bit sketchy" as they went back sixty years. "What I remember *vividly* is how impressed I was by her sincerity and total 'unphoneyness' compared with other celebrities of the day. Working with her was always delightful, on the road as well as in the studio or concert hall set-ups. Her voice, in all registers, was extremely microphone-friendly and did not require any electronic manipulations such as limiters or equalization. Joan required minimal editing, as most of her output was one-take versions."

Joan Baez was released in time for Christmas 1960 and would spend sixty-four weeks on the *Billboard* chart, peaking at No. 20 and eventually being certified Gold. The singer was not yet twenty but her performance is remarkably assured. The vocals are full of light and shade and color; dramatic here, exquisitely *sotto voce* there—a dynamic range that was both thrilling and rare. Her guitar playing is fluid and already sophisticated, skillfully underpinning the vocal line, sometimes picking out a harmony with it. Her diction, breath control, and phrasing are perfect—it would have been unsurprising to learn she had stepped out of a conservatoire.

"This album was for many youngsters the first encounter with 'House of the Rising Sun' and the second for 'All My Trials,' known to Kingston Trio fans as 'All My Sorrows' from its best-selling 1959 album *The Kingston Trio at Large*," wrote Michael Fremer of website AnalogPlanet, reviewing Craft Recordings' 2018 all-analog rerelease cut from the original stereo tapes on 180g vinyl. "Songs like the bleak 'Silver Dagger' and 'East Virginia' and the love-anthem 'Fare Thee Well' carried aloft by Baez's well-rehearsed and delivered performances resonated with a young generation of college and high schoolers eager to break free from their suburban chains. Helping greatly were Vanguard Records co-founder Maynard Solomon's erudite liner notes." Fremer had been taken by his mother to see Baez's November 1961 New York Town Hall debut. He was fourteen and only appreciated the experience in retrospect.

In March 2015, *Joan Baez* was added to the National Recording Registry of the twentieth century's historically and culturally important albums at the Library of Congress. The citation stated that it "preserves for posterity powerful performances from the Harvard Square coffeehouse repertoire that brought Baez to prominence as the folk revival movement was arriving on the national stage. Baez's haunting arrangements of traditional English and Scottish ballads of longing and regret, mixed with an eclectic blend of Bahamian, Yiddish, Mexican, and Carter Family favorite tunes, sent critic Robert Shelton 'scurrying to the thesaurus for superlatives.' The album's success was especially important for women in the folk music milieu who found a role model 'absolutely free and in charge of herself,' in the words of fellow folksinger Barbara Dane."

It was also important for people of *color* in a nation still defiantly segregated. For Baez was *brown*, not white, and a large part of her insecurity stemmed from the fact that at school she had often been made to feel "a dumb Mexican." There was Odetta and Harry Belafonte, and before them Josh White, who performed at President Roosevelt's third inaugural and who was invited by Franklin and Eleanor to perform his anti-segregationist album *Southern Exposure: An Album of Jim Crow Blues* at the White House. But the folk revival was overwhelmingly white—and, despite a small group of high-profile older women, overwhelmingly male. As of course was the music business itself, even if it was not yet a business.

Having moved in with a schoolfriend to a walkup near Harvard Square once her parents had left Boston, Baez herself soon headed west, settling into a one-room cabin in the Carmel Highlands with Michael New, the Harvard boyfriend she felt too insecure to leave, and who was jealous of her success. She would immortalize him in her 1979 song "Michael."

Meanwhile, her career was being managed from Boston. Manny Greenhill was promoting her with a flyer that featured the Eric Von Schmidt drawing from Club 47, Robert Shelton's "star was born" quote, plus a list of her appearances which, besides clubs and Newport, also included the universities of Harvard, Yale, Brandeis, Boston, and Massachusetts, as well as Wellesley College. "Available in 1960–61," it declared, above the Vanguard logo.

In New York, Baez had already played at Carnegie Hall, a hootenanny on October 14, 1960 to benefit *Sing Out!* magazine at which Lightnin' Hopkins was the main attraction, his first appearance beyond the South. Pete Seeger was the host for an evening that also featured The Clancy Brothers and Tommy

Makem. Baez's set included a rock 'n' roll send-up, as well as "Virgin Mary." Three weeks later, on November 5, she made her solo debut in the city at the 92nd Street Y. Shelton was there for the *Times*, and his review proclaimed her "enormous talent," concluding presciently: "Considering her time for growth as an interpreter, Miss Baez faces a glowing future."

The same year, 1960, she made her television debut in two shows by writer and producer Robert Herridge, creator of the esteemed arts series *Camera Three*. The first was *Folk Sound USA*, which also featured John Jacob Niles, Flatt and Scruggs, and John Lee Hooker. It aired in the summer. In December, she worked again with Herridge, alongside Lightnin' Hopkins, on *A Pattern of Words and Music*. She sang four songs, including "All My Trials." Actor Michael Kane recited poetry by William Blake and John Donne—"No man is an island," which Baez would later record on *Baptism*—and John Sebastian (father of the Lovin' Spoonful founder) blew a plaintive harmonica. Among those watching was a University of Minnesota freshman named Robert Zimmerman. "She was wicked looking," he would recall in *Chronicles*, forty years into his career as Bob Dylan. "The sight of her made me high. All that and then there was her voice. A voice that drove out bad spirits. It was like she'd come down from another planet."

In January 1961 came a brace of Sunday afternoon concerts at New York City's Fashion Institute of Technology, Baez sharing the bill with Earl Scruggs, Lester Flatt, and The Foggy Mountain Boys, "Direct from WSM Grand Ole Opry." A daring mix for its day! There were more concerts with Pete Seeger, whose consummate ease as a performer was in stark contrast to her own anxieties. Not only did he expand her repertoire (on her final tour, Baez was still featuring songs she'd learned from him), but he also demonstrated how life and work could be all of a piece. He was both hero and inspiration.

By now, she'd outgrown the Harvard Square and Boston scenes. A farewell concert at Club 47 in February prompted a four-page profile in *Cambridge 38* by Simon Lazarus III, who went on to be a lawyer in the Carter White House. His early career retrospective is perceptive: He describes her voice as "a stiletto of sound, slicing through the dark blur of smoke and people and darkness and talk," the singer herself "a mystery." Her talent was "deceiving in its apparent simplicity" and would take her far. He continued: "A mixture of timidity and arrogance, she stands, rather blankly, waiting for requests. The effect of this mien on the audience, combined with her manner while singing, is to make Joan seem at once innocent yet startlingly sophisticated, somewhat shy yet ready to do just what she damn pleases."

It was a bitterly cold winter, New York's coldest in twenty-eight years, and in late January '61, a chubby-faced dropout from the University of Minnesota waved goodbye to his ride at the Manhattan end of the George Washington Bridge. Robert Zimmerman had already reinvented himself as Bob Dylan, though the name change wasn't yet official. He headed downtown to Greenwich Village, to the clubs and coffeehouses where a group of aspirant singer-songwriters was already jostling for a spot on whatever passed for a stage. Gerde's Folk City, which had opened in January 1960 as The Fifth Peg, becoming Gerde's six months later, was already established as one of the pre-eminent clubs, and its Monday night hoots—open mic sessions—were a place to put down a marker.

Woody Guthrie's picaresque memoir, *Bound for Glory*, had cast its spell on the young student and while Baez had cast *her* spell, it was the Guthrie legend that drew him to New York. By the time he arrived, Woody was hospitalized with the Huntington's Disease which would kill him in 1967, but Dylan met his hero at the Sunday afternoon gatherings that Guthrie's friends arranged as a break from hospital. His "Song to Woody" was written following an early encounter.

Dylan's first break came on April 11, 1961, when he was booked for his first professional gig, playing support to bluesman John

Lee Hooker at Gerde's. Baez had already heard his name which is presumably why she headed to West 4th Street that night. She noted that he carried "an undignified amount of baby fat," wore a too-small jacket and seemed dwarfed by his guitar. His own songs were "original and refreshing if blunt and jagged" and she thought him "exceptional." He finished his set and was brought to the table where she was seated with Michael. "The historic event of our meeting was under way," she wrote a quarter-century later.

September saw the release of Baez's second album, simply titled *Vol. 2*, on which highly polished English balladry met American folk songs and Carter Family-style country and bluegrass. There was also "Plaisir d'Amour," which had so entranced her on that family excursion to Tulla's Coffee Grinder. The Greenbriar Boys, another Vanguard signing, featured on two of the tracks, adding their distinctive vocal harmonies, banjo, and guitars. The record prompted an early piece by the journalist and free speech activist Nat Hentoff, who, writing in *The Reporter* of folk's renaissance, suggested that, until Baez, "no one had appeared who could hold an audience by musical excellence alone." At first glance she "does not make a particularly strong impression . . . When she sings, however, Miss Baez, who is as spare with gestures as she is with smiles, draws the audience to her as if she were about to foretell the future. She communicates uncommon intensity . . ."

Baez played a score of concerts in 1961, including the thousand-seater Jordan Hall in Boston and, with The Greenbriar Boys, the all-important Town Hall in New York, the venue a way station between downtown Village clubs and uptown concert halls. *Variety* noted that "Joan Baez racked up an SRO gross of $4,100 . . . The 20-year-old folk chirper was a sellout three days after tickets went on sale." Two hundred people were turned away at the door. The reviewer observed that "Some extemporaneous patter on world affairs set an engaging tone for her work." Shelton, again in the *Times*, suggested she attend to "the pacing of material, differentiation of mood, and a need to avoid the drifting into reverie without bringing her audience with her. But she has made such strides in stage presence and interpretive depth that she has developed into a remarkable young folk musician."

Scarcely four years had passed since her Club 47 debut, yet May 1962 found Baez giving a solo concert at Carnegie Hall. The demand for tickets was such that two hundred people were given seats on the stage. In the *Times*, under the headline "Soprano and Guitarist Gives Second Major Concert," Shelton wrote that her voice was "shaded with an art singer's control. By combining splendid diction, understanding of her material and a gripping sort of reined passion, she delivered a series of interpretations that will not soon be forgotten." Baez was now "emerging from her youthful shyness and beginning to look at members of her audience, not singing in a detached semi-trance as she has in the past." Shelton once more offered a few words of criticism: "She appears, because she is gifted with such a great voice, to lean too heavily on vocalism alone." He again advised that she relieve the all-pervasive "monochrome mood of melancholy." The ballads themselves might be sad and tragic but between songs Baez needed to relax and have fun. That would take some time.

According to journalist and music historian Arthur Levy, whose insightful notes accompany each of Vanguard twenty-first-century reissues, it was Maynard Solomon's suggestion in late 1961 to "document all of her concert performances for a period of time, perhaps with a view to issuing concert albums, but perhaps just with a view to documenting material and determining what would be best on the next albums." Some forty concerts were recorded on three tours undertaken between October 1961 and spring 1963 at black colleges in Nashville, Atlanta, Mobile, Tuscaloosa, Tougaloo—parts of the Southern United States "sweltering with the heat of injustice, sweltering with the heat of oppression," as Dr Martin Luther King Jr. would put it in his celebrated speech at the March on Washington. The contracts expressly forbade segregation of black from white, so whites wishing to see her would have to go to a black campus where they would be shocked at the inferior facilities. Joan wasn't yet widely known among the black community, so at each stop Manny Greenhill and Solomon called local NAACP offices for volunteers to integrate the audiences. The signing of the Civil Rights Act was two years away and Baez was one of the first major artists to embrace the black cause.

Bill Fegan, a professor at Stillman College in Tuscaloosa and an old friend of Manny Greenhill, recalled a Baez concert there for Mitch Greenhill. "First, [the whites] had to come on campus, and they probably didn't know where the building was, and they probably had to speak to a black person and ask, 'Where would you get tickets for Joan Baez?' Our students were primed; might even take them to the building . . . And no white person asked—'Well, is this seat next to a black person?' Or 'Is this a white section?' . . . So, when the concert came, the audience was a wonderful sea of black and white. It was our little technique." Fegan asked Manny if Baez would sing with Stillman's gospel choir and she agreed to sing two numbers. Such was the exhilaration that half the concert featured the choir.

The evening didn't end there, for Professor Fegan had arranged a party, inviting a number of student leaders to his home. "In those days that was just not done—black and white in the same living room, enjoying food and drink together. But we did, and I still have the album cover—on which she wrote 'to the most integrated living room in Alabama.'"

Miles College, just outside Birmingham, Alabama, in May 1963, was a key date. The so-called Birmingham campaign was under way and during it King had been arrested, spending a week in solitary confinement and writing his Letter from Birmingham Jail. There had been months of sit-ins and boycotts, but the police, commanded by Eugene "Bull" Connor—who notoriously unleashed dogs and fire hoses on peaceful protesters—had agreed a truce. As an act of good faith, the protests had been called off as the city agreed to desegregate lunch counters, bathrooms, drinking fountains, and fitting rooms, and to instigate a program

Joan Baez painted by Russell Hoban for *Time*, November 23, 1962. He sketched her in concert in Tucson, Arizona, and at her home in Carmel, California. He remembers her driving a "little gray bomb"

of "upgrading Negro employment." A committee would be convened to monitor progress. But segregationists broke the truce and there were so many arrests that the jails were filled—rich whites donated their tennis courts as holding pens. The Baez party had arrived early, staying with King and his people at the Gaston Motel, the only place that would accommodate both blacks and whites—it was bombed a few days later and is now a Birmingham Civil Rights National Monument. Together they attended a local Baptist church, where Joan was invited to sing.

As they watched the audience arrive for the concert, Baez was told by Miles College regents that it was the first time ever that white people had stepped onto the campus. She admitted to feeling afraid, for herself and for those same white people who had come to hear her sing—these were dangerous times, the Birmingham summer was far from over. You can hear the nervous smile in her voice as she asks the audience: "Would you like to sing 'We Shall Overcome'?" The album movingly captures the moment when black people and white people sing together—tentative at first, growing in confidence, standing and linking arms: "*We are not afraid today.*" Whistles and cheers are audible in the applause. Years later, America's first black president would talk of "the audacity of hope." In May 1963, that was the sound of it.

The brace of *In Concert* albums, released in 1962 and '63, demonstrate Baez's growth as an artist and the clear direction of her career. Her repertoire is broadening to include protest songs (Malvina Reynolds's anti-nuclear protest "What Have They Done to the Rain" was put on the map) alongside traditional Anglo-American repertoire ("Geordie," "The House Carpenter," and "Matty Groves," three of the great Child Ballads), country and gospel, and three Brazilian songs. Woody Guthrie's "Pretty Boy Floyd" features alongside the first two of many Dylan songs, both of which would become concert staples: "Don't Think Twice, It's Alright" and "With God on Our Side." The first of the two albums begins with "Babe I'm Gonna Leave You," which as a concert-opener must have been challenging: The vocal is dramatic yet almost ethereal, and Baez truly inhabits it, her subtle use of *rubato* adding to the weight of emotion, while her guitar playing is sophisticated, an even tremolo throughout. Dick Zaffron was surely impressed. So too, when he caught up with it, was session guitarist Jimmy Page who took it to Robert Plant. Led Zeppelin was born and a much longer version of the song, written in the 1950s by Anne Bredon, featured on the band's 1969 tour.

In Concert Part 1 and *Part 2* are both very natural-sounding recordings—it's possible to imagine being *in* the audience, something few live recordings attain. (Further material from the concert series forms part of *Very Early Joan*, released in 1982.) In terms of reception, they reprised the success of her first two releases but they have a significance beyond either the aesthetic or the commercial. *Part 1* was released in September 1962, becoming Baez's third Gold album and gaining her first Grammy nomination, for Best Folk Recording.

Time took note of the Baez phenomenon with a short item on June 1, 1962 in its Music section, which led with a feature on Glyndebourne. A short column on "The Folk Girls" wrapped around a picture of the opera company's founder, John Christie. The magazine mused on the new folk fad: "It is not absolutely essential to have hair hanging to the waist—but it helps. Other aids: no lipstick, flat shoes, a guitar," it opened. "So equipped, almost any enterprising girl can begin a career as a folk singer." Baez was singled out as "the most gifted of the newcomers" and praised for her "pure, purling soprano voice, an impeccable sense of dynamics and phrasing, and an uncanny ability to dream her way into the emotional heart of a song." That week, she had "two albums perched high on the pop charts." *Time* recommended three "other newcomers": Bonnie Dobson, Judy Collins, and Carolyn Hester—all of them still active.

Six months later, November 23, Baez was on the magazine's cover, her portrait painted by Russell Hoban. The author of the cover story, uncredited as was the custom in those days, was John McPhee, who perhaps had something to do with the earlier article. For under the headline "Folk Singing—Sibyl with Guitar," the piece began in much the same tone, noting the emergence of "both an esoteric cult and a light industry" which had multiplied the sales of guitars—400,000 in 1961 alone. The "cultists" were contemptuous of "entertaining groups like the Kingston Trio and the Limelighters." Joan Baez was the real deal and McPhee waxed lyrical:

> Her voice is as clear as air in the autumn, a vibrant, strong, untrained and thrilling soprano. She wears no makeup and her long black hair hangs like a drapery, parted around her long almond face. In performance she comes on, walks straight to the microphone, and begins to sing. No patter. No show business. She usually wears a sweater and skirt or a simple dress. Occasionally she affects something semi-Oriental that seems to have been hand-sewn out of burlap. The purity of her voice suggests purity of approach. She is only 21 and palpably nubile. But there is little sex in that clear flow of sound. It is haunted and plaintive, a mother's voice, and it has in it distant reminders of black women wailing in the night, of detached madrigal singers performing calmly at court, and of saddened gypsies trying to charm death into leaving their Spanish caves.

There was a detailed biography, which revealed that her parents were now in Paris, where Albert Baez was a consultant for UNESCO, and several photos, including one of boyfriend Michael. Already Joanie was "under attack," McPhee continued, "by other singers, disorganized coffeehouse groups, and organized critics . . . sniped at for her failure to study, for not training her voice, for using folk material to express her own feelings, for singing nearly everything sadly."

Most likely she was under attack for becoming a successful woman.

Eric Von Schmidt's poster for the Baez and Dylan tour
in spring 1965. Commissioned by Manny Greenhill,
the poster took its cue from a photo at Club 47

4

WE SHALL OVERCOME

The new year began well for Joan Baez. In a review of *In Concert*, *High Fidelity* magazine declared her "a talent of the first magnitude," praising the "amazing purity" of her voice, "a silvery quality not unlike the sound of a light, flawlessly cast bell," and "the depth of vision and the inner integrity that transmute each of her ballads into a unique artistic expression." The reviewer, "OBB," thought her "a very important and very moving artist" whose style was "uniquely and profoundly" her own.

Yet for some traditionalists and their followers who'd been ploughing the folk furrow long before the 1960s revival, the Baez voice was too polished for folk music, which, in her hands, became something akin to art song. When Peggy Seeger, stepsister of Pete, observed that "Joan Baez has a beautiful voice. Mine is a character voice and that has helped me in singing different types of songs," she may not have meant it as a compliment. John Cohen of The New Lost City Ramblers, writing in *Sing Out!* in March 1963, seems ambivalent as he seeks to account for her rapid rise. He observed that when Baez sang in "her autobiographical first-person manner, she is telling her own story." With Peggy, on the other hand, "the singer is speaking about life experience, not revealing one way or the other as to whether this is biographical. At this point is the crucial separation between Joan and folk music, and it is here that her personality takes over." Cohen, who married into the Seeger dynasty, noted that "a segment of the traditionally inclined enthusiasts are very critical of her as a mis-interpreter" of folk music.

Arguments about "authenticity" swirled around all these "arriviste" folkies until the mid-1960s, when the urban folk revival became subsumed in folk rock, at which point there were charges of "sell-out." Such a charge could never be leveled at Baez, but there were those who felt that she and others like her could not be considered "authentic" because—unlike Jean Ritchie, for example, the so-called "Mother of Folk Music" who had grown up in a ballad-singing family—they had not trekked through the Appalachians collecting songs and their variants. Baez never claimed any great interest in a song's history and evolution: What mattered was whether it touched her soul. Perhaps her Anglo-Scottish ancestry accounted for a notable affinity with the great English and Scottish ballads. It was John Jacob Niles, with whom Baez played some early concerts, who was able to link the Child Ballads to the songs he learned as a young man growing up in Kentucky.

In any event, by spring 1963, folk music was big box office and ABC had launched a TV series. A pilot for *Hootenanny* had been filmed at the University of Syracuse in autumn 1962 and it was sufficiently successful that a series was commissioned. Six shows were filmed in spring '63, the first featuring Bob Gibson, Bonnie Dobson, and The Limelighters, who would headline several more episodes. While *Variety* thought it "lacked the spark and spirit that is found in 'live' college and concert dates," the *Times* judged the show to be "the hit of the spring." As the audience headed toward a peak of eleven million, ABC announced that *Hootenanny* would return in the autumn as an hour-long show. A craze had been born and it wasn't just concert bookers and record companies who piled in—there was clothing, shoes, and vacations; car dealers held "Hootenanny Sales"; amusement parks featured "Miss Hootenanny" contests.

No doubt ABC hoped that Joan Baez would be their real-life Miss Hootenanny, but then *Variety* reported that Pete Seeger would not be invited to appear because of his left-wing views, even though a seven-year battle with the House Un-American Activities

photo by Lars Speyer

"... Much of her music is from another time and place, yet she makes it immediate to the present, as if life itself were at stake in the urgency of her songs..."

Joan Baez

by John Cohen

So much has already been written about Joan Baez; we can read in the popular press the extent of her record sales, the attendance figures of her concerts, her family background, and all kinds of intimacies about her private life.

This article is an attempt to look briefly at what she has achieved in terms of affecting the current ideas of folk music, to see where her music

John Cohen is a member of the New Lost City Ramblers and a leading critic of the contemporary folksong scene.

has come from, and some of the forces that seem to influence her. Perhaps when these ideas are clearer we can have a basis for understanding where her music is unique, where it is different from her sources, and so, we can know her contribution, to see what it is that she has offered which has caused her music to reach so much farther than was ever expected or intended.

Perhaps the seeming incongruity of it all should be stated early; Joan Baez is a small and beautiful girl whose very simplicity creates a complexity of thought within her and the listener.

-5-

The opening page of John Cohen's *Sing Out!* appraisal from Vol. 13, No. 3, Summer 1963. Baez was the cover story

Committee had seen him vindicated. As a result, Baez refused to appear, as would The Greenbriar Boys, Tom Paxton, Barbara Dane, and Ramblin' Jack Elliott. Judy Collins and Theodore Bikel, having participated in earlier shows, refused future appearances. With the talent pool badly depleted, *Hootenanny* was not well placed to survive the Beatles-led British invasion and ABC cancelled the third season.

For Baez, who would attach conditions to any television appearance, the show's demise was neither here nor there. Her career was going from strength to strength. She was on the road again, a nationwide tour that saw her visit old stamping grounds in Boston and Stanford, and Washington, D.C.'s Coliseum with Pete Seeger. On April 19, she filled New York's Philharmonic Hall at Lincoln Center, Robert Shelton noting that her stage manner had become "exceedingly relaxed, warmer and communicative."

In the two years since their Gerde's introduction, both Baez and Dylan had been busy. Dylan had been signed by Columbia, but his eponymous debut had been a slow sell—only five thousand copies in its first year, leading to his being nicknamed Hammond's Folly, after producer John Hammond, whom Baez had spurned. He was managed by Albert Grossman, whom she had also rejected, and he'd been to London to appear in Philip Saville's BBC TV drama *Madhouse on Castle Street*, a visit more notable for his various folk club appearances than for the play itself. There was also a meeting with Martin Carthy, who taught Dylan two English folk songs whose melodies would appear on his second album, *Freewheelin'*.

Released in May 1963, *Freewheelin'* would establish the young singer-songwriter as a talent to watch, for it included songs that are now classics, including "Blowin' in the Wind," which Peter, Paul and Mary (another Grossman act) would soon take to the top of the charts. It also included "Don't Think Twice, It's Alright," which was already in Baez's repertoire and captured live on *In Concert, Part 2*, and "A Hard Rain's a-Gonna Fall," a song written with fierce urgency the previous October as the world held its breath during the Cuban Missile Crisis. Baez's own version of it would appear on *Farewell, Angelina* (1965), and both songs would feature in countless concerts, with "Don't Think Twice" the opener for her final performance in Madrid in July 2019.

There's little evidence that their paths had crossed since Gerde's, though in a *Hootenanny* magazine profile of the pair, Shelton—by now spending a good deal of time hanging out with Dylan in Greenwich Village—reported that they'd met again at a party in Boston, where Dylan had gone to sniff out the scene, failing to get a slot at Club 47 and instead filling in between Carolyn Hester's sets. Baez had admired his "Song to Woody," which he had sung that night in Gerde's, so it's reasonable to assume that Grossman made sure she got to hear Dylan's latest compositions, laid down in the celebrated Witmark Demos, not least because Grossman stood to benefit financially.

It was at the first Monterey Folk Festival in May 1963, which marked Dylan's West Coast debut, that "the Voice and the Poet" (as a *Hootenanny* headline put it) began to get properly acquainted. It appears he and Baez sang "With God on Our Side." Fariña, whose ambition may have outstripped his talent, both of which were thwarted by his tragically early death, fancied himself as a commentator at the royal court. In "Baez and Dylan: a generation singing out," published in *Mademoiselle*, he implies that Monterey provided Baez with her first proper exposure to Dylan both personally and professionally. As she grew in confidence and came to understand that she could harness her growing popularity to causes in which she believed passionately, she recognized that her repertoire needed to extend beyond traditional folk song and the few contemporary numbers (such as Malvina Reynolds's "What Have They Done to the Rain?") she had already incorporated. Yet where were the songs? Dylan's "strong-willed, untempered, but nonetheless poetic approach to the problem filled the gap and left her awed and impressed."

Their time together after the festival in Baez's Carmel Valley home must have been very fulfilling. He would return there with her at the end of the summer and again the following year. By all accounts, Dylan was productive, enjoying the seclusion and the swimming, the Pacific Ocean just a short drive away in the Jaguar XK-E she'd bought on a whim with cash and which the IRS would later seize and sell to offset the taxes she was withholding in protest against Vietnam. (She has always said Dylan was a terrible driver, so he may not have been allowed behind the wheel of the silver sports car, of which neighbor Hunter S. Thompson was envious.) They explored the spectacular Big Sur coastline and visited Cannery Row, Dylan thrilled to find himself in John Steinbeck country. Among the songs he wrote out west were "The Lonesome Death of Hattie Carroll," "Lay Down Your Weary Tune," and "Love Is Just a Four-Letter Word," which he left behind, apparently unfinished, to be retrieved by Baez from behind the piano. She told Dylan's biographer Robert Shelton that she tried to leave him undisturbed, and he responded by establishing some sort of routine, spending mornings at his typewriter or at the piano. "I tried to get Bobby to look after his health," she continued. "I tried to get him to cut down on his smoking and to brush his teeth and all of that." She and Shelton both worried that he was "killing himself."

By the time the Newport Folk Festival rolled around on the last weekend of July 1963, Peter, Paul and Mary's version of Dylan's "Blowin' in the Wind" was at No. 2 on the *Billboard* chart, with 300,000 copies sold in its first week of release. The music and lyrics were printed in the program. As to Bob Dylan himself, he was (as Shelton put it) "an underground conversation piece." The three-day lineup included Jean Ritchie, Theo Bikel, Judy Collins, Ian and Sylvia, The Freedom Singers, Mississippi John Hurt, and Ed McCurdy, best known for the anti-war song "Last Night I Had the Strangest Dream." Dylan had a spot on the opening evening, while Baez and Pete Seeger featured in the closing concert. Officially, there were no stars—everyone was paid $50 plus board and lodging.

It was at a Friday afternoon workshop hosted by Bikel that Baez and Dylan gave the first of their now-legendary Newport

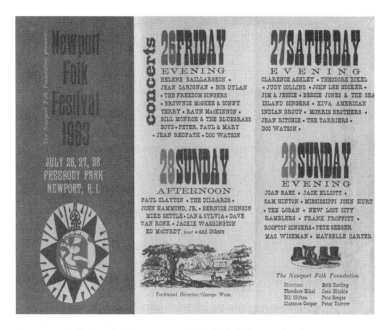

Newport Folk Festival program, 1963. Bob Dylan arrived "an underground conversation piece" and left a star, thanks to Baez

performances. Grainy live footage shows them sitting on folding chairs atop a crowded stage, Dylan fumbling both tuning and capo before launching into "With God on Our Side," which featured in his solo set later that evening. The finale saw Dylan center stage with Baez, Seeger, Bikel, Peter, Paul and Mary, and The Freedom Singers performing "Blowin' in the Wind" and then "We Shall Overcome," black musicians and white linking arms in a powerfully evocative image in that summer of George Wallace and Bull Connor. Baez's own Sunday evening set included "All My Trials," "Don't Think Twice," and, once again, "With God on Our Side," for which she called out Dylan, who again played the guitar. The grand finale was "This Land Is Your Land," the Woody Guthrie song known to generations of American schoolchildren.

Like Joan Baez four years earlier, Bob Dylan left Newport a star. If she was folk's reigning queen, he was now its crown prince.

Following Newport, Baez had a series of East Coast concerts and where once she had played with Flatt and Scruggs or Pete Seeger, now she would share the stage with the young man she would immortalize in song as "the unwashed phenomenon, the original vagabond." Their two managers agreed a formula and a deal which, according to Shelton, saw Dylan make more money than Baez. She would open each concert and then introduce Dylan, who would play a half-dozen songs, and then they would sing together. It's easy to forget that in the old analog world, few people would have known what was coming, and it's fair to say that not every audience was ecstatic. Nevertheless, Baez—always loyal to a cause—persisted, enabling Dylan quickly to acquire an audience. At Forest Hills Tennis Stadium on August 17, 1963, some fifteen thousand people were present to hear Baez introduce her protégé: "Bobby Dylan says what a lot of people my age feel but cannot say." In the *New York Times*, Shelton reported: "With dignified modesty the soprano folk singer devoted more than half her program to new songs by Bob Dylan, sung either by herself or by the young minstrel-poet in an unannounced appearance." In October, an even bigger audience awaited at the Hollywood Bowl.

Eleven days later, on August 28, 1963, Baez and Dylan shared a rather different stage, appearing on the steps of the Lincoln Memorial at the great March on Washington for Jobs and Freedom, when upwards of 250,000 souls converged on the nation's capital, conveyed aboard two thousand buses, twenty-one chartered trains, ten chartered airliners, and innumerable cars. In the sweltering heat, they gathered on the Mall, some able to cool their tired feet in the Reflecting Pool. Dr Martin Luther King Jr.—whom the young Joanie had first heard at Quaker summer camp—made a speech that remains one of the greatest in history, the rolling cadences of his celebrated "dream" as emotive as ever. Contralto Marian Anderson, a favorite from Baez's childhood who had sung from the Lincoln Memorial in 1939, was to have sung the national anthem but was unable to get there in time. She later performed the spiritual "He's Got the Whole World in His Hands." Mahalia Jackson and Lena Horne sang, as did Odetta, Josh White, Peter, Paul and Mary, and Dylan.

Baez sang at various points throughout the long day, rousing the growing crowd at 10am with "Oh, Freedom." During the course of the morning, she joined Dylan for "When the Ship Comes In" and led the singing of "We Shall Overcome." She and Dylan joined Len Chandler for "Keep Your Eyes on the Prize, Hold On," the last song before the official program. And between brief speeches by the Reverend Ralph Abernathy and Nobel Laureate Ralph Bunche, Baez sang "All My Trials." It had never sounded so poignant.

If the March held out the promise of a better and more equable tomorrow, events in Birmingham, Alabama, a couple of weeks later shattered the dream. Members of the local Ku Klux Klan bombed the 16th Street Baptist Church, killing four little girls and injuring twenty-two other souls as they prepared for church and a sermon titled "A Love That Forgives." The brutal attack marked a turning point in the civil rights campaign and the Civil Rights Act, which President Kennedy had advocated in a televised address earlier that summer, was signed into law by President Johnson in July 1964. Justice was long delayed—Birmingham had no black police and FBI Director J. Edgar Hoover quickly closed the files. Among the many tributes was the song "Birmingham Sunday," written by Richard Fariña and which Baez would record in 1964 on her fifth Vanguard album. She revived it in the latter portion of her American Fare Thee Well tour, when it formed a bitter companion piece to "The President Sang Amazing Grace," Zoe Mulford's song about the 2015 Charleston church shooting.

Baez was driving to the grocery store on November 22, 1963 when news broke that President Kennedy had been shot and killed. She had already accepted an invitation to sing at a gala for JFK, surprisingly given her reluctance to engage with politicians.

Perhaps at this early stage in her career she felt unable to refuse. According to *And a Voice to Sing With*, a telegram arrived on November 23 assuring her that the show would go on, only with a new beneficiary—the Johnson for President Committee. It took place at New York's Madison Square Garden the following May, when Baez—formal in high-neck white lace and heels— rubbed sequined shoulders with the likes of Ginger Rogers, Gregory Peck, Woody Allen, and members of the New York City Ballet. She sang three carefully chosen songs and, according to *Music Business*, was "totally aware that she had an audience with the President of the United States, and realized the significance of this moment to herself." She dedicated "All My Trials" to "one very brave young woman with whom we all share a deep grief: Mrs Jacqueline Kennedy." Then she turned to President Johnson, telling him: "I realize that 'we' are very young by your standards, but some of us like to consider ourselves serious thinking people. We are very involved in world conditions and we are particularly aware of changes which are difficult yet imperative. We've watched you begin to make some of these changes, and for this we are proud of you and honor you. This next song is for you." She then sang "The Times They Are a-Changin'," which urged "senators and congressmen" to "please heed the call" and not block youthful progress. Before the applause had faded, she launched into "Blowin' in the Wind." *Music Business* thought her performance a moment of "hope and inspiration and absolute beauty. A rare experience when one is reminded of the ability of art to heighten the dignity of man and elevate the spirit and comfort the soul."

Baez had been on a very steep learning curve and however anxious she remained as a performer, she had quickly learned the value of her position, acquiring confidence enough to take advantage of a situation for the greater good. Now, in a letter addressed to "Dear Friends" and released publicly, she told "the Eternal Revenue Service" that "I do not believe in war. I do not believe in the weapons of war." Thus, she was "no longer supporting my portion of the arms race" and was withholding the sixty percent of her income tax used for defense spending. Her stance was part of a great tradition of dissent—the Harvard poet, philosopher, and essayist Henry David Thoreau, in an essay that had influenced Walt Whitman, Mahatma Gandhi, and Martin Luther King, had advocated civil disobedience against an unjust state. In the 1960s, American Quakers were arguing for a peace tax.

Dylan's thoughts on the subject, if any, are unknown, though Baez had yet to understand he was not an activist. For the moment, they were still having fun together, offstage and on. Her diary for 1964 included around twenty concerts, the year beginning and ending on the West Coast, and now it was Dylan's moment to return the compliment and invite *her* onstage, which he did at Berkeley's Community Theatre in February. Richard Fariña (in that same *Mademoiselle* article) wrote: "Had a literary audience been confronted by Dylan Thomas and Edna St Vincent Millay the mood of aesthetic anxiety might have been the same . . . They claimed to be there not as virtuosos in the field of concertized folk music but as purveyors of an enjoined social consciousness and responsibility. They believed they were offering contemporaries the new musical expression of a tenuous American legacy, a legacy that threatened to become the most destructive and morally inconsistent in the nation's history," Fariña continued, casting himself in a role akin to Arthur Schlesinger at the Kennedy White House. "They felt the intolerability of bigoted opposition to civil rights, the absurdity of life under a polluted atmosphere, and they were confident that a majority of their listeners felt the same way . . . When they left the stage to a whirlwind of enthusiastic cheers, it seemed that the previously unspoken word of protest, like the torch of President Kennedy's inaugural address, had most certainly been passed."

The group—also including singers Bob Neuwirth and Paul Clayton, and Dylan's road manager Victor Maymudes—gathered the following evening in Carmel, en route to Los Angeles. The Fariñas must have been there too, for Richard describes them arriving "bearing gifts of French-fried almonds, glazed walnuts, bleached cashews, dried figs, oranges and prunes." There's no mention of alcohol, but Dylan was then partial to Beaujolais which would have gone well with the beef stew cooked by Joan Senior, who was visiting from Paris. They listened to Everly Brothers records and at some point Baez mentioned that she planned an entire album of Dylan songs. In fact, she recorded a *double* album, *Any Day Now*, released in late 1968.

In July, Newport was bigger than ever. Baez played the opening night, Dylan the closing. Each guested on the other's set and they hung out together, frolicking around the Viking Hotel's pool. "We were never more together than we were that summer," Baez would reflect. Afterwards, the couple went to Woodstock with Richard and Mimi, staying in the old farmhouse that was Albert Grossman's upstate retreat. In her memoir, Baez described Dylan as "turning out songs like ticker tape, and I was stealing them as fast as he wrote them." (He also wrote to Joan Senior, a parody of Baez's own letters. Her mother apparently never understood Dylan's allure.) In between they rode Dylan's Triumph 350, she preferring to have charge of the handlebars which, as it would turn out, was wise. They mooched around local antique shops and hung out at Bernard Paturel's Café Espresso with its chequered tablecloths and wax-encrusted Chianti bottles.

The summer sojourn was interrupted by Baez's annual concert at Forest Hills, and en route to Queens the musicians and their clan stopped over in Manhattan. Baez and Dylan returned to the Hotel Earle, on the corner of MacDougal Street and Waverly Place just across from Washington Square Park which Baez would later immortalize as "that crummy hotel over Washington Square." According to David Hajdu in *Positively 4th Street*, they played at being tourists and Baez bought everybody shoes at Allan Block's Sandal Shop on West 4th Street, a hub of the Village music scene and a place for jams—Block himself was a fiddler, and Music Inn was next door.

Despite his friendship with Dylan, Robert Shelton was highly critical of his Forest Hills appearance, noting "the lack of control of his stage manner, his raucously grating singing and the somewhat declining level of his new composition." Baez, whose political engagement drew praise, was "a much finer interpreter of Bob Dylan's songs than he was," her performance emphasizing their "power, perception and poetic wealth. She imbued his 'The Lonesome Death of Hattie Carroll' with a story-telling suspense that was masterful." Together on "With God on Our Side" they scored "a strong philosophical-musical point" but Dylan's solo performance "weakened the overall impact of the evening." The commentary is surprising, because Shelton was generally partisan, taking Dylan's side over Suze Rotolo, the girlfriend immortalized on the cover of *Freewheelin'*, and Baez. Even in the supposedly more enlightened 1980s and 1990s, he believed that male artists were entitled to rely on the woman as muse.

When they next sang together in New York it was at Philharmonic Hall, a big step up for Dylan, whose concert it was. It was Halloween and whatever spirits they were communing with, the result was a performance that quickly became the stuff of legend, one now happily available on CD. Photos show the two of them clearly having fun, Baez in a smart dark dress and Glengarry hat looking happy and relaxed. Princeton historian Sean Wilentz, who grew up over the family-owned Eighth Street Bookshop, a few paces along MacDougal from the Earle, was just into his teens but the concert made an indelible impression. In *Bob Dylan in America*, he reflected that what was almost forgotten amid the endless Baez–Dylan myths and their unmaking were "the rich fruits of their singing collaborations. Joan always seemed, onstage, the earnest, worshipful one, overly so, in the presence of the Boy Genius, and Bob would sometimes lightly mock that earnestness, as he did between songs at the Philharmonic. But when singing together they were quite a pair, their harmony lines adding depth to the melodies, their sheer pleasure in each other's company showing in their voices."

A Joan Baez–Bob Dylan concert tour was planned for spring 1965. Or was it Bob Dylan–Joan Baez? Eric Von Schmidt was commissioned to design a poster, each of their managers instructing that his star must have equal billing. Von Schmidt adapted a photo of the two of them at Club 47 and created a Toulouse Lautrec-inspired poster on which would be added the details of each concert. Several thousand were printed ahead of the first, scheduled for February, before Dylan decided Baez was too prominent and his nose too big. The posters are now collector's items. As to the tour itself, there were at least a half-dozen dates, all on East Coast campuses, where they took turns opening, each then playing a solo set before closing with duets. Baez apparently talked to the students about human rights and pacificism while Dylan largely ignored his political songs, to the disappointment of the audience. They apparently weren't talking much but in one of their few conversations he suggested they play Madison Square Garden because it would "be a gas." Baez was "scared" and suggested to Dylan that such a move would mean that "you'll be the rock 'n' roll king and I'll be the peace queen."

When Dylan had joked to his Philharmonic audience about wearing his Bob Dylan "mask," he was perhaps telling everyone that his days as a writer of socially conscious songs were over. At much the same time, Nat Hentoff, writing in *The New Yorker*, reported him as saying: "Those records I've already made, I'll stand behind them, but some of that was jumping into the scene to be heard and a lot of it was because I didn't see anybody else doing that kind of thing. Now a lot of people are doing finger-pointing songs. You know—pointing to all the things that are wrong. Me, I don't want to write *for* people anymore. You know—be a spokesman." Lest there be any doubt, he volunteered that he wasn't going down South to hold any picket signs and, besides, "The NAACP is a bunch of old guys." Founded in 1909, the National Association for the Advancement of Colored People was America's foremost civil rights organization and an organizer of the March on Washington.

It was against this backdrop that the king and queen departed a few weeks later for London. Baez had her own concert scheduled, at the Royal Albert Hall, but she'd never been to Britain and assumed that Dylan's invitation meant that he would reciprocate her artistic generosity. She addressed him directly in *And a Voice to Sing With*, the pain still raw twenty years on: "I had introduced you in the States, and to have returned the favor not only would have been natural, but would have given me the perfect leg up I needed before my own tour, which followed directly after yours." As D. A. Pennebaker's documentary *Don't Look Back* reveals, not only did he not invite her to sing—he and his hangers-on were rude and insulting. Her famous "farewell kiss," alluded to by Dylan in his 1966 song "Visions of Johanna," was captured by Pennebaker for posterity. Baez's own concert (for which her parents flew in from Paris) was a success and marked the beginning of a fifty-year relationship with British and European audiences, but it seems fair to assume that Baez was unable truly to savor the moment.

Amid all the personal *Sturm und Drang* of 1964 and 1965, Baez turned out for the Free Speech Movement in Berkeley, joined the Selma to Montgomery march in support of black voting rights, and founded the Institute for the Study of Nonviolence in Carmel Valley, while releasing two albums that demonstrated her own remarkable artistic evolution. *Joan Baez/5* is her last totally acoustic album and draws on the widest range of material. The cover features the singer in long-shot, leaning against a rock at Lone Cypress Point on the misty Monterey Peninsula. The notes are by Langston Hughes, poet, novelist, playwright, social activist, and a leading figure of the Harlem renaissance.

It opened with a song that would forever remain in her concert repertoire, "There but for Fortune," by Phil Ochs. Deceptively simple and gentle, it's one of the most humane songs ever written. There but for the grace of God go all of us, as Ochs knew better than most. Dylan is represented by just one song, "It Ain't Me Babe," its lyrics open to wide interpretation. "Birmingham

Sunday" is chillingly unambiguous, Fariña's account of the 1963 church bombing drawn from newspaper headlines and set to a traditional Scottish melody. Baez employs her full dynamic range, from *pianissimo* to a skillfully controlled *fortissimo*, expressing horror, sadness, outrage, and resignation, and supported by arpeggiated guitar accompaniment that is steady and understated. The studio echo enhances the affect. There are two Child Ballads, and a hint of country (more than a hint on the 2002 reissue) with the Johnny Cash number "I Still Miss Someone." John Jacob Niles and Richard Dyer-Bennet, two great old names of folk music, are represented with (respectively) "Go 'Way from My Window" and "So We'll Go No More a-Roving"—Byron would surely have been thrilled to hear Baez's soaring, impassioned reading of his lyric. And there's a thrilling "O' Cangaceiro," taken from the Brazilian movie of the same name, where for the first time Baez is double tracked.

The most surprising track—the most remarkable in all her repertoire—is her performance of "Bachianas Brasileiras No. 5," one of nine suites by Heitor Villa-Lobos each scored for different combinations of instruments and each a marriage of Bachian harmonic and contrapuntal techniques with Brazilian folk song. An aria for eight cellos and a soprano, "Bachianas Brasileiras No. 5" is a challenge for a trained soprano, its melody ranging across an octave and a half, much of it toward the top A on which it concludes, and with some difficult intervals and time signatures. Maynard Solomon in fact used twelve cellos, conducted by Maurice Abravanel who was signed to Vanguard with the Utah State Symphony Orchestra.

"I'd known 'Bachianas Brasileiras' for years from Bidú Sayao," Baez recalled, referring to the Brazilian soprano and a star at the Metropolitan Opera, when I asked her about the session in 1990. "From when I was tiny, it had been one of my favorite things. So I knew I just had to have the words taught to me. I have this image of me on that high note, on my tippy toes trying to get to it. Bearing wrong, head tilted back, *everything* stretched out of shape—but I was 23!" She agreed it sounded "pretty good," and it must surely have thrilled her parents. It also pleased the critics, with heavyweight *Musical America* remarking: "Anyone who doubts the aptness of Baez's voice, with its much-praised pathos combined with bell-like purity and lightness, to this rapturous and haunting music, is in for a thrilling experience."

Marc Aubort, the engineer who had worked on all Baez's records, told me: "It is indeed stunning, easily surpassing Bidú Sayao. I remember now a delightful moment when Joan interrupts Abravanel, saying: 'I don't know what you are doing with your arms'."

In comparison, *Farewell, Angelina*, released the following year, was positively conventional. In acknowledgment of the changing times it features, in addition to a string bass, an electric guitar, picked by Bruce Langhorne—he had played on Dylan's *Bringing It All Back Home* and was said to be the inspiration for the song "Mr. Tambourine Man." The cover photo, a black-and-white close-up of Baez in modish PVC, was by Richard Avedon.

The album is simultaneously milestone and stepping stone, for the tracks include folk songs (among them "The Wild Mountain Thyme," often sung in duet with Dylan) and country ("A Satisfied Mind," a song she helped put on the map), as well as Donovan's "Colours." (At Newport '65, perhaps to irritate Dylan, she had invited Donovan to join her for a duet.) For the first time she sings in French (Léo Ferré's "Pauvre Rutebeuf"), and in German (a translation of Pete Seeger's "Where Have All the Flowers Gone?"). Despite their breakup, Dylan's songs comprised the lion's share of the album, including the title track, which would remain a concert staple, and "It's All Over Now, Baby Blue," later a vehicle for her celebrated Dylan impersonation. "A Hard Rain's a-Gonna Fall," the magisterial closer, showed up live as late as 2019.

Farewell, Angelina, her sixth album, marked Joan Baez's first five years—an extraordinary opening chapter of a career nobody could have predicted. Her first three albums would shortly be awarded Gold status, while *In Concert* garnered a Grammy nomination. Nineteen-sixty-six would be a quieter year spent largely away from the concert stage, a time for reflection and consolidation.

"GIRLS SAY YES to boys who say NO," inspired by Aristophanes's play *Lysistrata*. The campaign, featuring the three Baez sisters, attracted anger from the new women's liberation movement. The poster, created by Larry Gates, raised funds for Draft Resistance

5

BRAND NEW
TENNESSEE WALTZ

By 1966, Robert Shelton was embarked on the first interviews for his Bob Dylan biography, though as it turned out the book would not appear for another twenty years. Baez was obviously going to be a key source and in April he hitched a ride in the car that was taking her from the Hotel Earle to Kennedy en route to Europe. "I'm giving up concerts for the rest of 1966," she told the journalist. "The last trip was England, and the concerts are just getting rougher and rougher. I just realized I didn't want to walk out on the stage." The main problem was in the States, "because I feel like I have to keep up with something. Europe is not that kind of a strain so I don't think it will be that difficult, say in Poland, for me to just get up and sing a couple of songs."

Shelton's transcript records that in the car with Baez were her manager Manny Greenhill and Ira Sandperl, who had tutored her in pacifism and nonviolence since she had met him at Quaker Sunday school, and with whom she had recently established the Institute for the Study of Nonviolence in Carmel Valley. The main purpose of their trip was for Baez to lead the Easter Day Anti-Nuclear March in Essen, Germany, and to participate in a festival of protest song.

The Institute—"the school" as she generally referred to it—had started life in her new home in Carmel Valley but soon ran up against zoning laws. So Baez bought a former one-room schoolhouse a few miles away. Neighbors feared an invasion of "hippies and free love subversives" would be "detrimental to the peace, morality, or general welfare of Monterey County," and would send property prices plummeting. The Board of Supervisors convened a hearing which took place in December 1965, Baez and Sandperl winning on a vote of three to two after five hours of discussion. Still, the relationship between the Institute and the local residents was uneasy and they must have felt relief when Baez moved north to the Palo Alto region, taking the Institute with her.

The initiative, facilitated by her earnings, grew out of her own quest for knowledge and a greater seriousness of purpose: "I did not want to remain an ignoramus forever and asked if [Ira] would consider tutoring me more formally," Baez recalled in *And a Voice to Sing With*. "The discussion evolved into a proposition that we form a school called the Institute for the Study of Nonviolence."

Sandperl earned his daily bread as a bookseller at Kepler's, one of three radical Bay Area bookstores. It was founded by a World War II conscientious objector named Roy Kepler, a Fulbright scholar who had worked for War Resisters' International and for the public radio station KPFA, which was the launchpad for the Pacifica Radio network. Looking for what he called "meaningful work," Kepler saw opportunities in the new paperback revolution—Lawrence Ferlinghetti had recently opened City Lights in San Francisco. He scraped together $4,000, found a storefront on El Camino Real, the San Francisco Peninsula's main artery, and opened for business in 1956, keeping late hours and stocking not only paperbacks but also literary magazines. Cody's opened the following year, and the three stores co-promoted titles such as Allen Ginsberg's controversial *Howl*. Sandperl, who ran the Palo Alto Peace Center, was Kepler's soulmate and first employee and the two men joined Stanford physicist Albert Baez in setting up the Peninsula Committee for the Abolition of Nuclear Tests. In 1957, the trio organized a demonstration outside the nearby Livermore Radiation Laboratory, at which Nobel Laureate Linus Pauling spoke.

Kepler's quickly became a hub for Stanford students, beatniks, and bohemians who could hang out over a ten-cent coffee from the ever-filled urn and maybe even buy books. Jerry Garcia and Phil Lesh met there, making it a locus for Deadheads. Having got to know Sandperl, Baez too became a regular and in due course they would all be part of a local peace movement that would, among other things, try to shut down the US Army's Oakland Induction Center. As Michael Doyle writes in *Radical Chapters: Pacifist Bookseller Roy Kepler and the Paperback Revolution*: "Throughout the first years of the sixties, in particular, the political and psychedelic threads were woven together at Kepler's."

The Institute for the Study of Nonviolence, or something like it, had been a notion in the back of both Kepler and Sandperl's minds for some time, the aim being to train activists and human rights workers and send them out into the world. Baez shared their ideals and had the profile and—most important—the wherewithal to make it happen. Sandperl was to be its president, doing most of the teaching, Baez its vice-president, Holly Chenery, who handled the Kepler's accounts, would oversee formalities. At Baez's urging, and with her financial support, the Fariñas would move west and Mimi would instruct the Institute's students in movement and dance, which she had long been studying.

Enrolling students were given an extensive reading list, prepared by Sandperl (Thoreau, Tolstoy, Huxley, Gandhi, Malcolm X all featured), and were required to learn meditation and the benefits of Quaker-style daily silence. Baez described them as "regular-looking, college-age people. Flower children, thank God, aren't interested." Students came from across the States and beyond, Baez an inspiration and a regular though low-key presence by all accounts. A Buddhist monk from South Vietnam came to teach, and she and Ira hoped that Thomas Merton, the Trappist monk, mystic, social activist, and best-selling author of *The Seven Storey Mountain*, might consider emerging from behind the walls of his Kentucky monastery to lead some classes.

The visit that she and Sandperl made to the Abbey of Our Lady of Gethsemani would, years later, inspire a song—recorded with The Grateful Dead, performed at a few concerts but never officially released. Merton had been writing openly about Vietnam and some of his many books were on the Institute's reading list. According to Robert Hudson's account—*The Monk's Record Player: Thomas Merton, Bob Dylan and the Perilous Summer of 1966*—Baez and Sandperl visited Merton at the Louisville monastery (the mother house of American Trappistine monasteries) en route to South Carolina to meet with Martin Luther King Jr. and members of the Southern Christian Leadership Conference to discuss organized nonviolence. They arrived to a warm reception from the brothers, Merton eager to leave his monastic surroundings for lunch. He chose a fast food joint and ordered two cheeseburgers, fries, and a chocolate milkshake. His hosts each had a hamburger and coke, their feast taken in a nearby field. "The three of us, sort of Piglet, Owl, and Pooh," Baez wrote. "Merton looked considerably like Pooh." They discussed Vietnam, nonviolence and discipline, and Merton's desire to travel, thwarted by his Abbot. Afterwards, they returned to his small cabin where the monk produced a bottle of Irish whiskey and admitted to having fallen in love with the young nurse who'd looked after him following recent spinal surgery. According to Hudson, both Merton and the nurse shared an enthusiasm for Baez's music, agreeing they would each listen to her recording of "Silver Dagger," a song of unrequited love from her debut album, every day at 1.30am. In his *Midsummer Diary*, Merton confided: "All the love and death in me are at the moment wound up in Joan Baez's song 'Silver Dagger.' I can't get it out of my head, day or night. I am obsessed with it." Did he tell the singer that day? In any event, Merton never made it to Carmel.

Nor did Martin Luther King who, as a Nobel Laureate, was more in demand than ever. He took his campaign north, the ambitious Chicago Freedom Movement demanding better housing, access to

Bob Muson's poster for the 1965 Big Sur Folk Festival, a sort-of West Coast Newport held in the grounds of the Esalen Institute, birthplace of the Human Potential Movement

education, health, jobs, and much besides. The year-long push was largely responsible for the 1968 Fair Housing Act. In September, Baez and Sandperl joined him in Grenada, Mississippi, as King sought to desegregate the schools. An economic boycott was beginning to bite and the city's fragile peace was being tested. A judge ordered the children be protected from attacks but news footage, still painful to watch, reveals the harsh reality. Baez, with King and leading a group of black schoolchildren, was called "nigger-lover" by a little white boy, while a woman backed abruptly out of her drive, forcing the marchers to break. A block from the school, twenty troopers barred the way: Only parents beyond this point, they were told. Baez explained she was there on behalf of parents who had asked her to carry application forms for their children to transfer to the formerly all-white school. The deadline had expired, but the parents wanted it extended. The evening news showed little black children being denied the right to education. Baez explained she was marching because of the guilt she felt for white America and the shame at its treatment of black America. Perhaps because her presence attracted the cameras, there was no violence that day.

Meanwhile, since the end of 1965, Baez had been on something of a musical vacation. Whether she needed much persuading to sign up for *The Big T.N.T. Show*, "a concert film" recorded live at L.A.'s Moulin Rouge on November 29, is unknown though she's scarcely if ever talked about it. Originally titled *This Could Be the Night*, its theme song written by Harry Nilsson, it was hosted by David McCallum (*The Man from U.N.C.LE.*) and featured The Byrds, Ray Charles, Bo Diddley, Petula Clark, Ike and Tina Turner, and The Ronettes. Amid the sequins and beehives, Baez is demure in a dark dress and heels, her hair long and glossy. She sings "500 Miles" and "There but for Fortune," the audience (including Frank Zappa) suspending its screaming during her performance but clapping wildly at its end. Donovan is at his most fey as he introduces Baez for the show's final song. "You've Lost That Lovin' Feeling" finds her seated at the piano, next to a flat-capped Phil Spector who plays and directs the orchestra. It's a classic song but not one that suits her voice, or not her mid-sixties voice, especially as the song reaches its denouement. It would have worked better with a second voice to provide both harmony and the call-and-response bridge that makes The Righteous Brothers' original so memorable.

Perhaps Baez did it to cock a snook at Dylan or perhaps she was egged on by Richard Fariña, because by the time the show aired in April 1966 she was in the studio under his direction recording "a rock 'n' roll album," though she told Shelton that "it isn't really all hard rock, it's a variety of things." The journalist asked if she'd heard about "the controversy in the east about electrification. The purists are screaming." Baez had been present when Dylan plugged in at Newport '65, though it was nothing to the brouhaha that lay ahead. Baez herself had received "letters, terrible letters, from people who are frightened. I'm not sure *why* they are frightened. Before I had even planned a rock record, only whispered it, I got letters saying please don't do rock 'n' roll. There's really not that much change in my voice—there's a little freedom with all the instruments but it's pretty much the same voice. I have found it a terribly liberating thing to record with other instruments."

Her comments are intriguing because it's not clear from *The Big T.N.T. Show* (released in 2016 on DVD), and from the unreleased tapes of Fariña's rock album, that she *felt* liberated. Richard and Mimi had been a hit at Newport '65, playing three different sets, most memorably the Sunday afternoon concert in the rain, when Baez joined them. Richard had contributed a song, and dulcimer accompaniment, to Judy Collins's *Fifth Album*, and he and Mimi had two folk rock albums out, Baez having helped secure their Vanguard contract by recording a handful of Fariña demos for Maynard Solomon. And his novel, *Been Down So Long It Looks Like Up to Me*, had a spring publication date, so Richard was probably on a high. Despite her oft-expressed doubts about him ("blatantly ambitious, lovable, impossible, charming, obnoxious, tirelessly active—a bright, talented, sheepish, tricky, curly-haired man-child of darkness," as she wrote in *Daybreak*), not to mention the whole Baez family's anxiety about Mimi marrying at such a young age, Joan herself had warmed to Fariña. They had wed secretly in Paris, in April 1963, then officially in California on August 24 with Thomas Pynchon as best man. Now they were all in Carmel and the three of them spent lots of time together—informal dinner parties where Fariña cooked and he and Joan play-acted and made mischief and listened to old records that she and Mimi had bought. In an interview for *Positively 4th Street*, Baez told David Hajdu they were singing along one night when Fariña suggested she make a rock album, a thought that had never occurred to her. "Dick got this brainstorm. He could be terribly persuasive and it started to sound like a good idea."

Solomon was probably aghast but Baez was Vanguard's best-selling artist so he suggested the inexperienced Fariña work with arranger Trade Martin. Recording began in New York toward the end of March with a seventeen-piece band and chorus. Exactly what they recorded is open to debate. The material in circulation doesn't include "Anyone Who Had a Heart" or "What the World Needs Now," which are frequently mentioned, but instead two less good Burt Bacharach and Hal David numbers, "Little Red Book" and "Always Something There to Remind Me," and in place of Paul Simon's "Sounds of Silence" there's "Homeward Bound." There's an early attempt at Dylan's "One Too Many Mornings," jauntier than the *Any Day Now* version, while Donovan's "Turquoise" would be revisited on *Joan*. A low point is a strange cover of Utah Phillips's "Rock Salt and Nails," a country song that would feature on *David's Album* but which is here badly popified and seems to have a verse of "Wagoner's Lad" grafted on to it. Lennon and McCartney's "Yesterday" would appear in acoustic form on *Live in Italy*, its universality likely a deciding factor in front of a rambunctious audience. Of Fariña's own songs, "Pack Up Your Sorrows" (co-written with Baez's elder sister, Pauline) was released as a single, while "Swallow Song" and "All the World Has Gone By" would form part of *Memories*, the album Joan and Mimi assembled after Richard's death.

Unusually, Baez undertook interviews about the work in progress, even allowing journalists and (according to the *Village Voice*) at least one photographer into the studio. Among them was Alice M. Bunzl, who wrote in Jerome Agel's monthly *Books* that the singer "didn't need to change her voice or style to be at home in the medium; her voice and her melodic lines are as musically phrased, as direct, as warm, as clear as anything previous." Bunzl, who mentioned seeing scores for Pete Seeger's "Oh, Had I a Golden Thread" and Dylan's "Chimes of Freedom," suggested that the new album would be "a happy integration of many musical elements." Another visitor was Dick Schaap of the *New York Herald Tribune*, who quoted Solomon as saying the record had "folk, rock and classical elements," while Fariña described it as "folk rock." Baez herself said: "I hate to call it anything. It's different. That's all."

Within a few weeks, and on his wife's twenty-first birthday, Fariña would die in a motorcycle spill in Carmel following the launch party for his novel. Would the album have been released had he lived to finish it? Possibly, but it seems more likely that Baez would have listened to it critically, alone, in the cold light of day, and with Solomon, and decided that it just didn't cut the mustard. When we spoke in Bristol in 2018, she referred to it as "that goofy album I did with Richard Fariña." A decade or so later, her voice mellower and her style looser, she might have handled such songs better. As it stands, it's akin to the uncomfortable excursions Kiri Te Kanawa and Jessye Norman made into the Great American Songbook—her voice was just too big for the material.

Instead, she returned to the studio to make a Christmas album, the first of three collaborations with composer and arranger Peter Schickele (the two later worked on the soundtrack of *Silent Running*), a Juilliard graduate who enjoyed a long career as a musical satirist, creating the character of P. D. Q. Bach, "the only forgotten son" of the Bach family, and writing such works as the *1712 Overture* and *Iphigenia in Brooklyn*. All that meant that *Noël* was not at all a typical Christmas album. There's not a Santa or a roasting chestnut in sight as Baez sings to Baroque-inspired arrangements of recorders and viols, lute, harpsichord, organ, woodwind, strings, and percussion. The selection included a number of well-known carols, plus the traditional-sounding "I Wonder as I Wander" by John Jacob Niles, and that modern classic "The Little Drummer Boy." Schubert's "Ave Maria" is impressive, the intonation perfect, but the tone too ethereal and the tempo too slow. Most memorable are "The Carol of the Birds" and "Cantique de Noël," where the youthful beauty of Baez's soprano, counterpointed against a lush arrangement, is perfectly demonstrated.

It was Schickele's "first major arranging gig," he recalled in a note for the 2001 reissue, and "Joan was a joy to work with. A natural musician. Even when she just sat down and made a junk tape of a song so that I would have something to work from, every note was in tune, and the crystalline vocal quality for which she is justly famous never deserted her." With *Noël*, it almost feels as if Baez was cleansing her soul having strayed to "the other side."

The sessions for *Joan*, her eighth album, took place in April 1967 at Vanguard's new West 23rd Street Studios, with release in August. She was "moving towards another style of repertory," Arthur Levy reported Maynard Solomon as telling him when they talked during Vanguard's millennial rerelease program. Again, Schickele observed her innate musicianship and they were able to record three or four songs a session. The best of contemporary songwriters were represented—Lennon and McCartney, Paul Simon, Tim Hardin, and Jacques Brel, whose "La Colombe," sung here in English, is magisterial, brass and drums adding an ironically martial air, while the strings seem to weep with the sadness of the lyric. "Annabel Lee," Edgar Allan Poe's last poem, set to music by Don Dilworth, finally makes it on to disc, while "The Greenwood Side" is the last Child Ballad she would record. Baez makes her debut as a songwriter with "North" and "Saigon Bride," the lyrics, by Nina Duschek, having arrived unexpectedly in the mail. And there's a tribute to her late brother-in-law, "Children of Darkness," which Richard and Mimi had recorded, in a very different style, on their second and final album, *Reflections in a Crystal Wind*.

There would be a handful of US concerts in 1967, plus one in Montreal, but the year began in Japan. Still an unhappy flyer, Baez had long put off a visit that would take her to four cities for nine concerts, including a benefit in Hiroshima for the victims of that city and Nagasaki, for which Hiroshima did not wish to share the proceeds. Baez and her party—including Mimi, and Ira and his wife—quickly became suspicious about the interpreter, for audience reactions to what he said in Japanese seemed to bear no relation to what she had said in English. Only when she was back home in California did she learn that the CIA had pressured the interpreter to mistranslate her political remarks. "If you don't cooperate, you will have trouble in your work in the future," *The New York Times* reported his being told.

Clearly, Baez was now regarded as a problem. Not only was she still refusing to volunteer her income tax in protest against American policy in Vietnam, she was also encouraging others to do so, and before the year was out she would be arrested and imprisoned twice, the second time with her mother, for blocking the Armed Forces Induction Center in Oakland and for aiding and abetting draft resisters. She was still in jail on her twenty-seventh birthday, and a couple of days later Martin Luther King Jr. visited with Andy Young, later President Carter's UN representative. So too a young cowboy-hatted Stanford student activist named David Harris, leader of Resistance, a movement dedicated to helping young men refuse the draft and to work together to oppose and end the war. (Their story is told in a documentary, *The Boys Who Said NO! Draft Resistance and the Vietnam War*, directed by Judith Ehrlich.)

The European Exchange System announced that sales of Baez's records would be banned from US army base shops, a move the American military denied was censorship. The Daughters of the American Revolution (DAR) denied her permission to use their Constitution Hall in Washington, D.C., as she knew they would. Instead she played a free concert to thirty thousand people in the shadow of the Washington Monument, permission surprisingly granted by the Department of the Interior.

Politically and creatively, Baez was busy. As she'd shyly told Robert Shelton, she was writing a book. An autobiography "sounds so pretentious," she said, so it would be "short little incidents of what happened to me."

Released from Santa Rita Rehabilitation Center in mid-January 1968, Baez was quickly in touch with David Harris. Not surprisingly, given their Stanford and Kepler's connections, they had Ira Sandperl in common and before long the three of them were on a college speaking tour for Resistance, Harris resigning his role as president of Stanford's student body to work full time organizing draft resistance. The three Baez sisters posed for a fundraising poster, "GIRLS SAY YES to boys who say NO," which angered the women's liberation movement, even though Joan, Pauline, and Mimi were clothed and casually assertive-looking. Intellectuals would have got the reference to Aristophanes's *Lysistrata*, which it turns on its head.

On March 26, Baez and Harris married at New York's St. Clement's Episcopal Church, speaking Quaker wedding vows. The groom wore a dark three-piece suit and tie, walrus moustache, and whiskers, the bride a Grecian-style floor-length dress. Judy Collins sang. The following day they gave a press conference, and their honeymoon was spent on a concert and lecture tour in support of draft resistance, a high-profile action that assured Harris would not be treated leniently.

The previous October, he had returned his draft card and shortly thereafter the draft board ordered him to report to the Oakland Induction Center in January. Harris didn't comply and so, on May 28, the Honorable Oliver Carter, who would preside over the notorious Patty Hearst trial, accused Harris of a "refusal to submit to a lawful order of induction." The jury retired for eight hours before the judge instructed that the only possible verdict was: guilty. Eventually, that verdict was handed down and Judge Carter told

Harris: "Normally, sentence is a question of rehabilitation. Your case is an exception. You don't need to be rehabilitated. You don't want to be rehabilitated. Perhaps you shouldn't be rehabilitated. But you will be punished." He was sentenced to three years and told he could appeal, which he did—unsuccessfully.

The period is chronicled in the documentary *Carry It On*. Baez was persuaded by Harris to leave her architect-designed home in Carmel Valley (which in 2009 was added to Monterey County's Register of Historic Resources on account of its vernacular style) and go to live in a commune, one of a cluster in Los Altos Hills. Its mission was "to provide an opportunity for peaceful and harmonious social commingling" and it had evolved out of the sixties counterculture. Many of the residents were draft resisters, and Baez named it Struggle Mountain. And it may well have been quite a struggle for her, at twenty-eight, to give up both her privacy and a home with so many memories. Nevertheless, it was there, on July 15, with all eyes on the Moon landing, that Harris was arrested, federal marshals arriving with a warrant. As he was being shackled, the communards affixed a "RESIST THE DRAFT" bumper sticker to the squad car.

A month later, Baez was at Woodstock, hair cropped short and looking very pregnant in a kaftan as she talked proudly about her husband. "This is an organizing song," she said before launching in to "Joe Hill," the union ballad that Paul Robeson had sung years earlier. "And I was happy to find out that after David had been in jail for two and a half weeks, he already had a very, very good hunger strike going with forty-two federal prisoners, none of whom were draft people." She sang "Swing Low, Sweet Chariot" *a cappella* and closed with "We Shall Overcome." Helicoptered in with her mother and Janis Joplin, she also sang from the free stage at the hog farm, hanging out for three days but worried that the food would be laced with drugs. Mitch Blank, a student who helped with the build and take-down of the vast rig, managed to swap the hot dog she was offered for watermelon.

Baez—among the highest paid artists at $10,000, but one of very few women on the bill—was the conscience of Woodstock, determined to put her message across even as dawn broke and everyone lay stoned. "Though a few people were singing about the war, like Country Joe, it was a joy festival," she reflected in *The New York Times*'s fifty-year retrospective. "A revolution, I would think, involves taking risks and going to jail and all that stuff that happened in the civil rights movement and the draft resistance. I was still in my own mode, which was talking about what was going on outside. David was in jail, I was pregnant, and it was all about changing the world and taking risks. I know people got bored with me talking about it, but my mission continued, even into this big festival." Essentially, the rain, isolation, and deprivation meant that for one long crazy weekend, everyone was caring and sharing, cops putting away their guns and helping hippies roast hot dogs.

Amid all this frenetic political activity, Baez had found time to finish her memoir and to record two albums. *Daybreak* received mixed reviews, her writing praised for its vivid portraiture of her parents and childhood, but criticized (by Richard Goldstein in *The New York Times*) for a style "somewhat like a cross between Kahlil Gibran and Winnie-the-Pooh." There was almost nothing about her career and, until editor E. L. Doctorow (later of *Ragtime* fame) intervened, nothing at all about Dylan. Perhaps as she herself had hinted, she was too young for such a project, or perhaps she simply lost interest as the tempo of her life increased.

There were two albums in 1968. The first of them, *Baptism: A Journey Through Our Time*, the last of the Schickele albums, was a collection of poetry, prose, and songs spanning centuries and continents. Maynard Solomon had made the selection, which Baez approved, and then Schickele set to work on the scores. The album hung around the charts for a few months but critics were for the first time harsh. *Rolling Stone* thought it "most ambitious" with "gorgeous moments" but "an effortful listen." Calling Baez "the matron saint of the hippies," *Stereo Review* loved "the waterfall-transparent soprano" but thought she "stumbles badly in the spoken portions of this splendidly produced and arranged album." While she may briefly have studied drama, Baez had no experience as an actress and her speaking voice is not yet resonant enough to convey the gravitas of the words.

In October 1968, she went to Nashville to make good on her promise of a Bob Dylan album. Indeed, what emerged was a *double* album, a rarity in those days and a first for Baez. The musicians— many of whom had played on Dylan's own Nashville excursions— were skeptical of her politics, and "WALLACE FOR PRESIDENT" stickers appeared on their equipment. They were quickly won over by her warmth and musicianship. Arthur Levy's reissue notes describe how Baez sat cross-legged on the studio floor, running through the songs she planned to record while the session musicians took notes and direction from leader Grady Martin. Then she'd stand at the microphone, tapes running, and the musicians took cues from both her and each other, the arrangements thus "a kind of collective improvisation at its very finest." It's hard to disagree with Levy's assertion that the original sixteen songs were arranged as a song cycle, the order as well as the songs themselves telling their own story about singer and songwriter. Dylan would later claim in song that he had written "Sad-Eyed Lady of the Lowlands" for his wife Sara, "staying up for days in the Chelsea Hotel," though all the evidence points to him writing it in Nashville, during the *Blonde on Blonde* sessions—and tapes of Robert Shelton interviewing Dylan in Denver in 1966 indicate he was working on it even earlier. Whatever, this epic—which Baez sang in concert at Wembley in 1973—contains lines that could be said to allude to both Joan *and* Sara. As *Renaldo and Clara* would later reveal, the two women were interchangeable in Dylan's mind.

Baez too had now "gone electric," but without any of the drama that had attended Dylan's plugging in. *Any Day Now* is an album with a distinct country accent and it features some characteristically brilliant playing from musicians who, despite all, are clearly simpatico. Baez is discovering her lower notes and the voice is mellower now, more expressive. The album, which would be declared Gold, was surely a nice Christmas present for her husband, whose love of country music went deeper than the cowboy hat and boots he routinely sported. It was her next opus, recorded at the same time in less than a week in Nashville and released in May '69, that bore his name. *David's Album* was "a gift" to the man to whom she had been married for a year. They were a power couple before the term was invented, each struggling for equilibrium and space in a very public life beset by internal and external stresses.

The songs on *David's Album* were easy pickings for the musicians Baez quickly came to regard as "good ol' buddies." There was old country ("The Tramp on the Street," "Poor Wayfaring Stranger," and "Will the Circle Be Unbroken") and new country (Gram Parsons's "Hickory Wind" and "If I Knew," Baez's elder sister, Pauline, having written a melody to more words by Nina Duschek). "Green, Green Grass of Home" was a favorite of David, while the exuberant "My Home's Across the Blue Ridge Mountains" came from The Carter Family, whose music Baez had admired way back in Boston. From her earliest days onstage, Baez had mixed folk with country, and there had been city concerts with Flatt and Scruggs at a time when country music was regarded as hick outside the South. Now she was merging both those musical sensibilities with soft rock.

Come summer, with Harris in jail, Baez continued her tour, including Madison Square Garden where, as on every other date, the maximum ticket price permitted was $2. Filming for the documentary that would become *Carry It On* was wrapped up. In September, Baez, six months' pregnant, returned again to Nashville.

One Day at a Time would be released to mixed reviews the following year, yet its fusion of country and rock has stood the test of time. Baez is in fine voice, supported on a couple of tracks by the mellifluous tenor of Jeffrey Shurtleff, one half of the Struggle

Mountain Resistance Band from Woodstock. (The 2004 rerelease features two additional duets that should never have been cut from the original.) The album is notable for two songs written by Baez: "Sweet Sir Galahad," about sister Mimi emerging from the grief of losing Richard to find love again; and "Song for David." From The Rolling Stones' *Beggars Banquet* she plucked Jagger and Richards's "No Expectations." Quietly powerful but much less known, "Ghetto" by Bonnie Bramlett, Homer Banks, and Bettye Crutcher is redolent of the sense of resignation, hopelessness, and fear that engulfed America's poor amid the violence of 1968: You can smell the smoke and feel the latent violence. As to the title song, life surely was "one day at a time" as she awaited the birth of her son.

Gabriel Earle Harris arrived on December 2, 1969, and he would meet his father at Safford Prison, Arizona, the following month. Harris was paroled in March. Forty years later, Baez told the *Sunday Times*:

> Gabe arrived at a pretty intense time. I was thrilled to be a mother, but there was so much other stuff happening in my life I thought it would be selfish of me to take time off. For the first year of Gabe's life, David was still in jail and I toured almost constantly. Things became even more complicated after David was released. We were living in a commune in California. Not a hippie commune—we were all political activists. But it was at that point that David and I started to drift apart and eventually we got divorced. Of course, poor Gabe was caught up in the middle of all this. I had no idea what to expect from motherhood. It's a bit like getting old. You don't know what it's like until you get there.

In 1970, Baez was giving concerts across Europe, including a headlining appearance in August at the Isle of Wight Festival, which Dylan had played the previous year. From now on, she would tour abroad annually. Gabe was an international traveler at the youngest age, dandled on some celebrated laps and living a gypsy life, just like his mother; a life that she would enshrine in song.

The tour included concerts in Rome and Milan, the latter at the city's football stadium where, on the second night, Italy's many political factions battled it out while Baez, marooned onstage in the middle of the pitch, tried in vain to keep control of the audience. Amid the chaos, an incredible storm broke; the electricity died; and the singer was carried bodily to safety by a tall bearded student in a scene she depicts vividly and with good humor in her memoir.

Was it on this trip that film composer Ennio Morricone asked her to write the lyrics to his score for the movie *Sacco and Vanzetti*, the celebrated story of the two Italian-American anarchists executed in 1927? "Here's to You," sung over the credits, would be a staple of many concerts, the words taken from Bartolomeo Vanzetti's pre-execution statement that "the agony is our triumph"—indeed, the song would have many lives beyond the film, beyond Baez. "The Ballad of Sacco and Vanzetti" quoted from Vanzetti's letters to his father, and from Emma Lazarus's poem "The New Colossus," inscribed on the base of the Statue of Liberty. Baez also quoted from Christ's Sermon on the Mount—which suggests that within the film project lay the seeds from which her next album would grow.

Blessed Are . . . would be her last album for Vanguard and the only one not produced by Maynard Solomon. To record it she returned to Nashville—and to the new Quadrafonic Studios opened that year by Norbert Putnam. In an interview with Rick Clark of *Mix*, Putnam recalled: "I had introduced Kris Kristofferson to Baez, and he was originally supposed to produce it. After some thought, he ended up talking with Baez, and they both felt I should do it. I asked her, 'Would you do it in my new studio?' 'Sure,' she said. I called [pianist] David Briggs and said, 'Wow! We've got a star coming to our new studio.' She had warned me, 'I've got twenty-four sides to record, and we need to do it in five days.' I said, 'That means we are only doing a song-and-a-half per session, and we are used to doing four.'" She told Putnam she wanted a hit record and she believed he and his Muscle Shoals friends could help achieve it.

The double album brought together songs from a wide variety of writers: Jagger and Richards, Lennon and McCartney, and Stevie Wonder the most celebrated among them, Baez picking personal favorites. Quad had become a place to hang out, its well-stocked bar doubtless an attraction, and Arthur Levy reports that the Baez sessions became a magnet for lesser-known songwriters. Mickey Newbury, Jesse Winchester, and David Patton were among those who would see their credits on *Blessed Are . . .* And there was Kristofferson's "Help Me Make It Through the Night," which the Silver-Tongued Devil, to whom she had grown close, complained had languished in her unopened mail for a year or two. But the most notable feature of the set was Baez's emergence as a truly natural songwriter, with nine songs including the title track. Each was as direct as Dylan's were so often obscure; about friends, family, lovers; about chance encounters; the spiritual and the temporal. There was a lullaby for Gabriel, a charming song about Marie Flore, a little girl she'd met in Arles and with whom she would forever remain friends, and a striking bluesy lament for her husband, whose artwork adorned the sleeve.

And the hit record? "The Night They Drove Old Dixie Down," with all of Quad's aspirant songwriters and hangers-on adding their voices on the chorus. Robbie Robertson's song from The Band's second album was a Top 10 hit for Baez on both sides of the Atlantic which found new life in 2017 on the soundtrack of the award-winning movie *Three Billboards Outside Ebbing, Missouri.* It was a Gold single from a Gold album. Over their eleven years together, Maynard Solomon and Joan Baez had done well for each other. They parted in style.

A concert, at New York's Felt Forum, marking the third anniversary of the Chilean coup. Orlando Letelier, who had been Salvador Allende's Ambssador to the US, was stripped of his citizenship on the day of the concert

6

ONE DAY AT A TIME

By the time *Carry It On*, the movie and the album, were released, Baez and Harris had separated, and they would divorce in 1973. It's difficult to imagine many couples surviving such tempest-tossed times and both of them, and probably their son, were bruised by the experience. But they were dignified in public, and when they appeared on camera together in *How Sweet the Sound* (2009) it was clear the spark had not been entirely extinguished.

The Joan Baez that emerged from their time together was now a mature thinker and speaker, light years away from the young woman who once told an audience that she had something to say but didn't know how to say it, or from the fey author of *Daybreak*. It seems reasonable to assume that Harris, and some of his Resistance friends, helped in that process—the documentary revealed him to be an eloquent speaker. Baez, tempered by age (though still only thirty) and experience—and no doubt by the exigencies of communal living—had grown in confidence and was learning how to use her voice and her presence to best effect. The couple continued to work together on antiwar projects, including Stop Our Ship, a West Coast movement which sprang up as US military tactics in Vietnam shifted from ground to air war. Designed to prevent the dispatch of aircraft carriers to the Gulf of Tonkin, it won a good deal of public support and a number of sailors joined the protestors and refused to sail with their ships.

Baez would soon relocate to a modest home in Woodside, on the San Francisco Peninsula, to begin a new life. Both parents shared custody of Gabriel. Joan was assisted by her old friend Christine Coffey, a blunt Yorkshire woman who had been in the Signal Corps during World War II, settling in California for health reasons. They had met in Carmel in 1961 when Baez came to sing at a birthday party for a terminally ill young woman for whom Christine was then caring. After an emotional encounter, Coffey invited the singer into the kitchen for a restorative cup of tea. They hit it off. "I told her I was having a brunch the following Sunday and she was welcome to come—as long as she didn't wear blue jeans, which always remind me of Communist China," Coffey told me. So began a relationship with the Baez family that lasted until Coffey's death in May 2002. She was cook, "general factotum," and nanny to Gabriel, ensuring his speech did not acquire the American slang of his school friends; chewing gum was discouraged. Coffey never failed to speak her mind, something Baez appreciated.

Baez devoted much of 1972 to various causes but early in the year she returned to Nashville and Quadrafonic to record a new album, her first for A&M Records. This time she co-produced with Norbert Putnam. *Come from the Shadows* had more than a few country overtones and the six Baez originals were a mix of the personal and the overtly political. One of them, "Myths," was explicitly about the marriage breakup and it was preceded by "Love Song to a Stranger," a public confession of what Harris presumably already knew. Two other songs which she did not write mused on their situation: "A Stranger in My Place" on mistakes made, a love gone bad, of her having "fallen short"; and "Tumbleweed" acknowledged the pain and suggested a search for direction, though Baez was hardly "just a slave to the wind."

"All the Weary Mothers of the Earth (People's Union #1)" would have made Mother Jones proud, while "Prison Trilogy," based on stories she'd learned from her ex-husband, challenged America's penal system. But the most viscerally harrowing track was "Song of Bangladesh," about the March 1971 massacre of Bengali students, many in their beds, by the American-armed

Pakistani army—a slaughter of the innocents which marked the beginning of the genocide. It was preceded by "To Bobby" in which Baez pleaded for Dylan to return to the fray. (On Bangladesh as on much else he was silent, though he did lend his presence to George Harrison's Concert for Bangladesh in August 1971.) John Lennon's "Imagine," then new and relatively unknown, closed the album, the title of which came from lyrics to "The Partisan," a song from World War II. Baez had sung it for Melina Mercouri and her husband Jules Dassin the previous October at a Berkeley benefit for the Greek Resistance—Greece was suffering the agony of military dictatorship.

The album's back cover showed a contemplative Baez in the woods with her dog. Running down the side of the photo, her liner notes talked about Vietnam and concluded with a call for action. "What I'm asking you to do is take some risks. Stop paying war taxes, refuse the armed forces, organize against the air war, support the strikes and boycotts of farmers, workers and poor people, analyze the flag salute, give up the nation state, share your money, refuse to hate, be willing to work . . . in short, sisters and brothers, arm up with love and come from the shadows." The front cover showed an elderly couple giving peace signs as they are arrested at Oakland Induction Center.

With a little boy to look after, Baez probably wasn't keen to return to jail, so instead she worked—for much of 1972—with Ginetta Sagan. A Jewish-Italian woman who had been arrested and tortured for working with the Italian resistance during World War II, she had narrowly escaped execution. Later, while living in the San Francisco Bay Area, she discovered that Baez was a near neighbor and showed up unbidden on her doorstep with "a big messy bundle of documents," persuading her to help set up a West Coast outpost of Amnesty International. The human rights organization was founded in London in 1961 and had an office in New York, with eighteen chapters and just a few hundred members nationwide.

The Berkeley concert with Mercouri and Dassin—an idea cooked up by Sagan when everyone found themselves together in Paris—provided the launchpad. The ten-thousand-strong audience at the famed Greek Theatre on the university's campus chanting "Free Greece, Free Greece" were all potential supporters. By the end of 1976, Amnesty International USA had seventy-five West Coast chapters and seventy thousand members nationwide. Sagan said she had asked Baez for help and she "promptly responded and has been our greatest help . . . We needed a voice and Joanie was the first one to join me."

Sagan's guest room was their office, Baez answering the phone, stuffing envelopes and, crucially, fundraising, sometimes with small dinners at her home. Soon she was on the organization's Advisory Board. Following the CIA-sponsored coup in Chile, which removed the democratically elected President Allende and installed General Pinochet, the two women concentrated on raising funds to send doctors into the country from where came widespread reports of torture. There were concerts, vigils, and demonstrations, leafleting at San Francisco screenings of Costa-Gavras's harrowing *State of Siege*. Baez attended the inaugural gatherings in New York and Paris of Amnesty's Campaign to Abolish Torture. Its goal was a UN resolution to "outlaw the torture of prisoners throughout the world." The petition for it would garner one million signatures from eighty-five countries, and in London for a concert in April 1973 at Wembley's Empire Pool, Baez was the first to sign. At an intensely political event reflecting her recent trip to Hanoi, she publicized Amnesty from the stage and with leaflets.

Spring 1972 was the occasion for a Washington, D.C. demonstration sponsored by Baez. Ring Around Congress was Ira Sandperl's idea and the aim was a "symbolic act of solidarity with the women and children of Vietnam" and a demand that no more tax dollars go toward the war. Baez attempted to bring together a number of high-profile figures and organizations, initially with great success. Then came threats, recriminations, and ultimately sabotage—years later the Watergate hearings would reveal the true story. Finally, Hurricane Agnes all but put the kibosh on proceedings, though 2,500 women *did* march on the Capitol and, with a stretch, joined arms to encircle Congress.

In November, Baez joined B.B. King, The Voices of East Harlem, and her sister Mimi Fariña for a Thanksgiving concert at Sing Sing Prison, her performance of "I Shall Be Released" inevitably winning the biggest cheer. Did the concert contain the seeds of Bread and Roses, the organization Fariña founded just a couple of years later to bring free music to institutions?

The invitation that would test her courage, commitment, and resolve arrived out of the blue the following month from Cora Weiss, an early member of the Women's Strike for Peace, with which Baez had worked, and head of the Liaison Committee, which was dedicated to maintaining friendly relations with the Vietnamese people by sending American visitors to North Vietnam. The singer, who would deliver Christmas mail to American PoWs in Hanoi, would be a guest of the Committee for Solidarity with the American People and she would be traveling with Telford Taylor, a former brigadier general and lawyer who had been a Nuremberg prosecutor; an Episcopalian minister; and a Vietnam Veteran Against the War. It was to be a short visit and they would be home in time for the holidays. Nobody had expected President Nixon would shortly unleash Operation Linebacker II, an air campaign that would see twenty thousand tonnes of bombs dropped, mostly on Hanoi, leaving more than a thousand people dead. The first B-52s discharged their load on December 18, the group's third night in the city, and continued bombing for twelve days. North Vietnam would effectively be bombed to the negotiating table: The Paris Peace Accords were signed in late January 1973.

Baez would arrive home on New Year's Day, clearly traumatized by the experience about which she proceeded to speak and write. "If there was ever a time when I would give up my nonviolence it was sitting under the B52s and scared to death," she told me a decade later. "I had never had to face my own mortality before and I didn't like it a bit. I was not ready to die, but there I was." The fifteen hours of recordings she had made during the trip would form the basis for her next album, and before heading back to Nashville and Norbert Putnam she made her own rough edit.

Where Are You Now, My Son?, released in May 1973, was her second outing for A&M and both parties had been expecting more commercial fare. It featured one side of mostly Baez originals, including "Rider, Pass By," a powerful if opaque song about the burgeoning gay liberation movement. Side two, the title track, was a twenty-two-minute song-poem spoken and sung by Baez to a sound collage of her twelve days under the bombs: children singing, women crying; air raid sirens; talk and laughter in the shelters; her own singing, including the midnight Mass that was interrupted by a raid. The song's refrain was taken from the chant of an elderly bombing victim: "Oh, my son, where are you?"

Before the end of the year Baez was in the studio again, this time in Los Angeles, fired up by events in Chile to record an album in Spanish. *Gracias a la Vida* carried a dedication "to my father who gave me my Latin name and whatever optimism about life I may claim to have" but it was conceived as "a message of hope" for those suffering under the American-backed military junta which had ousted and executed a democratically elected president. The album itself was a political statement, and as other countries in Latin America fell to brutal regimes, it found a ready audience. Among the songs featured was "Te Recuerdo Amanda," a love song with a subtext by Victor Jara, the Chilean singer-songwriter tortured and murdered in the days following the coup, and "No Nos Moverán" ("We Shall Not Be Moved"), but the overall tone of the album—not least VioletaParra's title song, henceforth a concert staple—was joyous. Despite positive reviews (*Stereo Review* noted Baez's "fabulous natural musicality and that electrifying intensity with a lyric") *Gracias a la Vida* was not a Stateside success, though it did inspire Linda Ronstadt to explore her own Latino heritage.

The album was backed up by a tour of Latin America, her first, taking in Buenos Aires, where she played two concerts, each with audiences of more than twelve thousand, Mercedes Sosa joining her for one of them; Rosario, to which Baez traveled by a slow train, giving an impromptu concert on board; and Caracas. John Wasserman of the *San Francisco Chronicle* reported that while on tour she practiced her Spanish and met with journalists, academics, students, workers, radicals, and political prisoners—"anyone who could give her information. Anyone who could disseminate her information."

No one had thrown any eggs, or worse, which Baez regarded as a triumph. "In Latin America, everything is violence," Wasserman reported her as saying. "The right wing is busy crushing one country after another down there and their [people on the left] response to that is this tremendous physical violence and murders and political assassinations . . . I don't know what it means. I'm a pacifist. I'm very practical. I'm not passive. I hate passivity. I'm a nonviolent soldier. For six thousand years, violence has *not* brought brotherhood nor peace nor liberty. It has brought chaos and fear. That's what I tried to say. We must look for another way of fighting."

A decade or so earlier, Baez had gone out to buy a flashlight and returned with an XK-E, paid for in cash. She'd spent the years since funding family, friends, and the causes in which she passionately believed, picking up the tab for all the organizing. Music and politics had happily fused on many of her albums but in the early seventies it was clear which took priority. Suddenly, her albums weren't selling so well and there was less money to live on, let alone give away. To A&M's relief, she decided to revitalize her career, and her bank balance, with the commercial album she had long promised.

Inspiration for the task arrived quite out of the blue—a phone call from "a booth in the Midwest." As she recollected to Arthur Levy, Bob Dylan rang and read to her the entire text of "Lily, Rosemary and the Jack of Hearts," a lengthy and surreal song that would appear a few months later on *Blood on the Tracks*, still regarded as among his finest albums. "I couldn't figure out what it was about, or anything about it except the words were cool." Pretty soon, Baez would be coaching Dylan as he learned the lyrics for live performance. "That phone call, and hearing his voice, brought everything back and that's when the song 'Diamonds & Rust' came about."

"Diamonds & Rust," without which no Joan Baez concert henceforth would be complete, is breathtaking in its emotional honesty, the listener transported back in time to "that crummy hotel over Washington Square," the Hotel Earle—"the perfect dump," as she described it in a backstage chat with The Indigo Girls. The intricate E-minor guitar riff, a shimmering cymbal, a hint of drum, the synthesizer (with which Baez had just begun to have fun), and then, after a few bars, the declarative vocal opening: "Well, I'll be damned / Here comes your ghost again." The extraordinary Baez–Dylan relationship laid bare in four verses and a bridge, whose passing chords take the song into a different realm, as the vocal melody changes to triplets for the almost breathless recollection of Dylan, snow in his hair, the brown leaves falling, as they walk in Washington Square Park. "As I remember your eyes were bluer than robin's eggs / My poetry was lousy you said"—a cliché, deliberately inserted, in order to make a joke against herself. It's all there—he "the unwashed phenomenon," she "the Madonna"; the cufflinks she bought him . . . As the song plays, the synthesizer wails like a banshee under that full moon; a cry in the night that echoes down the foggy ruins of time. "Diamonds & Rust" is a *perfect* miniature—raw, romantic, and intense, the best song she ever wrote, as Baez has acknowledged. "It's just a freak, it just came out. It didn't have any formula to it," she told the Indigos, as they rehearsed at the Greek. "It just happened, and I know it's because the subject matter was profound. It came from *way* deep."

Yet, astonishingly, not everyone got it. A *Melody Maker* review of the single release described it as "exceptionally sentimental

. . . this descends to the depths more suited to *True Confessions.*" Reviewing the album for the same paper, Karl Dallas, who had followed her career from the outset and should have known better, suggested the song was written about her ex-husband!

Diamonds & Rust—released in April 1975, curiously enough at much the same time Saigon fell and the last Americans were hurriedly evacuated—was certified Gold before the year was out. Arthur Levy's liner notes for the 2003 box set of A&M recordings report that the celebrated title track was the first song to be recorded when the sessions began in late January. Just a few days earlier, Bob Dylan, the song's subject and inspiration, had released *Blood on the Tracks*, an album Baez immediately loved and from which she plucked "Simple Twist of Fate," singing a verse in Dylan's voice. It's a brilliant recording, Baez relaxed and rocking along with the band, who between them lay down some memorable solos. While her version of "Fountain of Sorrow" by her old friend Jackson Browne doesn't quite convey the desolation of the lyric, she gets to the heart of the matter with Stevie Wonder's "Never Dreamed You'd Leave in Summer," the arrangement complementing her voice, and there's something almost unbearably poignant about her reading of "Jesse" by Janis Ian. "Children and All That Jazz" had begun life with Baez "messing around on the guitar," and challenging herself to work outside familiar chord sequences. Pianist Hampton Hawes dropped by the studio and they jammed together, working out the riff. She wrote the words the next day. The free association lyric she wrote to the riff they worked out is to, and about, Gabriel, and her multitracked vocal is agile and gossamer-light, revealing a new-found versatility. Hawes's solo is the *piece de résistance*. As to "Winds of the Old Days," the song was written on tour in Australia in response to Dylan's announcement of his 1974 return to the stage after a long absence. It has none of the musical or lyrical sophistication of "Diamonds & Rust"— indeed, its folk-like simplicity is probably intentional, even if some of its gloopier rhymes are not. It's a *mea culpa*, a sort of retraction of the earlier "To Bobby," in which she acknowledges "those eloquent songs from the good old days / That set us to marching with banners ablaze," and an admission that she has for too long sat in self-righteous judgment.

Dylan's call must have been a testing of the waters for his next project, the traveling medicine show that became The Rolling Thunder Revue, which he had conceived over the summer when he was hanging out in the Village. He was writing songs (including "Hurricane") with Jacques Levy, songwriter and theater director, who had worked with Sam Shepard on his one-act play *Red Cross*, staged at two celebrated downtown spaces, the Judson Poets' Theatre and the Provincetown Playhouse. Levy was also a clinical psychologist—probably useful when it came to directing the first of the two tours, which was considered the most successful and enjoyable.

With the show newly on the road, Baez told Larry Sloman in *Rolling Stone* that "Bob called up and asked what I was doing for the month of November. I had a tour lined up. Usually I'm not working with a dollar sign in front of my face, but this time I was, so I had to give it considerable thought. But I'm bright enough to know what this tour will mean. I didn't trust a lot of it," she continued, to the journalist she nicknamed Ratso, a soubriquet that stuck permanently. "I've known these guys a long time and I love them dearly, but everybody *is* slightly unstable. But it's delightful to be working with Bobby again. He's relatively impossible to follow and that's a challenge, but I need that." Lawyers drew up a detailed contract and Baez's only complaint appears to have been the injunction that the tour staff and crew eat separately from the musicians. "That *is* segregation."

The plan for Rolling Thunder was a spiritual reunion, and to get into the mood Dylan led his merry band into Gerde's Folk City, where he'd been playing a residency when Robert Shelton's career-defining review appeared in *The New York Times*. It was owner Mike Porco's sixty-first birthday and the Dylan and Baez duet of "Happy Birthday" and "One Too Many Mornings" must have seemed a special present. Ramblin' Jack Elliott, Phil Ochs, Eric Andersen, Patti Smith, and Bette Midler were among those who performed on the tiny stage, in front of the familiar old painting of a flamenco dancer. The cameras rolled. A week later, the first Rolling Thunder Revue concert took place at the War Memorial Auditorium in Plymouth, Massachusetts. The ragtag group of pilgrims had landed on Plymouth Rock.

They played more than twenty shows in the five weeks that followed, mostly in smallish venues at short notice: Everything would be spontaneous. The great Baez–Dylan reunion ten years after their public split helped ensure widespread media coverage on both sides of the Atlantic and beyond. The final concert, at Madison Square Garden, was renamed The Night of The Hurricane and it was a benefit for Rubin "Hurricane" Carter, the boxer wrongly convicted of murder. It was preceded by a concert at New Jersey's Edna Mahan Correctional Facility for Women, a setting which did not discommode Baez.

At the outset shows ran for around three hours, each of the headline acts performing his or her own set. The second half generally opened with the sound of Baez and Dylan duetting, often on "Blowin' in the Wind" and sometimes "The Times They Are a-Changin'," from behind the Rolling Thunder Revue curtain, which would rise slowly to reveal the two of them, cheek-to-cheek behind a single mic. The intensity and the thrill is evident in the concert footage in the recent Martin Scorsese documentary and even more so in *Renaldo and Clara*, the four-hour "giant mess of a home movie" (as she described it) written by Dylan with Sam Shepard in which Baez was billed as The Woman in White—essentially a whore, like all the Rolling Thunder women. "I Dreamed I Saw St. Augustine," "Deportees," "The Water Is Wide," "Railroad Boy," "Never Let Me Go," and "Dark as the Dungeon" featured prominently throughout both tours. Their set was always "a hazard," she told Nat Hentoff of *Rolling Stone*, which

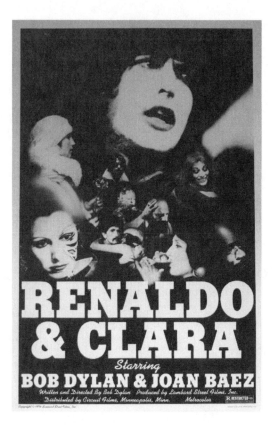

Dylan's home movie, *Renaldo & Clara*, 1978. Film critic Pauline Kael wrote that Baez "never takes what's going on seriously enough to be embarrassing . . . she just seems to be humoring Dylan"

devoted innumerable pages to Rolling Thunder. "It's hard singing with him because he's so devilish. There are times when I don't know what song he's plucking on that guitar until he starts singing. And he can be tricky. On one song we'd been doing two choruses all along the tour but one night, just as I'm about to belt the second chorus, the song was all over. *Done!* Thanks a lot. Bob had worked out the new short ending with the band and hadn't told me."

After their joint set, Baez would perform a handful of songs solo and with the band. At the first day of rehearsals, Dylan had told her that he'd like to hear "that song off your new album. You know,

'Diamonds & Rust.'" No one in the audience could have failed to understand its eerie significance. Other songs she played included "Swing Low, Sweet Chariot," "Long Black Veil," "Please Come to Boston," and "The Night They Drove Old Dixie Down." The Revue would come together for the closing song, often "This Land Is Your Land." Every night, Baez watched from the wings as Dylan performed. "I didn't want to miss a note. I didn't want to miss a word."

She and Dylan dressed in near-identical clothing: boots and jeans, dark waistcoats over shirts. Dylan wore a flower-bedecked hat and white face (occasionally a mask) and on a few occasions Baez did too, even going so far as to *perform* as Bob, with his agreement, at Madison Square Garden, a concert notable for her inclusion of "Dancing in the Street," the old Martha and the Vandellas hit.

Following a second Hurricane Carter benefit in January 1976 at the Houston Astrodome, the Revue rolled south for a further twenty or so dates, the final show taking place in Salt Lake City on May 25, by which time, as Janet Maslin put it for *Rolling Stone*, "The Rolling Thunder Revue, so joyful and electrifying in its first performances, had just plain run out of steam." Baez was less than enthralled, and Dylan's telling her that she would sell more records if she grew her newly cropped hair can't have helped. She was beginning to feel that "my life was being wasted in a madhouse." Dylan tried to persuade her to stay, talking already about a sort of never-ending tour on which they could all bring their kids. She declined, but in a bizarre dinner-table ceremony, at Dylan's drunken suggestion, they took a steak knife to each other's wrists, allowing the trickles of blood to commingle. Blood brothers for life, he declared.

In June 1982, Baez would introduce "Robert" during her set at a Peace Sunday concert at the Pasadena Rose Bowl when, among other songs, they revisited "With God on Our Side." But by 1984, Dylan had clearly forgotten their Rolling Thunder pact. On tour in Europe with him and Santana, Baez is once more treated badly; relegated to opening act, her name in the smallest type. Grainy film exists of their last ever performance together, in Munich, Baez dancing during a guitar solo and trying to look happy as they sing "Blowin' in the Wind." She bows and walks out of Dylan's life once more. They would appear on the same stage in January 2010, as the newly elected President Obama and Michelle celebrated the music of the civil rights era at the White House. Not a word was exchanged.

Prior to Rolling Thunder, Baez had been on the road, performing a half-acoustic, half-electric concert that would be recorded and released as *From Every Stage*. Among the new songs were "Natalia," Shusha Guppy's song about the Russian poet Natalia Gorbanevskaya who was imprisoned for protesting against the Soviet invasion of Czechoslovakia, and "Boulder to Birmingham," in which Emmylou Harris, writing with Bill Danoff, attempted to come to terms with the death of Gram Parsons. And there was Dylan's "Lily, Rosemary and the Jack of Hearts." It was Baez's first tour with a band and she felt compelled to explain to the audience that she was having "a vacation." She had worried what the public would think if she simply entertained them. The response surprised her: "They thought I was human. And *I* liked it too," she told Hentoff. "I found myself dancing during concerts and I love to dance. I'd never been so spontaneous onstage. The audiences were having fun and so was I."

Baez's final album for A&M was *Gulf Winds*. It was advertised as her first, in that it was the first (and as it turned out only) album comprised entirely of her own songs. Inspired by her tour with Dylan and his band of merry pranksters, it appears she began to write it around the midpoint of the second Rolling Thunder tour. Her liner notes indicate she was in Corpus Christi, where her father and his family had lived when they first came to the United States. The Revue had played the city's Memorial Coliseum on May 10, 1976. Baez is wakeful, feeling the urge to sing and write: "I walk out on the narrow cement jetty, about 200 yards into the

Gulf . . . The breeze is warm. It comes from Mexico . . . I make up words in my head until just before dawn and then return to my room to write them in a note pad."

The clear implication is that the song which would give the album its title was the first to be written. "Gulf Winds," at more than ten minutes the longest she ever wrote (leaving aside "Where Are You Now, My Son?"), tells in concise and vivid imagery the story of her childhood and family life. It's the most succinct of autobiographies. "My father turned down many a job just to give us something real / It's hard to be a scientist in the States when you've got ideals / And Mama kept the budget book, she kept the garden too / Bought fish from the man on Thursdays, fed all of us and strangers too." It's accompanied only by Baez's acoustic guitar, a distinct, disciplined, and rhythmic motif for which the bass E-string has been dropped to D, giving a particular tonal color. The echo around her voice is entirely appropriate—it's almost as if she's singing in her grandfather's church, to which she alludes. It has greater resonance now, but the soprano is still intact.

Of the other eight songs, at least two return to her relationship with Dylan: "Oh, Brother," an angry response to his "Oh, Sister," and "Time Is Passing Us By." Given the infrequency of his calls, the reference in "Sweeter for Me" to the red telephone that "practically bore your name" suggests another, more chatty, lover, though probably not "the pirate" of "Stephanie's Room." It's often been suggested that the affair recalled here is a gay one—but the song's title refers to Stephanie Barber, the legend of Lenox, whose Wheatleigh mansion near Tanglewood was a home from home for many musicians. As the sounds of waves and birds suggest, "Seabirds" was one of several songs written at the Cliff House, a restaurant on the rocky San Francisco headland of Point Lobos. It's all about ambience, the daydreamy lyrics sung high over special effects. "Caruso" was written there, too, a surprisingly MOR number for the Neapolitan tenor, even if he doesn't measure up to Baez's musical hero Jussi Björling. As to "Kingdom of Childhood," it's hard to pin down but rather magnificent, the musical layers accreting as the song progresses, the singer vocalizing over her own multitracked voice.

Sadly, *Gulf Winds* did not fare well in the charts, cresting at sixty-two on *Billboard*. Reviewers were generally not kind—*High Fidelity* wrote of "self-conscious poetics and clumsy phrasing," though *Stereo Review* thought Baez was "back in very secure stride as a composer," her voice "still the shimmering, satiny soprano." Yet the best of the songs on the album are strong indeed and because it's clear that energy and imagination have been expended—Baez still engaged with making music and working with a more sophisticated palette—the reception must have been a disappointment to her. Despite the success of *Diamonds & Rust* and her high profile with Rolling Thunder, the reality was that tastes were changing along with the times. Joan Baez had become unfashionable, her combination of music and activism unpalatable in a music business where money trumped morality.

In any event, Baez was quickly immersed in a cause. Northern Ireland's Troubles had raged since 1969, taking hundreds of lives and devastating countless others. In 1976, Betty Williams witnessed the death of three young children, one just six weeks old, hit by a car driven by an IRA paramilitary. Outraged and distressed, she launched a petition calling for an end to violence in the Province. Within a few days, more than six thousand people had signed. With Mairead Corrigan, the children's aunt, and journalist Ciaran McKeown, the three meeting for the first time on an RTE current affairs program, Williams formed the Peace People. It was McKeown who wrote the declaration which included the words: "We reject the use of the bomb and the bullet and all the techniques of violence." The trio set about structuring an ongoing peace movement, a key stepping stone on the long road to the Good Friday Agreement of 1998.

Over the following weeks, an office was opened, and groups organized. Marches brought thousands on to the streets in Belfast, Enniskillen, and Ballymena demanding an end to violence. But to ensure the world's attention, the Peace People needed to march in London, from where Northern Ireland was run. A date was set, November 27, 1976, and Baez was approached.

The invitation made her cry, for the movement was "so pure. It didn't have any purpose except that they didn't want to see any more children get killed," she told Geoffrey Levy of the *Sunday Express* as she arrived from California. She praised the women's courage, admitting her own fear at going to Northern Ireland where, a few days later, she joined ten thousand marchers from North and South as they met at a new bridge over the Boyne. Some fifteen thousand marched on Trafalgar Square, where Baez sang "We Shall Overcome" and "Ain't Gonna Let Nobody Turn Me Around." The Archbishop of Canterbury and the Cardinal Archbishop of Westminster were among the speakers. Also present was Jane Ewart-Biggs, widow of the recently murdered British Ambassador to Dublin. In an open letter to the *Socialist Worker*, former MP Bernadette McAliskey alleged that the Peace People was "a propaganda adjunct of the British military machine in Ireland," while Pat Arrowsmith, co-founder of the Campaign for Nuclear Disarmament, told Baez in a private letter that there would be no peace "until Britain withdraws from Ireland and removes her troops." The singer responded by saying that "Peace—I prefer the word nonviolence—frightens people." The very existence of the Peace People proved "there is some hope in this world."

Meanwhile, Baez had been persuaded to leave not just A&M but her longtime manager, Manny Greenhill. She signed with the new West Coast-based Portrait label and entered the studio to record a new album. *Blowin' Away* was released in June 1977 to some fanfare, half-page ads for both the album and the supporting tour appearing widely. "In the beginning there was her voice . . . Now on this new album we see Joan Baez in her ultimate role of musician—a singer's singer, who captures the essence of every kind of song." She would later judge it "a good album with a terrible cover." Half the songs were her own, Baez proving once again that she is strongest as a songwriter when she's telling a story, as with "Luba the Baroness." The Stevie Wonder-inflected "Miracles" is musically engaging, Baez once again having fun with a synthesizer, but it's weighed down by some clunky lines. "Altar Boy and The Thief" is an understated gem, the vocal line borne aloft on flattened sevenths and ninths which only resolve on the final chord. She smolders exquisitely on the old torch song "Cry Me a River" and, as she duets with Tom Scott's sax, you sense a whole new Joan Baez anxious to break out.

Baez's inner-sleeve cartoon can be read as both explanation and apology, while her donation of proceeds from her British concerts to the Commonweal Collection (a library of works on peace and nonviolence founded in the 1950s by activist David Hoggett), Operation Namibia, and the Campaign Against the Arms Trade suggested that nothing much had changed.

Nineteen-seventy-eight was a mix of music and politics, with concerts in Norway, Germany, and London, as well as in the US, where Baez appeared on behalf of the Nuclear Freeze movement and turned out to defeat legislation that would have barred gays from teaching in California schools. There was also an appearance at the memorial for San Francisco mayor George Moscone and Supervisor Harvey Milk who had been assassinated in City Hall, where she gave a free concert on Christmas Eve.

Baez had been due to join Santana, The Beach Boys and others for an American Independence Day celebration in Winter Palace Square in what was then Leningrad, but at the last moment Party apparatchiks cancelled the concert. Visa in hand, Baez decided to visit the Soviet Union alone, the plan to meet Andrei Sakharov and other dissidents. She traveled again with John Wasserman, the pair joined by Grace Kennan, Soviet expert and Russian speaker. Baez took photographs and letters from Sakharov's stepdaughter Tatiana, recently settled in Boston. The Nobel Laureate told her he was "perhaps too old to be a pacifist."

Her second and last Portrait album was released in July 1979, with cover photography by Karsh of Ottawa in which Baez sported a perm. Recorded in the celebrated Muscle Shoals Sound Studio, *Honest Lullaby* featured an eclectic mix of songs, three of them (including the title track) Baez originals. Twenty years on from her coffeehouse days in Cambridge, one of them reflected on the folk scene there and her first real love, the troublesome Michael, while "For Sasha," sung to her solo guitar, was inspired by German friends, still carrying the guilt thirty years after the war. Once again, the standout track is a torch song, this time from the 1930s. "For All We Know" is sung with palpable emotion to Barry Beckett's piano, clearly in memory of Wasserman, to whom the album is dedicated. Wassie, as she called him, had died on a California highway a few months earlier. It sounds as if it was recorded in one take, for there are a couple of fluffs on the piano. Baez's voice is rich and sonorous, the lessons she had begun with vocal coach Robert Bernard already paying dividends.

The reviews were more positive, noting the new qualities of the Baez voice. *Stereo Review* thought it "quite an achievement . . . Even though the waterfall-pure soprano has clouded, and the impetuous dramatic earnestness has mellowed into a calm sincerity, it is the sense of wisdom that permeates Baez's new work that is so striking." Yet despite her touring to promote it, *Honest Lullaby* would linger just outside the Top 100 for seven weeks and then vanish, the last Baez original to be released in the States until 1987.

Baez assumes it was sidelined on the day of release after she had called the then president of CBS Records (presumably Walter Yetnikoff) to discuss the album, mentioning in passing that she had pulled out of a music festival because it was in Egyptian territory occupied by Israel. Her views were anathema to him and it appears she learned a brutal lesson as to her "place" in the new music industry hierarchy.

Baez has said often that "action is the antidote to despair" and she threw herself into action. There had been disturbing news about human rights violations in Vietnam—arrests, torture, and re-education camps—some of it first-hand reports from those lucky enough to escape. With her old friend Ginetta Sagan, she set up a study group which led to the founding of the Humanitas International Human Rights Committee, which would advocate for human rights and nonviolence in a way the Institute was not set up to do. The immediate findings led Baez to publish An Open Letter to the Socialist Republic of Vietnam, a controversial move since many on the left did not wish to revisit the issue, much less criticize the Vietnamese government. Of the 350 people asked to sign, only 85 did. On a concert tour to raise money for the Boat People, as the fleeing refugees were called, Baez was frequently jeered. "Don't follow Joanie's baloney," they chanted in Seattle, though in Hyannis Port, Rose Kennedy made a rare show of support. In Washington, President Jimmy Carter promised to send the Seventh Fleet to rescue Boat People at sea. A joint appeal by Humanitas with Bay Area TV and newspapers raised one million dollars for the cause, while Linda Ronstadt, James Taylor, and The Grateful Dead were among those who played fundraising concerts in San Francisco. A March for Survival to the Thai–Cambodian border ensured food and medicine reached the camps. Organized by the International Rescue Committee and Médecins Sans Frontieres, it was led by Baez with such figures as civil rights leader Bayard Rustin, British MP Winston Churchill, Holocaust survivor and historian Elie Wiesel, and actress Liv Ullmann.

While the music business ignored her, a variety of organizations and institutions honored Baez's commitment to peace and human rights. In 1979 she received the Earl Warren Civil Liberties Award, and in 1980 the Jefferson Award from the American Institute for Public Service. The universities of Rutgers and Antioch each made her an Honorary Doctor of Humane Letters. Many more would follow, at home and abroad.

In 1981, Baez, film crew in tow, traveled to Latin America for a concert tour and Humanitas-sponsored fact-finding mission. As *There But for Fortune: Joan Baez in Latin America* showed, her efforts at both were repeatedly thwarted. The 1980s was the high-water mark of US-supported totalitarianism and no one was safe—in El Salvador in 1980, four Maryknoll nuns, American missionaries, were raped and murdered, and Archbishop Óscar Romero was shot while saying Mass. Baez met with the Mothers of the Disappeared in Buenos Aires, where a press conference was interrupted by a bomb scare. She was forbidden to give concerts in Chile but sang informally for students in Santiago. Two concerts were cancelled in Brazil. Only in Nicaragua was she welcomed, allowed both to perform and to discuss human rights. PBS aired the documentary in 1982. It also received a theater showing in London.

Beyond the French Legion of Honor, the highlight of 1983 was surely her *Concert pour la Non-Violence* in Paris's Place de la Concorde on July 15, the permit finally approved by President Mitterrand himself. Songs were dedicated to Gandhi, "the father of nonviolence," to the Mothers of the Disappeared, to Lech Walesa, and others fighting the good fight. Police estimates put the crowd at 120,000—but still Baez had no record contract. The summer's concerts in Europe—five in Germany and one each in Belgium and Portugal, in addition to Paris—became *Live Europe '83: Children of the Eighties*. It went Gold in France where it received the Académie Charles Cros Award for the year's best album.

"Children of the Eighties" and "Warriors of the Sun" had both been inspired by the new, engaged young audiences Baez had encountered in Europe, notably Germany, where the Green Party had unified a variety of movements comprised of people disillusioned by mainstream politics. Petra Kelly, one of the founders, described the Greens as "the anti-party party," and its alternative agenda embraced environmental concerns, feminism, human rights, and peace at a time when President Reagan was unveiling his so-called Star Wars initiative and planning to base a new generation of nuclear weapons on European soil. Both songs were staples of Baez's 1980s concert repertoire, while the album's third original, "Lady Di and I," was a charming fantasy written shortly after the wedding of Prince Charles and Lady Diana Spencer. At home in California, she'd set her alarm early in order to watch it live with friends.

Music and politics mingled over the next few years. In 1984, a visit to the Greenham Common Women's Peace Camp attracted widespread media coverage, Baez singing arm-in-arm with the women and chatting round a campfire as they baked scones. That was uplifting. The Glastonbury CND Festival was not: She had been expecting a socially engaged audience but instead found everyone zoned out in the sunshine. There were two Amnesty International tours, the first in 1986, Conspiracy of Hope, with Peter Gabriel, Lou Reed, and The Neville Brothers, resulting in 25,000 new American members.

In winter 1985, she and Ginetta Sagan went to Poland, Baez keen to meet Solidarity founder Lech Walesa. The movement had been driven underground: Martial law had officially been lifted but many political prisoners remained in jail until 1986. Staying in the parish house of St. Bridget's Church, a place of sanctuary for Solidarity members, Baez visited the Walesa family at home, the living room concert including "Happy Birthday, Leonid Brezhnev," written by her as Russia crushed the Polish uprising. She also gave free concerts at St. Bridget's and at the Catholic University of Lublin. A couple of years later, she would contribute the title song to the film *To Kill a Priest*, about Father Jerzy Popiełuszko, the priest and supporter of Solidarity murdered by government operatives in 1984 and later beatified.

Extraordinarily, Baez was not invited to participate in the making of "We Are the World." When it came to 1985's Live Aid, promoter Bill Graham, with whom she'd often worked, surely realized it would be rude not to include her, even if there had been fallout over the abortive Dylan and Santana tour. But she was granted only the 9am Philadelphia opening spot and given six minutes to perform. Introduced by Jack Nicholson, she declared: "Good morning, Children of the Eighties! This is your

A late 1970s
Spanish
concert poster

Woodstock, and it's long overdue," before singing "Amazing Grace" and (somewhat ironically) a couple of verses of "We Are the World."

"I was thrilled and terrified," she told me a few years later. "It's very clear that I have this position that nobody else has. I'm the link with real social-political work, the only one who's been really serious about it for a long period of time. But the problem is always: 'What's the old girl gonna sing?' It would be nice to be back in a position where I could actually do a set with my band and the kids would recognize me and recognize the music."

Still, Live Aid gave her profile a much-needed boost and a hook for her autobiography, published two years later. *And a Voice to*

Sing With was a bestseller on both sides of the Atlantic, its success translating into several languages. It was widely reviewed, often by high-profile critics. Some found it too honest for comfort, and while others were bothered by its self-absorption, there was wide acknowledgment that she was also self-critical and hard on herself. Barbara Goldsmith spoke for many when she wrote in *The New York Times Book Review* that the author was "possessed of rapier-sharp observation and recalls events in bright snapshots."

Meanwhile, Baez had at last signed a record contract, with Gold Castle Records. The new label, owned by journalist turned music business manager Danny Goldberg and Julian Schlossberg (co-producer of *No Nukes*), and co-founded with Paula Jeffries, provided a welcoming home for established artists who found themselves out in the cold. She would make three albums over three years, all of them produced by Alan Abrahams, whom she described at the time as having "the combination of a tremendous musical savvy, wild enthusiasm, and the kind of irreverent sense of humor I needed to keep me from my own self-importance, and to in fact cause hysterics, which are a no-no in vocal discipline, but essential to the soul. His production work was brilliant and as a result of all the above, together we produced three of my favorite albums."

Abrahams told me: "I was approached by Paula, my former assistant from RCA Records. My first response to her was 'I don't think that would be a good fit for me, she might be a bit stuffy.' Paula immediately said 'You are absolutely wrong, I insist you meet her, you will fall in love with each other. She is wonderful.' And it was the best thing that ever happened to me, professionally, creatively and personally. Joan was an absolute producer's dream."

Recently, the first fruit of the Baez-Abrahams creative partnership, was "all about what we created together," said Abrahams. "The repertoire was easy, from her wonderful originals to an impromptu *a cappella* intro to 'Do Right Woman, Do Right Man'—I heard her singing it in the shower and was gobsmacked! 'Asimbonanga', Johnny Clegg's homage to Mr Mandela, was brought to us by a

South African friend of Joanie's . . . Of course the Gospel rendition of 'Let Us Break Bread Together/Oh Freedom' with the L.A. Mass Choir was a no-brainer to me, and we let the spirit move and reveled in its beauty . . . 'Biko' she was already doing live, and Joan had a unique tapping-the-strings-and-body-of-the-guitar approach. Because we were open to everything together creatively, the notion of adding the bagpipes as a mournful intro was: *let's give it a try*. We did, it worked beautifully. Our spirits were high and joyful, and the material just flowed in terms of decisions. The results speak for themselves."

Released along with the book in 1987, *Recently* is mature, sophisticated, and cohesive, the production elegant. Her voice is at her mid-period best, and the arrangements complement it perfectly. "Brothers in Arms," "Asimbonanga" (which received a Grammy nomination), "MLK," and "Biko" are each stylistically different yet all of a piece, no doubt inspired by the Amnesty tours, and they work unexpectedly well with the live medley of "Let Us Break Bread Together/Oh Freedom." "Do Right Woman, Do Right Man," which appeared in *Carry It On*, is bluesy and mellow, Baez finally able to swing.

As to "The Moon Is a Harsh Mistress," Jimmy Webb, the song's celebrated writer, told Abrahams that Baez's version was his "absolute favorite" among myriad recordings. The producer speaks of it as "that Jimmy Web gem . . . beautifully enhanced by the late great Gene Page's string arrangements. She got the whole thing in one take, and when she asked me `What do you think?' I said: `We're not touching it, it's beautiful . . . Brilliant!' I have a picture of us sitting together listening in the studio as Gene conducted the strings. But the centerpiece is that magnificent vocal."

Two years later, *Diamonds & Rust in the Bullring*, recorded live in Bilbao, Spain, found her digging deep into her song bag. The career-spanning collection includes some new numbers: "Famous Blue Raincoat" was always a feature of Judy Collins's repertoire but a rarity for Baez. Cesar Cancino's piano infills and the cello counterpoint he arranged for John Acosta add a new dimension to the Leonard Cohen classic. "Txoria Txori," a Basque staple by Joxean Artze and Mikel Laboa, and Sting's "Ellas Danzan Solas" are both previously unrecorded, while Mercedes Sosa, with whom Baez had sung in Argentina, gives new life to "Gracias a la Vida."

Speaking of Dreams, which marked Baez's first thirty years, closed both the decade and the Gold Castle chapter. A mix of the personal and the political, it's an album full of surprises, among them George Michael's "Hand to Mouth" and Paul Anka's "My Way," sung in Spanish as "A Mi Manera" in rumba-flamenco style with The Gipsy Kings. Abrahams recalls "a brilliant night," Baez "like part of the band, duetting with Nic Reyes, joyfully toe-to-toe." It is boisterous and joyous, the consummation of a long-distance love affair with their music which had finally resulted in dinner in Paris, and a statement of intent: "This is my moment to do it my way, their way—any way but the way it was written," she would tell me later. "China," which opens the album, is bold and ambitious, the arrangement mixing Western rock with hints of Eastern pentatonicism. But the standout track is the lush and dreamy production ballad that gives the album its title. "Speaking of Dreams" began life at the piano, the words—addressed to a young French lover—following a year later. The string arrangement is again by Gene Page, its colors as rich as "the paintings of Paul Gauguin" at which the lovers gaze.

"She first played it to me at home on the piano," explains Abrahams. "She composed it on the piano and the day of the recording she played it to our brilliant pianist for the session, John Hobbs, and he put all the feeling and nuance into it . . . It was also, most importantly, a true story. Or as Arthur Levy said in his impeccable notes about the Gold Castle collections, 'No woman can map the arc of a love affair with a (much) younger man with quite the dreamy textures as Joan Baez.' It was all true! I still take a breath when she sings 'I am the Queen of Hearts and the Daughter of the Moon.' I just wanted us to create a sonic movie of it. We are most proud of that unexpected gem—and it is truly a fine musical and lyrical composition. Inspired. It defies any category."

"Fairfax County," a traditional-sounding ballad, was the work of David Massengill, a Tennessee-born writer and dulcimer player with whom Baez had sung at the silver anniversary of Gerde's Folk City, in New York in 1985. They'd met again at Newport where, in an informal singing circle at the Viking Hotel, she'd heard Massengill perform the song. "She seemed so surprised that someone was writing in an old style again," Massengill told me in the Village, where he has lived since the 1970s. "When she first heard it, she thought it was an old song, because it was long and it was beautiful and someone died! So it sort of took her by surprise . . . Hers is a great version."

With little promotion and scarcely any review coverage, the three eighties albums came and went, all but unknown until their rerelease in a box set in 2016. It included two powerful songs that failed to make the original cut: "Lebanon" by David Palmer from the *Recently* sessions, and Billy Joel's "Goodnight Saigon" from *Speaking of Dreams*. Taken from Joel's 1982 album, *The Nylon Curtain*, "Goodnight Saigon" is multilayered and carefully constructed, a song that explores the anguish and trauma of Vietnam through the eyes of a young Marine, hope turning to ashes in the jungle. Abrahams remains as perplexed as anyone that it never made the original album and added as an aside: "When we did the choruses of 'and we will all go down together,' we were at Capitol Studios and Studio A was being rebuilt, stripped right down to the studs, and so there was a natural ambience, echo that we used after we gathered up people from the building—friends, parking lot attendants—all to sing in unison and in a spirit of camaraderie as Billy Joel's lyrics suggest."

The song never takes sides—which made it controversial in some quarters and perfect for Baez. "Seeing through both eyes" had been the *raison d'être* of Humanitas. Life and art come together in perfect harmony.

"Nobody in his right mind should volunteer tax money, 82% of which goes to build weapons of death" - Joan Baez, *Jazz & Pop*, August 1968

7

AIN'T GONNA LET NOBODY
TURN ME AROUND

Shortly after Saigon fell on April 30, 1975, and the last American helicopter had lifted unceremoniously off the roof of the US Embassy, 100,000 people filled the Sheep Meadow in New York's Central Park for a War Is Over rally. Pete Seeger, Odetta, and Joan Baez were among the performers. The event was organized by Phil Ochs—writer of "There but for Fortune"—a troubled man who would shortly take his own life. It was intended as a celebration of the end of America's controversial involvement in South-East Asia. Vietnam had galvanized American youth, had been both fuel for the protest movement and the glue that held it together. When the war "ended," most of those who'd sung and spoken so eloquently against its injustices moved on.

Baez did not. She'd served two jail terms for "aiding and abetting" draft resisters and had spent twelve days in Hanoi during Nixon's Christmas 1972 bombing campaign, "the biggest aerial operation in the history of warfare," according to a military official in Guam, where the B-52s were based. When she returned to the States, her pacifist philosophy unshaken, Baez spoke and wrote and sang about her experiences in North Vietnam. As the years passed, she also undertook a good deal of work with the veterans whose lives had been torn apart by their experience—"after all, we paid for their trip over, and they've paid for all the years in between," she observed to the *Houston Chronicle* in 1987.

By 1979, Baez, too, was trying not to think about Vietnam. However, confronted with the evidence and two refugees who came to a study group at her California home to ask what had happened to all the Americans who had marched in solidarity with the Vietnamese, she could no longer stand aside. Her campaign for the Boat People brought opprobrium from the left, who felt she was letting the country off the hook over the war, and praise from the right, presidential candidate Ronald Reagan applauding her stand and noting that she'd finally "seen the light."

The episode goes to the heart of what preoccupied the world's youth during the 1960s and demonstrates the depth of Joan Baez's convictions and the degree to which both those on the left, with whom her causes *coincidentally* aligned her, and those on the right, who'd condemned her as "an outside agitator" and a communist, misunderstood her.

Baez was no "spring vacation revolutionary." Nor was she ever a rent-a-quote celebrity for this or that cause. Not until Barack Obama did she lend her support to a presidential candidate, though at various times she worked with like-minded elected officials. The key to understanding how she evolved into a sort of modern-day Joan of Arc, carrying a guitar rather than a spear into nonviolent battle, lies in her background. It's not clear how much Joanie saw of her grandparents—the family was after all peripatetic—but their influence on her own parents is clear and the legacy of "Father B" and "Mother B," as her paternal grandparents were known, lives on in downtown Brooklyn. Big Joan had been educated at a Quaker school and when her husband's conscience was troubled by matters of war and peace it was she who led the family to the Quaker meeting house. One imagines conversation around the family dinner table was not trivial.

The Baez family had joined one of America's central traditions of dissent, and however much Joanie, and her sisters, hated the Sunday silences, she attended until she left home and has done so sporadically ever since. As a teenager she made friends with members of the American Friends Service Committee, working with it down the years. Though she may now call it meditation, Baez routinely "keeps silence," alert to "the still small voice" of God, whatever she may call him. Silence was a central part of the day at the Institute for the Study of Nonviolence—the school Baez founded in 1965 with the help of Ira Sandperl. Students could learn about civil disobedience and discuss thinkers such as Gandhi, King, and Thoreau, whose celebrated essay *Civil Disobedience* was on the school's reading list. A lifelong abolitionist, Thoreau was a key influence on both Gandhi and King, as well as Baez. He wrote that "Law never made men a whit more just; and, by means of their respect for it, even the well-disposed are daily made the agents of injustice" and suggested it was "not too soon for honest men to rebel and revolutionize."

One way of doing so was by withholding taxes, he wrote, questioning whether it was right for "a citizen to resign his conscience to the legislator." While he was anxious to be "a good neighbor," paying for schools and highways, Thoreau wished to "refuse allegiance to the state . . . I do not care to trace the course of my dollar, if I could, till it buys a man a musket to shoot one with . . . But I am concerned to trace the effects of my allegiance." His fellow Americans should not pay tax out of self-interest, "to save his property, or prevent his going to jail." He wished to remind his fellow countrymen "that they are to be men first, and Americans only at a late and convenient hour." Sentiments with which Joan Baez has always concurred.

By the time she left high school and headed east with her family, Joanie was already a devotee of Pete Seeger and Harry Belafonte. Seeger had stood firm even during the worst years of Senator McCarthy's red scare, lucky to find in Manny Greenhill a manager prepared to stand up to the witch hunts. Banned from the airwaves, Seeger took to the summer camps, his mission to bring back the five-string banjo and, later, to clean up the Hudson River long before anyone began seriously to consider the environment. His advocacy of folk music among teenagers was a key building block in the 1960s folk revival. Belafonte, "king of calypso," was superficially more commercial, but he was an early supporter of the civil rights movement and, in the 1960s, a confidant of Dr King, who stayed at his apartment when he was in New York City. Belafonte bankrolled the 1964 freedom summer, the year of *Mississippi Burning*, when three young activists were ambushed, tortured, and killed by the Ku Klux Klan, and in August that year flew into Greenwood, Mississippi with $70,000 in cash to support the Student Nonviolent Coordinating Committee (SNCC). He and Baez were on the great Selma to Montgomery march.

In 1960, Baez appeared alongside Seeger at a SANE rally (the inspiration for the Committee for a SANE Nuclear Policy had come from Britain's Aldermaston marches). The folk consciousness of the 1930s had been all of a piece with the anti-fascist groundswell. As the children born during and after the Second World War came of age—the baby boomers—folk music was discovered anew, dusted off for use in protest against all aspects of the so-called military-industrial complex. Baez was frequently quoted saying she sang to "troubled intellectuals with the Bomb on their minds."

Reflecting on her burgeoning social action years later, she said that, following SANE, "one thing led to another, and I got involved in the civil rights movement." She and King and his lieutenants were close. "Sister Joan," privy to some of their most private moments—meetings in motels, cars, and diners—was disappointed to discover the talk was rarely serious, just guys together letting off steam. She was at conferences, an unhappy witness to the inevitable behind-the-scenes tensions and division

Joan Baez performs at the Golden Vanity in Boston, *c.* 1960. She was one of only a few performers to play on both sides of the Charles River

At the 1960 Newport Folk Festival: Joan Baez with Maynard Solomon, co-founder of Vanguard Records and her long-time producer

Joan Baez performing at Mandel Hall at the University of Chicago, October 18, 1961, on her first national tour

The voice and the poet: Joan Baez and Bob Dylan, Newport Folk Festival, July 24, 1964. During the weekend, each guested on the other's set

The March on Washington for Jobs and Freedom, August 28, 1963. Baez sang at various points during the day, beginning with a 10am performance of "Oh Freedom"

A workshop at the Southern Christian Leadership Conference's annual retreat at the Penn Center, Frogmore, South Carolina, 1966. Dr Martin Luther King, Jr. is seated third from left. Music was crucial to the movement and Baez was the balm between sometimes fractious meetings

The Baez clan at the 1967 Newport Folk Festival. Albert with, from left, Joan, Pauline Marden, Joan Senior, known as Big Joan, and Mimi Fariña

Baez with Manny Greenhill, her first manager, who guided her career for over a decade

Reunited after her husband's release from prison: Baez with David Harris and their son Gabriel, at home on Struggle Mountain, 1971

"Diamonds & Rust": with Bob Dylan for the Rolling Thunder Revue – The Night of the Hurricane, Madison Square Garden, New York City, December 8, 1975. Each sported whiteface and near-identical clothing

Backstage at The Bottom Line, during the Ring Them Bells sessions, April 11, 1995: Baez with Mary Black (left) and Janis Ian

At Jalazone refugee camp near Ramallah on May 12, 1988. Baez spent a week in Israel and the Occupied Territories

Arriving in Sarajevo, April 11, 1993, accompanied by UN Commander Major-General Philippe Morillon. Baez played a concert for peacekeeping troops and gave impromptu performances across the besieged city

Joan Baez and former Czech President Vaclav Havel at a concert commemorating the 20th anniversary of the Velvet Revolution on November 17, 2009, in Prague, Czech Republic

September 28, 2018: Baez addresses demonstrators gathered in Washington DC to protest the nomination of Brett Kavanaugh to the US Supreme Court

Farewell to Boston, September 14, 2018: Baez on stage at the Wang Theater, Boch Center with, from left, Dirk Powell, Grace Stumberg and Gabriel Harris

"The folk grannies": with Betsy Siggins celebrating 60 years of Club 47/Club Passim at Boston's Folk Americana Roots Hall of Fame, November 14, 2019

"Gabriel and Me": mother and son backstage at London's Royal Albert Hall, May 28, 2018

"Adios, amigos, adios": a final farewell at the Teatro Real in Madrid, Spain, July 28, 2019. El Pais described her as "emotional, serene, humble and extraordinarily generous"

that beset the Southern Christian Leadership Council (SCLC). On such occasions, her music must have been a balm. And she saw King at some of what he called his "valley moments." Grenada, Mississippi was one of them. When she was summoned to a local preacher's house where King was staying, to sing him awake when all other measures had failed, it was clear he wasn't simply exhausted but also despondent, according to Taylor Branch in his magisterial biography of King, *At Canaan's Edge*.

As a pacifist, King agonized over Vietnam, which FBI wire taps revealed he considered "immoral," recognizing also that the money spent on the war meant there was less available to fight domestic poverty. But the SCLC executive was worried that taking a stand against Vietnam would cause a reduction in the organization's funding and rupture relations with President Johnson's White House. However, by the end of 1966, King felt he could no longer stay silent and in a sermon at New York's Riverside Church on April 4, 1967, exactly a year before his assassination, he brought the issues of poverty and the war together—"my conscience leaves me no other choice," he declared. Nevertheless, in a 1970 interview with Nat Hentoff for *Playboy*, Baez—despite her love for King—was critical of his delay. "I think King was an American first, a good citizen and a preacher second, and a black man third and an exponent of nonviolence fourth." She was also careful to acknowledge the pressures under which he was working, and her admiration for the man and his achievements remains undimmed.

Baez was an American only at Thoreau's "late and convenient hour," but of course, unlike Dr King, she was beholden to no one. Though she would cease withholding her income tax when the Vietnam War ended, she had been a consistent advocate of the protest, in 1966 putting her name to an advertisement by the Committee for Non-violent Action which declared that none of the undersigned would pay that percentage of income tax which was earmarked for military purposes. The IRS responded that "in fairness to the millions of taxpayers who do fulfil their obligations" it would make efforts to collect the taxes in other ways.

In an open letter published in August 1968 in the journal *Jazz & Pop*, Baez urged her fellow musicians to join the boycott. "Nobody in his right mind should volunteer tax money, 82% of which goes to build weapons of death." By then, Baez was withholding *all* her income tax, having discovered, for example, that roads were formally part of the nation's defense system. However, she believed everyone was duty-bound to contribute toward that which was of genuine public benefit, and her way of doing so, she pointed out, was to give charity concerts. In 1974, in a letter addressed to "Dear Friends at the IRS," she recapped her position, noting also that "I don't feel it decent to help to finance a government which supports a military junta in Chile, recognizing the new dictatorship immediately as it is executing, imprisoning, and torturing people *en masse*." She concluded: "I feel we are morally obligated to tax ourselves in a world where there is such blatantly unfair distribution of wealth." Her self-taxation benefited chosen causes at home and abroad but the IRS always collected eventually, though Baez made it an initiative test by spreading her money between various banks.

By the mid-sixties, youth had found its voice, raising it most notably on the nation's campuses. The Free Speech Movement challenged the authority of the universities, and the University of California, with its links to business and the military, was perhaps more authoritarian than most. In 1964, students returning to Berkeley after the summer recess were told they could not set up tables along Telegraph Avenue, one of the campus's main arteries, to promote "off-campus" activities. Student Mario Savio, who'd spent the summer helping civil rights workers in Mississippi and wanted to raise money for the SCLC, recognized "another phase of the same struggle . . . In Mississippi, an autocratic and powerful minority rules, through organized violence, to suppress the vast, virtually powerless minority. In California, the privileged minority manipulates the universal bureaucracy to suppress the students' political expression." For Savio, who had considered the priesthood, the key question was: "Are we on the side of the civil rights movement? Or have we gotten back to the comfort and security of Berkeley, California, and can we forget the sharecroppers whom we worked with just a few weeks back? Well, we couldn't forget."

Berkeley's activist tradition dates back to the 1950s, when there were vigils in protest against the death penalty and against the House Un-American Activities Committee. By 1963, civil rights had become a campus issue and, in 1964, the candidacy of Barry Goldwater and President Johnson's increasing involvement in Vietnam further galvanized students. The university administrators' attempts to curb activism met with further protests. Names were taken, protesters suspended, but the students were undeterred and the Free Speech Movement—midwife to the antiwar movement—was born. A couple of years later, Governor Roland Reagan would vow to "clean up the mess at Berkeley," which he regarded as a nest of social and political deviants.

When police were called to a rally, several hundred students simply sat down around the squad cars, so preventing arrests. The night passed in speeches and song, Baez summoned from her home in Carmel. After some thirty hours, Berkeley's regents agreed to meet the activists: The university would examine the free speech issue and not press charges. But the promise was reneged upon and the protests renewed. At their height, the students again called on Baez, who suggested they occupy Sproul Hall, Berkeley's administrative building. She told them: "We're going to go in there now and we're going to sit down and we're not going to move until they return us our rights. But when you go in there, go with love in your hearts." Once inside, the students held informal seminars, discussing civil disobedience with Baez and Ira Sandperl, all of them awaiting arrest. By the early hours of the morning, with no sign of the police, Baez returned home, at which point the police moved in and arrested 814 students, some of them resisting.

Thus did Baez's life became all of a piece, music inseparable from her social concerns. She was an increasingly visible symbol of dissent against the status quo, at home and abroad. In May '65 she was in London to lead a march demanding a break with America's policy on Vietnam, and in August she appeared at a commemoration of the twentieth anniversary of the bombing of Hiroshima. The following year, in addition to joining King in Mississippi, she led an Easter Sunday anti-war march in West Germany, gave a benefit concert in support of Cesar Chavez and striking farm workers in California, and joined a Christmas vigil at San Quentin urging the commutation of death sentences on sixty-four prisoners. The security services took an increasing interest in her, at home and abroad. Despite the long hair and frequently bare feet, despite the fey utterances of her early career, Baez was not a hippie, nor a flower child. Rather, she was part of "the Movement," which was all about rethinking politics, challenging the old order. Whether or not she'd read the Port Huron Statement, Baez would have agreed with its precepts. The 25,000-word document, the "agenda for a generation" that emerged from a five-day convention of the newly formed Students for a Democratic Society, was published in 1962, drafted principally by Tom Hayden, then a student at the University of Michigan. It stated in part:

> We are people of this generation, bred in at least modest comfort . . . looking uncomfortably to the world we inherit . . . As we grew, however, our comfort was penetrated by events too troubling to dismiss. First, the permeating and victimizing fact of human degradation symbolized by the Southern struggle against racial bigotry, compelled most

of us from silence to activism. Second, the enclosing fact of the Cold War, symbolized by the presence of the Bomb, brought awareness that we ourselves, and our friends, and millions of abstract "others" we know more directly because of our common peril, might die at any time.

Authority, bureaucracy, the military-industrial complex, consumerism: All were to be challenged as "we the people"—not the power elite—took control of political and economic affairs. Its call for participatory democracy, both as means *and* end, and based on nonviolent civil disobedience, finds a strong echo in our own times—the questioning of the so-called war on terror, the Occupy movement, Extinction Rebellion. "If we appear to seek the unattainable," it concluded with a rhetorical flourish, "then let it be known that we do so to avoid the unimaginable."

Yet Baez was never truly part of the New Left. Indeed, in an era of polarization, she was consistently radical. Movements that were exclusive, such as women's liberation, or potentially violent, such as the various black power groupings, drew only a negative response. What engaged her was what we had in common, not what set us apart. Libertarian in matters of sex, she was puritanical when it came to drink and drugs and generally skeptical about the whole student lifestyle. At a time of indiscipline, she urged discipline and commitment, personal risk over complacency.

Inevitably, her causes naturally aligned her with the left, but her philosophy was apolitical and she has remained true to it. "I am neither right nor left. I am a nonviolent activist and, supposedly, my job is to speak out against injustice and violence wherever and whenever it happens," she explained in 1980, in the wake of praise from arch-conservatives William F. Buckley and Ronald Reagan over her criticism of the Hanoi government. Reactionary violence or revolutionary violence—a rubber-hose beating felt the same whoever administered it, she explained, not for the first time. "I believe in people, not systems." To her, all life is sacred.

As the sixties wore on, movements which had been "unviolent"—nonviolent by chance rather than by design—became violent. The torch of which President Kennedy had spoken in his inaugural address was no longer a metaphor. In an essay entitled "The Folk Music Movement of the 1960s: Its Rise and Fall," Daniel J. Gonczy suggested that Baez was "more of a presence in the protest fervor of the Sixties than a polemicist for it . . . it was the emotional force of her music more than her ideology that often made an impact . . . Sustaining Baez's place in the movement, two forces, discipline and emotion, seemed always to be at work. Frequently, her control and self-containment reinforced her ability to move and to persuade listeners."

Her headline appearance at the 1969 Woodstock festival was a case in point and it is interesting that, in the (original) movie, Baez was represented by a performance of "The Ballad of Joe Hill," about the songwriter to the trades union movement whose 1915 execution on trumped-up charges made him a martyr. From death row, Hill wrote a telegram urging his supporters, "Don't waste any time mourning. Organize!" As Baez stepped out in that Woodstock dawn, her husband David Harris was newly in jail and organizing a hunger strike. Her set was highly political and she and musicians Jeffrey Shurtleff and Richard Festinger had called themselves The Struggle Mountain Resistance Band, named after the Los Altos, California commune that she, Harris, and their fellow Resisters called home. "Nobody was really thinking about the serious issues," she reflected to *The New York Times* on Woodstock's fiftieth anniversary. "I was graceless enough just not to accept it."

No matter that youth the world over seemed to have turned on, tuned in, and dropped out: Baez was still an influence. According to the *Woodstock Census*, "a nationwide survey of the Sixties generation" conducted by Rex Weiner and Deanne

Stillman in 1978, 44% of the 1,005 respondents said they had admired and/or been influenced by Baez. That figure put her at number eight, behind (in order) The Beatles, Dylan, John F. Kennedy, Martin Luther King, John Lennon, Ralph Nader, and Robert Kennedy, and above Eugene McCarthy and Janis Joplin. Baez, like Dylan, Lennon, and Joplin, was perceived as strong because she was sensitive.

Not surprisingly, she was more important to women than to men—52% to 39%. Said one: "Reading about Joan's beliefs in nonviolence impressed me greatly. I admired her stand against the war. She helped influence me toward nonviolent means of protest." Another said, "Baez in the Sixties became my alter ego. I wanted to *be* Joan Baez. Her continuing involvement in social issues is still inspiring." Less seriously, 32% of women admitted to having ironed their hair to get "the look."

In 1978, having pulled out of the Nuweiba festival in the Sinai oasis town after learning it was in Israel-occupied Egyptian territory, Baez instead played concerts in Lebanon and in Jerusalem, where there was a bomb threat and placards demanding "Joan go home." She explained her politics, telling the audience: "I am here because I love to sing with Israelis, like I love to sing with Arabs, Germans and other nations." There were songs in Hebrew, Russian, Spanish, and Arabic, "in case there's an Arab in the audience"—at which point the audience began clapping in time to the music. Offstage, she met with representatives of the Israeli and Palestinian communities.

Ten years later, Baez spent a week in Israel and the Occupied Territories, talking to Israeli peace activists and visiting the refugee camps in the West Bank and Gaza Strip. She had come *because* of the Palestinian uprising, which over its six months had led many artists to boycott Israel in its fortieth anniversary year. She spoke with care, the *Los Angeles Times* reporting that she told Palestinians gathered in Arab East Jerusalem: "I must have the humility to admit that I will never understand what it would be like to be a Palestinian Arab living in occupied territory. And on the other hand, I will never understand what it is to be Jewish [and] feel two thousand years of homelessness, fear, persecution and desperation." What she called "the dialogue of death" should cease. We should heed the advice of Gandhi, she said. He had told India that "In order for this to be a real revolution, we must free ourselves from being at the receiving end of the guns and free the British from being at the other end of the guns." Baez took the same message to a multicultural audience at the Caesarea Amphitheater and then to Tel Aviv, proceeds going to Peace Now, whose thirty thousand members were demanding that Israel withdraw from the Occupied Territories. On her last evening in Israel, she attended a rally by Yesh Gvul, a group of soldiers who were refusing to engage in "suppressing the uprising and insurgency in the Occupied Territories."

Such visits were not without risk. So too, in a different way, her 1978 visit to the Soviet Union. Baez had been due to perform with Santana and The Beach Boys at a concert in Leningrad's Winter Palace Square. Its cancellation left her with a visa and a clear diary, so Baez decided she'd go to Moscow anyway and visit Andrei Sakharov, then the world's most celebrated dissident, who was under house arrest. She traveled with John Wasserman of the *San Francisco Chronicle* and Grace Kennan, Soviet specialist and Russian speaker, as fixer, photographer, and translator. Kennan was horrified to discover that Baez had taken with her a considerable amount of money, stuffed into her guitar case, planning to give it to Jewish dissidents. It was a naive and foolhardy move which would have had serious consequences for everyone involved had not Kennan acted quickly. Sakharov and his wife scarcely knew who Baez was and, with problems of their own, had no wish to discuss human rights abuses elsewhere in the world. Nevertheless, they appreciated the gifts she brought and the songs she sang.

Doubtless the Soviets kept an eye on her but in Czechoslovakia in 1989, she outwitted them, smuggling dissident Václav Havel first of all into her hotel room and then into her Bratislava concert as a roadie. He was only recently out of jail, and she had invited him from Prague with nine other dissidents—the playwright and soon-to-be president called it "making mischief." From the stage, she talked about her friend Lech Walesa and sang about Solidarity. The audience was already going wild when, in Czech, she welcomed Charter 77 and "my friend Václav Havel," now secreted in a balcony seat. Finally, she invited singer-songwriter Ivan Hoffmann onstage. Baez had neither met him nor heard him; he'd been banned for eight years. "He took his time, and the audience cheered and yelled and finally got seated and he started playing this Dylanesque harmonica and then screaming into the microphone, this *ferocious* song," Baez told me a year later. "I'm amazed that he got two verses out before the sound was cut but the authorities were probably in such a state of shock . . . Afterwards four hundred police stormed the backstage area—I don't know why exactly, nobody was arrested. Eventually we herded everyone together and went back to the hotel and celebrated all night. They said it was the human rights event of the year."

Havel later claimed it was one of the key events which helped shape Czechoslovakia's Velvet Revolution, commenting: "The spirit of the Sixties was somehow revived there with Joan Baez, a symbol for the nonviolent peace movement." Baez and Havel met on many occasions and in 2006 she was a surprise guest at the annual Forum 2000 Foundation conference, a joint initiative between Havel, Japanese philanthropist Yōhei Sasakawa, and Nobel laureate Elie Wiesel. In November 2009, she performed at a concert in a thirteenth-century Prague church to mark the twentieth anniversary of the Velvet Revolution, with Suzanne Vega, Lou Reed, and Renée Fleming also on the bill. Baez sang "We Shall Overcome" in English and Czech to an audience that included Madeleine Albright, former US Secretary of State. The four rather ill-matched voices came together for "Oh, Freedom."

Yet Baez did more than preside publicly at some of history's big moments. She worked hard behind the scenes, rolling up her sleeves and dirtying her hands in often difficult terrain. William Lenderking, a US press attaché and information officer in Bangkok during the period she visited the Thai refugee camps, was keen to put on record how dedicated and hard-working Baez was. "She was very savvy; she had one or two people with her, helpers who were also savvy and focused and knew how to deal with people and how to push their agenda in an effective way . . . she was effective and impressive." Speaking for a Washington oral history project, Lenderking recalled that on one visit she gave a concert for American and Thai officials: "There was a lot of nervousness because the new president and some of the senior coup leaders and government officials were there. From the stage Joan Baez gave him a dazzling smile, saluted him and then sang a song of protest. She did it so gracefully that no one's back was raised and the hackles stayed put."

When she testified in Washington before the Senate Judiciary Committee following a fact-finding mission to the region, chairman Edward Kennedy found Baez "an extremely articulate spokesman for humanitarian concerns."

Few of those who marched and sang in the sixties have raised their voices in the years since, and fewer still did more than march or sing. In "Give Peace a Chance," John Lennon gave the movement its most memorable anthem and he certainly made some memorable gestures—the Bed-Ins for Peace, the War Is Over poster campaign. But then he embarked on a long lost weekend from which he recovered to retire to domesticity in the Dakota. Had he lived, perhaps he would have returned to the fray. Only Joan Baez appeared to see protest, in whatever form, as a vocation. Charges that she merely jumped on the protest bandwagon simply don't stack up. Her record sales, while impressive in the 1960s, were never enough to undermine her credibility. Nor has she abandoned her principles as musical tastes have changed. She has lived well, though not in the Hollywood sense, and enjoyed many of the trappings that come with celebrity, but she uses that celebrity to promote her ideals and beliefs.

If over the last couple of decades she has been less hands-on, Baez has been no less eloquent, and from platforms around the world—often in countries such as Bosnia, which she visited in their darkest hours—she has advocated in speech and song for the dispossessed and disenfranchised. That Baez is sincere is not in doubt. When she sang at the March on Washington, for example, she wasn't just lending her celebrity but using song to inspire the public's political consciousness. She has marched against twenty-first-century America's misguided missiles just as she did in the 1960s, and lent her support to a range of causes, at home and abroad, including Occupy, the Innocence Project, whose aim is the exoneration of the wrongly convicted, and Greta Thunberg, whom she praised for "coming to this country to speak truth to the most powerful nation on earth." And of course she has marched against President Trump, speaking out, singing out. It may even be time to go to jail again!

Baez has said that departing the stage amid a time of such peril gave her pause for thought, but the torch has to be passed; she will do what she can. "We couldn't have scripted this, *nobody* could have scripted this," she told me in Bristol, England in 2018, agreeing that the situation now is more dangerous than it was in the 1960s. "Nobody could have imagined it . . . The whole conservative agenda has nothing to do with much except self-service. *Money.* And you teach your kids to go out and make more money."

Music alone won't change the world, but without music Baez believes no movement can succeed. As she told *The Guardian*'s Kate Kellaway in 2019, "Music lifts the spirits, crosses boundaries and can move people to do things they would not otherwise have done."

MAGGIE GERRAND PRESENTS

AN EVENING WITH
JOAN BAEZ
THE LEGEND RETURNS

*'Spellbinding...
her voice is as clear
and distinctive as
it ever was.'*
THE INDEPENDENT, 2014

*'Baez switched
between ballads,
political songs
and gospel in a
remarkable show
that earned her a
standing ovation.'*
★★★★
THE GUARDIAN, 2014

2015 NATIONAL TOUR
CANBERRA 17 Sep Canberra Royal Theatre
SYDNEY 20 & 21 Sep Sydney Opera House
MELBOURNE 24 & 25 Sep Arts Centre Melbourne
HOBART 27 Sep Theatre Royal
PERTH 30 Sep Perth Concert Hall
BUNBURY 1 Oct Bunbury Regional Entertainment Centre
DARWIN 4 Oct Darwin Entertainment Centre
BRISBANE 7 Oct Brisbane Concert Hall QPAC
ADELAIDE 12 Oct Adelaide Festival Centre
JOANBAEZAUSTOUR.COM

CityNews, Canberra: "it was always Baez's revolutionary spirit that
has carried her career and that spirit has never been compromised."
Her final Australian dates

8

RING THEM BELLS

Spring 1990, and en route to Europe for a short concert tour, Joan Baez stopped off in London to talk up *Speaking of Dreams*. Meeting over afternoon tea at the Halcyon Hotel in London's Holland Park, our first encounter since 1984, I was introduced to her new manager Mark Spector, the man tasked with revitalizing her career and reinventing the woman trapped within the legend. "The legend idea was kind of nice but I was getting bored, and so were my audiences."

Baez had been through the long years of what she called "silence and ashes" and while politics and social justice had sustained her, she was and always would be a musician. Despite some pleasant surprises—in Turkey, *Recently* had sold more than twice the number of copies it had sold in America, and 25,000 had traveled to see her in Ephesus—life as a musician was increasingly difficult. The States was practically missionary territory, unsold seats even at modest venues. "I didn't know why I was bothering," she conceded. What got her through was meditation. She recognized she had "nobody but myself to blame, really" and she'd been "bitter with no real right to be bitter." She'd "lost confidence" and considered quitting, but friends in France persuaded her not to, so she'd cut *Speaking of Dreams*. "It didn't dawn on me until it was happily made that no one would hear it if I didn't find a manager."

She was forty-nine, an age when many of us angst about unfulfilled ambitions. A mid-life crisis. "I'm more open to the idea of a career now," she confided. "You've known me in the past, and you know that the *last* priority has always been my musical work. Whether it's been meeting other musicians . . . I've always been very isolated." During a sleepless night came "the sudden realization that I wouldn't have the voice for ever." There had, she agreed, been "a big dip" in its qualities and flexibility, "and then I got to work on it. And I guess I worked long enough and hard enough that there aren't many surprises left." I asked her about a classical album, which we'd talked about previously, but that was "off the table for the moment," though some classical repertoire was part of her "maintenance" regime. "I could do an album of some of the things I've loved all my life—we probably talked about Kathleen Ferrier. She makes it sound like a breeze but I don't think I could do it to my own satisfaction. I wouldn't want to listen to the playback."

Baez's career was then thirty years old. With good health and good luck, she hoped she might have another ten years but she wanted to bow out at a time of her own choosing, not merely fizzle—a comment we reflected on in 2018, a few weeks in to her Fare Thee Well tour. The world in 1990 seemed a better place than it had been when she started out. The Cold War having been ramped up, Ronald Reagan and Mikhail Gorbachev had recently signed the Reykjavík accord limiting nuclear weapons, and at home and abroad the Soviet leader was embarked on a program of democratization. The Brezhnev Doctrine, which had justified Soviet interference in Eastern Europe, was abandoned. The Berlin Wall had come down, and her old friend Václav Havel was President of Czechoslovakia. The words *perestroika* and *glasnost* had entered the Western lexicon. Environmental concerns were creeping up the world agenda.

"Maggie said 'Euphoria is a bad master,'" Baez laughed, imitating the then British prime minister, Margaret Thatcher. "*Hell*, I'll buy that at the moment! Compared to the Cold War, threats of World War III and the Evil Empire, let's have a little euphoria," she said, observing that with the old certainties gone, new struggles would emerge. But right now, after all that happened in 1989, there was hope—was that why she felt able to shift her focus from politics to music? "Yes, I think my change in attitude has to be connected to world events."

While her new manager got to work, Baez began collaborating with other musicians, notably the Indigo Girls and Mary Chapin Carpenter, then new kids on the block. It was a learning experience for all concerned, putting each performer in front of a new audience. The women first came together in 1992, a Humanitas benefit, as Four Voices for Human Rights, the first of many performances that continued throughout Baez's career. Her own touring schedule was now heavier in Europe and in the US, where she played gigs at old haunts such as the Bitter End in Greenwich Village, the Troubadour in L.A., Tanglewood, the Newport Folk Festival, and Esalen in the Big Sur highlands. The ground was being prepared and the focus now—for the first time since the very early 1960s—was on music. Pure and simple.

Following three original albums and a compilation with Gold Castle, *Brothers in Arms*, Baez signed with Virgin Records. *Play Me Backwards* was released in 1992, garnering a Grammy nomination for Best Contemporary Folk Recording. It was her most high-profile release in many years, *Billboard* summing it up as "a carefully constructed collection that keeps a reverent eye on Baez's history as an artful, poignant storyteller, while dabbling lightly in quasi-mainstream acoustic rock." The project took her back to Nashville, where she had thrived two decades earlier, teaming her with producers Wally Wilson and Kenny Greenberg, with whom she co-wrote four songs, including the title. "Mark went hunting for the right producers," she told me, the album newly released with a showcase at Virgin's London studios. "Many people said, 'Yeah, great idea, Joan Baez.' But the first to fly out to meet me were Wally and Kenny, who hung in there through lots of thin. By the time we got to recording it was fun, but I fought a lot of it kicking and screaming because I have so many old habits to deal with.

"I fought *anything* new!" she continued. "The things in me that needed to be challenged were all habits from age nineteen: not enough rhythm, not willing to cut loose, not willing to put enough time into my music, not willing to co-write, not willing to subject my music to other people's criticism. These were all things that needed to be dealt with, so naturally I was terribly resistant. I was saying that's too lively, there's too much drum, too much of this, too much of that. In the end, I really understood that my own instincts were not trustworthy in a lot of departments, which was what was holding me back. Each time I'd let go another notch, there it would be. I'd let go of another tired old habit and the music would just fall into my lap." She was even persuaded to make a video of "Stones in the Road," the song Mary Chapin Carpenter had given to her, a remarkable folk rock ballad about how a generation brought up to care had become selfish and preoccupied with material success. "I went through *all* my bullshit but in the end I had a wonderful time. We kept it elegant, dignified, slick and full of rhythm. What a kick!"

While British and American audiences were receptive, in France and Germany, where Baez had a young socially conscious following—"the children of the eighties"—journalists at least were initially skeptical. "In Germany it was horrible—they said my fans would be so disappointed. That I used to care and now I didn't. I just hung in there for two days, did about ten interviews like that." Then came the concert, featuring Fernando Saunders on bass and Paul Pesco on guitar, their pedigrees including Miles Davis and Madonna. "If I knew how to surf, I'd say it was like surfing. They *loved* it. The most rewarding thing afterwards was that people felt *not* as though I'd abandoned them but as though I'd come back."

Proof that Baez had abandoned neither her audience nor her convictions arrived swiftly. The promise of 1989, the year of revolutions, was soon dashed and when Lionel Rosenblatt, President of Refugees International—with whom she'd traveled to the Cambodian refugee camps—invited her to accompany him to Sarajevo, she didn't hesitate. The city had been under siege for a year, with well over a thousand killed and fourteen thousand wounded; some 62,000 children were trapped, and water, food, and electricity were scarce. George Soros, the controversial billionaire philanthropist, was bringing in not only humanitarian aid but musicians and actors in an effort to lift local spirits.

Traveling with guitarist Paul Pesco, Baez spent a week in Sarajevo in April 1993, a dangerous trip which required crossing the front line that separated the Bosnian Army from the besieging Serbian forces simply to get from the airport to the city. The be-ribboned skinny plait that snaked down from her gray crop dangled somewhat incongruously over a flak jacket as she toured the streets, on foot as well as in an armored car, clambering through the rubble to hug and chat with the locals trying to go about their daily lives. She visited hospitals, danced with firefighters, joined the cast of *Hair* which had been running for six months, and gave impromptu performances and a concert, for which she learned "Sarajevo, Ljubavi Moja," a popular song. She knelt before Vedran Smailović, the Cellist of Sarajevo, whose daily performances commemorated "the bread-queue massacre" and, in an act of great symbolism that flashed around the world, sat on his chair to sing "Amazing Grace." "The best thing I could have done was just to be there, because they are for the most part no longer afraid of dying, they are afraid of being forgotten," Baez told the *San Francisco Chronicle* as she arrived home.

The following month she was back on the road, with summer concerts in Europe bookended by Stateside gigs, a pattern repeated in 1994. Vanguard released a three-CD box set, *Rare, Live & Classic*, one third of the tracks previously unreleased. They included family tapes and tracks from the Grateful Dead sessions of spring 1982, the album planned and recorded at drummer Mickey Hart's Novato ranch but never released. Sadly, "Gethsemani," Baez's song to Thomas Merton, was not among them.

After two years of groundwork, in April 1995, Mark Spector made a clever and eye-catching move. Instead of taking Baez into a studio, he booked four nights at the Bottom Line, hallowed ground on the corner of West 4th Street and Mercer in Greenwich Village, where the likes of Lou Reed, Bruce Springsteen, and Van Morrison had played. Before an audience of four hundred people a night, she would record a live album with friends old and new: Kate and Anna McGarrigle and Mary Chapin Carpenter; Mary Black and Janis Ian; Mimi Fariña and The Indigo Girls; and Dar Williams and Tish Hinojosa. Percussionist Carol Steele joined Saunders and Pesco on the club's small stage.

It was twenty years since Baez's last live album, *From Every Stage*, and there would be three more before her final bow. Grapevine and Guardian, respectively the British and American independent labels she had signed with, created a major event around the *Ring Them Bells* sessions, the first two of which I covered for *Mojo*. You could argue that it would have made more sense to return Baez to Cambridge, or at least to Boston, but it was to New York City that she had come to record thirty-five years previously. Her first major concerts had been in Manhattan—and of course it was on the narrow, crooked streets of the Village that she and Bob Dylan and their friends had made history. That once-crummy hotel over Washington Square was but a few minutes' walk across the Park. Singing "Diamonds & Rust" those four nights must have felt unbearably poignant.

Of the women chosen to perform with her, only Janis Ian had spent time in the Village in the 1960s, though she's a decade younger than Baez. "Society's Child," her controversial debut, was released when she was just sixteen. With the exception of Baez's sister Mimi, whose last recording this is thought to be, all the other musicians emerged in the 1970s and 1980s. The concerts were a celebration not just of Baez herself but of the folk continuum and her place in it; of Baez as mentor and her fellow players as mentees though she has always seen it as "co-mentoring," everyone having something to teach and something to learn. A nod to the past that simultaneously acknowledged the present, torches passed back and forth.

The concerts were spine-tingling, the excitement palpable, and the press was out in force. The intimacy of the club heightened everything, the audience as up-close as it's possible to be. Given how much was riding on the first night in particular, it was hardly surprising that Baez displayed a touch of nerves at the outset and the tiny fluffs added authenticity to the album. The audience was fascinating. Gray hair, bald pates, and bifocals were much in evidence, but while quite a few looked as though they'd enjoyed "breakfast in bed for 400,000" at Woodstock, a fair number could have been conceived during the long lie-in. A mother and daughter had come from Brazil specially. A young couple held hands at the bar throughout, tears coursing down the woman's face during "Suzanne."

With Spector's blessing I was at the next day's rehearsals. I walked into the darkness of the club from bright afternoon sunshine just as Baez was organizing a coffee round. "Cappuccino?" she queried, as the familiar figure of tour manager Crook Stewart added me to his list and headed out. Janis Ian bustled in and, after exchanging hugs, sat down at the grand piano. "I notice the pedal still squeaks," she said to no one in particular. She and Baez worked first on "Jesse" and then "Amsterdam," a highlight of *Play Me Backwards*. It was written specially for Baez, who spent a few days with Janis and her partner at their home in Tennessee during the album's gestation period. Ian herself had never performed it and she tried a few riffs and experimented with vocal harmonies before suggesting some new touches from percussionist Steele.

Mary Black arrived with pianist Pat Crowley and they set to work on "Ring Them Bells," from Bob Dylan's 1989 album *Oh Mercy*, the religious imagery ideal for them both. They marked up the lyric sheet: who would take the lead where, who the harmony. Baez wanted to do an Irish song and suggested Van Morrison's "Carrickfergus," a favorite of Joan Senior. Black thought it overdone and proposed instead Phil Colclough's "Song for Ireland," which she sang, Crowley at the piano. Baez, seated on the floor, cried as she listened. In a late-night, up-town diner, everyone eating sandwiches after the show, Black remarked that "It's just so easy—she's really open to suggestion. We've never sung together before but it just seems so natural."

The album, released five months later, captured the wonderful spirit of the evening and the musicianship, with Baez solo (the standout being Eric Bogle's magisterial anti-war ballad "And the Band Played Waltzing Matilda") and in duet with each of her guests, the songs showcasing their own writing. The remastered version (2007) came as a double CD with six new songs. Most notable among them were "Stones in the Road," Baez singing with Chapin Carpenter, and "The Water Is Wide," a traditional ballad sung with The Indigo Girls in harmony so tight it gives you goose bumps. "Gracias a la Vida," performed at a languorous tempo with Tish Hinojosa, acquires new depths along with some subtle and delicious guitar chords.

Material remains in the can still, and from the first two nights alone there's "When I'm Gone"; "Song for Ireland"; "Pilgrim of Sorrow," *a cappella* and complete with quarter-tones, in response to a shouted request; and "Angel Band" with Chapin Carpenter. With Ian, there's "Amsterdam" and the wonderful burlesque of "On the Street Where You Live," from *My Fair Lady*, Joan starting and Janis joining in with gusto as the audience erupts.

"It was probably the first or second time we'd performed together," Ian reflected to me, twenty-four years later. "Joan is an absolute pro, not afraid to take a chance. She lets other performers shine. I'd work with her again any time; she's really a joy to me, as a performer. Ditto in the studio: she was a pleasure when we cut 'Amsterdam' . . . Joan always puts her heart into what she sings."

The album's innate quality, and its showcase of up-and-coming singer-songwriters at a time audiences were tuning in once again to that style of music-making, ensured widespread coverage for both the album and Baez herself, including a fourteen-page cover story in *Goldmine*, which would once have been unthinkable. She spent much of the next couple of years out on the road, and some of the dates were unusual for her—the Beale Street Music Festival in Memphis and the New Orleans Jazz & Heritage Festival, as well as concerts in Rabat, Budapest, and Bucharest. There was also another Bread and Roses benefit on Alcatraz, this time with The Indigo Girls and Dar Williams—in 1993 Baez had been the first artist to perform professionally at the former penitentiary. She suggested that in order to understand society everyone needed to spend some time in jail. It was a good thing for people to see inside and to recognize that problems didn't end in prison—they began there.

When it came time for the next album, Baez returned to Nashville to work once more with Wilson and Greenberg. This time, however, the three co-wrote only one song—"Lily," about Baez's childhood friend from Buffalo, whom she had recently visited. Instead, *Gone from Danger*, released in 1997, highlights work by new young writers, notably Richard Shindell, Betty Elders, and Sinéad Lohan. Shindell's three contributions have stood the test of time particularly well and "Reunion Hill," told from the perspective of a Civil War widow, "Fishing," an intricate and chilling song about the interrogation of a Mexican migrant, and "Money for Floods" are standout cuts. The selection demonstrates an unerring eye for a good lyric, and Baez's ability in this period to truly put her voice at the service of the song. The two-CD Collector's Edition released in 2009 featured live versions of the same songs plus a handful of additions. Most striking is "Long Bed from Kenya" by Elders who, with Shindell, joined parts of the *Gone from Danger* tour. With its folk-like simplicity and carefully wrought storyline, it's a song that deserves a far wider currency. That it scarcely ever showed up elsewhere is to be regretted.

Offstage, Baez remained socially engaged. On Earth Day, 1999, she and Bonnie Raitt joined Julia "Butterfly" Hill's Luna tree protest to protect California's giant redwoods, which were threatened by loggers. A few years later, Baez was up another tree, this time in South Los Angeles, supporting Hill's initiative to save a community garden where 350 local farmers had tended crops for more than a decade. There were a number of Honor the Earth concerts with Raitt and the Indigos. And as always she could be relied on for good-neighbor support: A range of hand-made, hand-painted pottery, created by her at the Petroglyph Ceramic Lounge, was sold in a silent auction for the East Palo Alto Tennis and Tutoring Program. "I've always thought this end of University Avenue, the wealthy end, needed to do something for the other end of University Avenue, the end that has nothing. Then I came across this program which is trying to combine the two types of people in Palo Alto," she explained. She also led a painting class for local kids. Immediately after 9/11, she played a free concert for local firefighters grieving their lost brothers and sang at an interfaith service for peace, justice, and healing. There was also a benefit for her cousin Peter Baez, to help pay the legal costs incurred while defending his Santa Clara County Medical Cannabis Center, and another for the Peninsula College Fund.

In July 2001, Baez's younger sister, Mimi, lost her battle with cancer, her legacy one of music but, chiefly, Bread and Roses, the organization she had founded in 1974 to bring music to hospitals, prisons, senior centers, and children's homes. "Mimi filled empty souls with hope and song," Baez said. "She held the aged and forgotten in her light. She reminded prisoners that they were human beings with names and not just numbers." The family led a memorial service the following month at San Francisco's Grace Cathedral, musicians, writers, artists, and politicians among the two thousand who gathered to remember a gracious woman who had known much sadness.

Amid the sorrow and anguish of Mimi's last weeks, Baez had escaped for an evening at Teatro ZinZanni, a circus-cum-cabaret which had been running in a tent on the San Francisco waterfront since the previous year. Following Mimi's passing, she called the director to ask if she might join the show's growing list of special guests, among them Maria Muldaur, Liliane Montevecchi, and Robin Williams. A three-week run as La Contessa began in

October, Baez as her fans had never seen her, variously in feathers and sequins, top hat, tuxedo, and blonde wig, dancing the tango and singing such numbers as "Falling in Love Again" and "What'll I Do?." She hammed it up with Yevgeniy Voronin on "Some Day My Prince Will Come." It was, she told me, "really fun and I got to be somebody else." Her mother went one night with producer Alan Abrahams, now a firm family friend. "I was Big Joan's date and we were sitting with about ten people. Joan in character was working our table and one of the patrons said to Big Joan, 'I heard that Joan Baez was supposed to be starring in this'. And with her daughter standing right there, Big Joan said, 'Oh really? I never liked her.' She was a hoot and lived to be a hundred." Baez would return to Teatro ZinZanni between concert tours over the next few years and doesn't discount a further appearance now she is free from touring commitments and the admonishments of her manager, who told her she should have "grown out of running away to join the circus fifty years ago."

Musically, Baez stayed focused, the long political raps that had characterized her concerts for so long replaced by ironic comments and jokes. Bizarrely, since her views were hardly a secret, some fifty people walked out of a concert when she told a joke about three microsurgeons, a horse's ass, and George W. Bush. A guy in the front row asked her to sing "God Bless America," which she refused to do, explaining, "I really love the human race." Offstage, however, if it wasn't quite business as usual Baez was still active. Over the next few years, she was vocal about the various wars the United States was prosecuting. In March 2003, she wrote an open letter to Secretary of State Colin Powell, "respectfully" urging him to resign his position from "this monstrous Administration," suggesting: "Your rightful place today, and in history, could and should be as a gifted, respected diplomat and a man of integrity, not as a member of a clique of elite, shortsighted warmongers scorned by sane peoples the world over." The month before, she had been among the leaders of San Francisco's march against the Iraq War (Pete Seeger turned out in

New York). There were also concerts with Steve Earle, Emmylou Harris, Chrissie Hynde, and Billy Bragg for the charity Landmine Free World and, in the run-up to the 2004 presidential election, she joined filmmaker Michael Moore's *Slacker Uprising* tour aimed at encouraging voter turnout among twentysomethings. In August 2005 she again joined anti-Iraq War protesters, this time at Camp Casey, near Bush's Texas ranch.

In 2003, she returned to the studio, Mark Spector producing *Dark Chords on a Big Guitar* in the cathedral-like setting of the brand-new Allaire Studios up in the Catskills near Woodstock. Released in the autumn, it showcased work by a range of mostly new, younger writers, among them Gillian Welch and David Rawlings, Natalie Merchant, and Josh Ritter, who would join her on tour. There were also songs from Joe Henry and Steve Earle, each of whom would later produce a Baez album. *Dark Chords on a Big Guitar*, its title taken from a line in "Rexroth's Daughter," bridges folk and alt-country (by now rebranded Americana) and adds a hint of grunge. In tone and content it does indeed feel dark. Baez's voice is darker too, bluesy when required, and she inhabits its lower range throughout. The atmosphere, which is key to this album, is full of foreboding: We are *all* now suffering through a dark night of the soul, and *Dark Chords* is its expression. She and the musicians complement each other perfectly: George Javori's percussion is always distinctive, while Byron Isaacs's bass and Duke McVinnie's lead guitar are masterly. "Christmas in Washington" closes the album, Earle's song in her hands becoming both a lament for what, and who, we've lost and the gentlest of calls to the barricades.

Josh Ritter gave up neuroscience for music, studying American history through narrative song at Oberlin College before going to Edinburgh for a postgrad on the Scottish ballads. He remembers being invited to open for Baez, and their first encounter was in New Hampshire. "I had the feeling that I was meeting a person who was of historic importance to the music I loved," he told me, on tour in Britain in 2019. "At that time, I just had a couple of records out and she treated me like a peer . . . When my manager called to say Joan Baez is going to record 'Wings' I couldn't wait to tell my parents. They couldn't believe it and they were *so* proud."

Touring with her, in Britain and Italy, was Ritter's first experience of "being on a bus, being with a crew of people. Joan took care of everybody in such a great way." They remain in touch and he pays tribute to her as "a mentor. I remember her saying you have so many voices inside you and one day the real voice is going to come out. That was something I needed to hear . . . She saw there was some unique artistic vision which hadn't come out yet . . . It was wild. When Joan Baez, who has introduced so many cool artists, takes you under her wing, that's a wonderful thing."

Baez's fall 2004 tour closed with two concerts at New York's Bowery Ballroom, a couple of days after the election that returned George W. Bush to the White House. On the second night, *Bowery Songs* was recorded live, opening poignantly with "Finlandia," Sibelius's beautiful melody given words by Lloyd Stone and Georgia Harkness in 1934, the height of the Depression, and featured in the movie *Slacker Uprising*. The songs spanned her career, surprises including "Seven Curses" (which, as Baez points out, Google attributes to Dylan), "Dink's Song," which would feature prominently in her final tour, and Steve Earle's "Jerusalem."

It is now fifteen years since she thought she had perhaps a decade left to sing that her voice begins to show its age. The break between chest voice and head voice, a problem overcome with lessons and daily exercises, is evident. She can sing in one or the other or make a leap for a high note or two, but melodies that require her to proceed seamlessly across the range are becoming a problem. The slightest cold or sore throat will of course exacerbate it, as will tiredness, all enemies of the singer. While natural musicianship and the adrenaline of live performance, not to mention her charisma, often carried Baez through, it was hard sometimes (as a longtime admirer who knew her work so well) to feel comfortable.

Still, when she toured Britain in spring 2006, the critic from the *Financial Times* gave her a five-star review and reflected on her ability still to "possess" a song, seeing "no hint of vulnerability of fragility." For *The Independent*'s reviewer, Baez's voice "retained all its old purity, but was mellowed by age . . . her stage presence amounted to an aura of nobility."

Nevertheless, her 2008 album, *Day After Tomorrow*, was both a critical and commercial success, marking a half-century of performing. "Dedicated to my Mom in her 96th year"—her father had passed away in 2007—it was an acoustic affair. Recorded in Nashville with Steve Earle producing, it included three of his songs, among them "God Is God," which would open many concerts. Unadorned, somber, spiritual as well as political, as befitted the times, it revealed a huskier voice which suited much of the material and conveyed a sense of wisdom and gravitas. The title track, penned by Tom Waits and his wife, Kathleen Brennan, is ideal Baez territory, the song told from the point of view of a young soldier whose hope and idealism have died on the battlefield. "Scarlet Tide," written by Elvis Costello and T Bone Burnett and sung by Alison Krauss on the soundtrack of the Civil War epic *Cold Mountain*, was another high point, though like "Mary," Patty Griffin's song for Everywoman, and Eliza Gilkyson's "Rose of Sharon," it exposed Baez's vocal difficulties. On the other hand, "Henry Russell's Last Words" worked perfectly, a beautiful song by up-and-coming writer Diana Jones, folk-like in its simplicity as it draws on letters found next to the body of an immigrant Scot who perished in a West Virginia mine disaster.

Once again, Baez was on the road for half the year, her schedule including Glastonbury and an appearance at the ninetieth birthday concert for Nelson Mandela in London's Hyde Park. Back in the States, there were some impromptu performances for organizers of Barack Obama's presidential campaign. For the first time ever she had endorsed a political candidate because it seemed "the responsible thing to do," as she wrote in a letter to the *San Francisco*

Chronicle. "If anyone can navigate the contaminated waters of Washington, lift up the poor, and appeal to the rich to share their wealth, it is Barack Obama. If anyone can bring light to the darkened corners of this nation and restore our positive influence in world affairs, it is Barack Obama. If anyone can begin the process of healing and bring unity to a country that has been divided for too long, it is Barack Obama. It is time to begin a new journey." Naturally, she was intrigued that a picture of Gandhi hung in his office. She would attend the inaugural ceremonies and sing at the Peace Ball—and at the White House a year later when the Obamas celebrated the music of the civil rights movement.

In 2009, in weather gray but less inclement than in 1959, Baez marked fifty years since her Newport debut with a return to the festival. In addition to her own set, she added harmonies to Judy Collins's performance of "Diamonds & Rust" and joined the closing hootenanny which included Pete Seeger, at whose Madison Square Garden ninetieth-birthday celebration she had recently sung. PBS marked her half-century with a documentary, *How Sweet the Sound*, directed by Mary Wharton. The two-hour film featured concert footage and took Baez back to the people and the places that had marked her life. Bob Dylan talked of her "heart-stopping soprano" and a guitar style he tried and failed to master, saying she was "at the forefront of a new dynamic in American music." Referring to her throughout as "Joanie," he said she had been "swept up in the madness my career had become" and that he felt "very bad" about what had happened. "I was sorry to see our relationship end." In a touching scene, she was reunited with David Harris, sharing memories of their whirlwind time together both heartfelt and natural. There was also remarkable footage, discovered in a freezer, of Baez performing at Club 47: She was seventeen, her talent all but fully formed.

Having put the stage fright behind her, Baez was having fun onstage, not least because she was now touring with her son, Gabriel, as percussionist. He had studied in Africa with master drummers, notably Babatunde Olatunji, returning to California to play with various ensembles before founding Rhythm Village, which leads workshops in schools, churches, hospitals, and corporations, promoting music as a healing art. With Dirk Powell, who played just about everything else, Baez had finally found "my big band" who would tour with her until her final bow. It was a family show and she felt privileged. The tours took them to places that were sometimes less familiar: Morocco and Ecuador in 2012; Argentina, Chile, Brazil, and Mexico in 2014; Australia and New Zealand in 2015.

More young singers enjoyed the warmth of the Baez spotlight. Marianne Aya Omac had been playing her gypsy-inflected music on the streets of Montpellier for several years when she met Baez in 2009. Incredibly, she was invited to sing at her concert on the city's historic Promenade du Peyroux, and the two women would go on to share the stage at more than thirty other concerts, including the Fez Festival of World Sacred Music in 2011. Baez and Harris invited Omac to San Francisco to record an album, *Solo*, to which they contributed, and she performed at a series of Gabriel's own concerts in California. Grace Stumberg, a young singer-songwriter from Buffalo, joined Team Baez as guitar tech and assistant in 2012. Coaxed and coached by Baez, she was soon adding backing vocals. Ultimately, Stumberg was billed as "co-singer," taking a verse on songs such as "Me and Bobby McGee," when her fine bluesy voice won appreciative applause.

In 2016, a big birthday loomed, one that surely concentrated her mind. Baez celebrated her seventy-fifth with an all-star concert at New York's Beacon Theatre, gathering old friends and new for a concert that was filmed for PBS and released as a live double album. Along with Chapin Carpenter and the Indigos, guest artists included Judy Collins, Jackson Browne, Emmylou Harris, Richard Thompson, and Paul Simon, as well as Mavis Staples, with whom Baez had shared many a civil rights gig. They dedicated "Oh, Freedom" to Harry Belafonte who was in the house. One of the evening's highlights was the duet with Irish singer-songwriter Damien Rice on the ever-mysterious Irish ballad "She Moved Through the Fair." After a final encore which secured Grace Stumberg a *Rolling Stone* namecheck, she told the audience: "See you in ten years!"

After the seventy-fifth birthday concert, which was released as both a CD and DVD, the rest of the year was a busy one, a long series of American dates broken up by a summer tour in Europe. She endorsed Bernie Sanders, who had "won my heart. He supports causes in which I have been personally involved for decades. I take great strength from his firm stance against the death penalty (amazing!), his belief that Palestinians should have a place at the bargaining table (unheard of!), his understanding that the prison system must transform its agenda from punishment to rehabilitation, his desire to treat immigrants as human beings, and of course by his grass roots funding and astonishing refusal to sell himself to the devil on Wall Street, or anywhere else for that matter." When she could no longer turn out for Sanders, she raised her voice at several anti-Trump rallies and even wrote a song, "Nasty Man," which went viral.

The following spring, Baez was inducted into the Rock and Roll Hall of Fame in a televised ceremony at Brooklyn's Barclays Center. Some felt it absurd but many thought it a long-overdue recognition of her importance to the wider rock ecology, her career opening the way to the first generation of female singer-songwriters, and to British folk rock bands such as Fairport Convention and Steeleye Span. There was Jimmy Page's admission of his fixation with her guitar playing on "Babe, I'm Gonna Leave You" and of course there was Bob Dylan, to whom she provided many a stage. How would the young Joan Baez have felt, I asked her when we met a few months after the ceremony? "I'd probably have refused," she laughed. "I'm sure I wouldn't have accepted. I was *such* a snoot. But it was fun. And you can look at it either way: 'What's *she* doing in the Hall of Fame?' or 'About time.'"

And it *was* about time. Coincidence or not, it dovetailed with Baez deciding it was time to hang up her guitar, or at least to decommission the tour bus. In November 2017 came the announcement of a final album, her first in ten years, and what the singer called "my last year of formal extended touring." She was, she said, "looking forward to being on the road with a beautiful new album about which I am truly proud. I welcome the opportunity to share this new music as well as longtime favorites with my audiences around the world." It was not a surprise, and sad as it was to think that she was leaving the stage, it was the right decision—to bow out at a time of her own choosing, as she'd told me in 1990, and on a career high. Who would deny her a retirement after sixty years!

Released in March 2018, *Whistle Down the Wind* was recorded at United Recording Studio B in three phases: two days in February, five in May, and three in September. The dedication is to Gabriel, her granddaughter, Jasmine, and "to my friend and soulmate, Pam. The Mom." The producer was Joe Henry, who had worked with old friends Bonnie Raitt and Ramblin' Jack Elliott. Carefully wrought and cohesive, the songs are all new yet linked inextricably to what's gone before. Timeless, more a closing of a circle than a linear signing-off. We may be "down to the wire, runnin' out of time," as Baez sings in Eliza Gilkyson's "The Great Correction," but she's "still got hope in this heart of mine."

Anyone familiar with the Baez *oeuvre* would have recognized instantly the resonances with songs recorded long ago: "Silver Blade," written by her protégé Josh Ritter, harking back to "Silver Dagger"; "I Wish the Wars Were All Over," adapted by Tim Eriksen, alludes to the folk tropes of "Jackaroe" and is a reminder of the singer's lifelong pacifism. Anohni's "Another World," a meditation on ecological disaster, sounds appropriately world-weary, freighted by older age—a resigned sense, perhaps, that nothing will improve in her lifetime.

Zoe Mulford's hymn-like and poignant "The President Sang Amazing Grace" would be a standout anywhere, anytime, but to hear Baez sing it as America reeled from the Parkland massacre was moving indeed. As Florida buried its dead, President Trump played golf and advocated more guns. In that Charleston church in summer 2015, President Obama had stood as comforter-in-chief, crying with his people and singing the age-old spiritual.

That, and the two Waits songs, are the highlights of an album that has plenty. "I can't stay here but I'm scared to leave," she sings on the title track, which probably summed up how she felt about her leave-taking, no matter her spiritual and temporal hinterlands. "Last Leaf" is a song about survival, sometimes against the odds, through fair weather and foul; about tenacity, faith, inner strength. Age and use had given her voice a wonderful patina that spoke of wisdom and experience. Its grain and gravitas were comfort and warning on songs that were personal, universal—and relevant.

No Depression summed up: "*Whistle Down the Wind* may be Joan Baez's best album, for it showcases her way with a song: her emotional engagement with the lyrics, her passionate delivery of the story in the song, her somber or soaring musical setting of the lyrics. There are moments of purity, clarity, and grace on Baez's album delivered powerfully and poignantly through her vision and her voice." The public responded enthusiastically, and the album debuted at No. 18 on the *Billboard* chart, her highest placing since *Diamonds & Rust* in 1975, and it sold well throughout Europe.

The Fare Thee Well tour began in Stockholm on March 2, 2018 and, with breaks, wound its way through Europe, including a ten-day season at Paris's celebrated Olympia in June. America would keep her busy from September through to Thanksgiving. In New York City, Bill and Hillary Clinton were in the audience, Baez clearly forgiven for supporting Bernie. Before the first baby boomer president, for whom Vietnam had caused campaign controversy, she and the band took a knee to a recording of Jimi Hendrix's Woodstock version of "The Star-Spangled Banner," Gabe's idea.

We spoke backstage at Bristol's Colston Hall in May 2018, the first date in the second leg of her British tour. She had a bad back, the consequence of years standing with a guitar slung round her neck and a fall from her treehouse, where she likes to sleep under the stars. Bumping around on the bus didn't help. She looked well, her silver hair still thick, lines of time and laughter etched into her olive skin, her brown eyes twinkling behind rimless specs. "We've been on this amazing ride . . . I said to Mark I feel as though we short-changed people, because tickets sold out in just a few hours. So in the States I'm adding the Deep South. Mark said you can't make any money there but I said treat it like Sarajevo. It's one of the things I *have* to do."

In fact, a whole second tour was mapped out, another month in Europe preceding further US dates. The returns to Selma and Birmingham in spring 2019 were emotional, not least because the nonviolent battles fought and seemingly won in the 1960s turned out not to be over, as Charleston (where she had sung at a memorial) and Charlottesville tragically showed. Baez dusted off "Birmingham Sunday," Richard Fariña's song from 1963 about the Sunday school bombing, which she also sang in her final New York City concert on May 1. It was no longer a report on a distant war—bombs were once again primed, guns loaded—and this time there was no moral outrage from the White House, just the "Nasty Man" trying to excuse violence on both sides.

A core repertoire, heavy on the new album and on Bob Dylan, pertained through the tour's entirety, Baez adding songs particular to each locale—"No More Auction Block" in the South, and in Bristol, where the slave trade had funded much of the city. "Deportees" remained horribly topical, seventy years after Woody Guthrie wrote it. "This is not the time to build a wall. It is time to feed the hungry and put clothes on the naked and take care of the most vulnerable, and those are the children," she would say by way of introduction.

At last, keys had been lowered and songs skillfully reworked, even "Diamonds & Rust." Grace Stumberg's harmony offered support and discreet cover where needed. We talked about "the voice"— which she has always regarded as "a gift," taking credit only for its maintenance and delivery. I suggested that it had taken her a long time to come to terms with its inevitable changes. "It *did*—that's why I didn't make an album for ten years. I think it took me *that* long to accept it. Embrace it, actually. I like the noises that came out on this album." As to what she calls "the old Joanie voice," she is, she said, "in awe" when she runs across it. "I don't take any credit for it. I'm just gobsmacked: *is that me?*" She was gratified that "young folk singer types are always very appreciative of whatever it was I did, sometimes through their parents. I've had an influence on their lives. Generally, it means politically as well as musically."

Baez would "miss the gang, so we're making the most of this trip. The halls are all filled up so it's double the excitement of any tour." She could understand that musicians retired and then wanted to go back out and do it all again but her voice was telling her and, though she was fit, so was her body. While she didn't entirely discount the possibility of turning out for a benefit or a guest spot, she wanted to go home and paint—she'd just staged her first exhibition, *Mischief Makers*, a celebration of those who helped bring about social change, including of course Václav Havel. The collection had been bought by the Federated Indians of Graton Rancheria for installation in the future Social Justice Learning Center at Sonoma State University. Maybe she'd travel a little. "You get only one life. I might end up going to see some places I haven't had a chance to explore. It'll be open to me. I don't know what I'll feel like."

The last month of Fare Thee Well took place in Europe, where her audience had kept the faith when Americans had not. Switzerland, Belgium, Germany, France; Germany again, Italy, back to France; and then finally into Spain. Three concerts at summer beach festivals, TV news chronicling her progress. The final one, Sant Feliu de Guíxols, delayed by a deluge, followed by one last, long bus journey—450 miles—to Madrid and the bijou grandeur of the Teatro Real. Catching a little sleep after the soundcheck at the nearby Hotel Ópera, a charming and unpretentious family establishment chosen for its proximity to the stage door, as the tour bus and driver had been returned to base. The gypsy life would tax people half her age.

In this most late-night of cities, the curtain was nine-thirty. Photographers and a TV crew crouched at the back of the stalls. "This is the last concert of the last tour. Of my life," she said, a few songs in. "I'm sad about it, but I'm happy about it." There was an ovation, shouts of "*brava!*" It was, of course, an evening of Baez classics, including "Gracias a la Vida," Violeta Parra's glorious hymn to life. Songs such as "Oh, Freedom" and "Ain't Gonna Let Nobody Turn Me Around" resonated in Madrid as much as in Montgomery, for less than fifty years ago Spain was a dictatorship. Only when General Franco was dead did Baez play in the country, and on her first visit she broke a decades-long taboo by singing "No Nos Moveran" on live television. The dedication was to La Pasionaría, the woman who had declared "*No Pasarán!*" during the battle for Madrid in November 1936. Baez sang it again as an encore, the audience—some of them old enough to remember the bad old days—singing along: "*Unidas en la lucha, no nos moveran.*" A rebel song in the opera house!

There was a surprise guest, Amancio Prada, the Leonese singer-songwriter, poet, and cultural historian whose song "Adiós Rios, Adiós Fontes," a setting of Rosalía de Castro's poem, Baez had occasionally featured in her concerts. De Castro, a mid-nineteenth-century figure, wrote in Galego, the Galician language. Despite the deprivations of her own life, she fought for the poor and defenseless, a champion of women's rights who challenged authority. Someone to whom Baez could relate. Together she and Prada sang the song they had practiced only briefly that afternoon. It was slightly ragged but there was no mistaking the emotion, onstage and off.

After the concert, after the backstage celebration, the two musicians hugged. Prada turned to leave. "Wait, I have a present for you," said Baez, returning with one of the two guitars that had accompanied her around the world. "Take it, it's my gift," she said as Prada resisted. "I couldn't imagine that she offered me something as valuable and personal as her guitar, one of the Martin guitars whose sound, by the way, had impressed me so much," he wrote the next day. "But she insisted. 'The guitar is yours, I don't need two guitars now.'"

"Dink's Song" was the final encore, closing a concert that *El Pais*, in a full-page review, described as "emotional, serene, humble and extraordinarily generous." Baez alone onstage, as she had begun sixty years ago; as she had been for so much of her career. The tremolo accompaniment rang out from her custom-made Martin 0-45JB, her voice soaring, the emotion palpable.

If I had wings like Noah's dove
I'd fly up the river to the man I love
Fare thee well, my honey
Fare thee well
Some one of these mornings, and it won't be long
You'll look for me and I'll be gone
Adiós, mis amigos
Adiós.
Some one of these mornings, bright and clear
I'm gonna spread my wings
I'm gonna fly from here
Adiós, mis amigos
Adiós.
Woke up this morning it was drizzling rain
And in my heart was an aching pain
Fare thee well, my honey
Fare thee well
If I had wings like Noah's dove
I'd fly up the river to the man I love
Adiós, mis amigos
Adiós.

"Adiós!" she said. And with a final wave she left the stage.

Still singing out: The eight-city tour raised funds and awareness to support education for displaced people via the Jesuit Refugee Service's Global Education Initiative

POSTLUDE

It's hard to imagine what it must have felt like for Joan Baez, as she, her band, and crew left Madrid early the following morning. Happy and sad, as she had said onstage. Doubtless a little tearful as they said their goodbyes—the camaraderie of the road is close and familial. "Retirement"—not a word she used—for an artist it is not like giving up the nine-to-five. Musicians are defined by what they do, and for singers, *real* singers, it's hard not to worry about the voice itself, yet without being too precious. A cold or a throat infection is always a nightmare prospect, and as singers get older there are fewer places to hide. Sleep, that great cure-all, is often hard to come by. The adrenaline that gets you on stage means you need time to unwind and decompress after a concert—but so often there's an early start and it's on to the next stop in the tour.

For sixty years, Baez had known little else, though the pace of her touring in the last couple of decades was far higher than earlier in her career. For much of her life on the road, she traveled without a crew, just with her guitar and a small handful of friends and associates who, in the 1970s and 1980s, when music played second fiddle to politics, were there to support her human rights work as much as anything else. Glamorous and grueling in equal measure, sometimes dangerous, it was the life she chose—or perhaps that chose her. It was, I believe, a vocation; a calling.

"There must be something I can do with my life that will be worthwhile," she worried to Nat Hentoff in one of their many encounters during the Rolling Thunder tour. "There are four of me, right? A mother, a woman, a musician, and a politician." Often those elements were in conflict with one another—in 2009's *How Sweet the Sound*, by which time her son, Gabriel Harris, married with a young daughter, was part of her band, she admitted she hadn't always been the most attentive mother, though she had thought she was. And in answering so many calls to action she believed she was helping to build a better world for him and his friends. Whatever the inevitable parent-child difficulties, they clearly talked them through and Gabriel's own chosen career path as a musician involved in the healing arts suggests he's more than a chip off the old block, as she is herself, and her parents before her.

Musician and activist. Activist and musician. Joan Baez has led a remarkable life and she's not done yet. In the months following that final concert, she popped up here and there: hanging out backstage with The Rolling Stones at Levi's Stadium; accepting an invitation from Lana Del Rey to step out for a couple of numbers at a concert in Berkeley; attending the Latin Recording Academy Awards in Las Vegas to be honored with a Lifetime Achievement Award; and joining a singalong, onstage and off, celebrating sixty years of Club 47 (now Club Passim) at Boston's Folk Americana Roots Hall of Fame. In the city where she truly fell in love with folk music, and where she took her first steps as a professional singer, Baez presented her old friend and fellow BU dropout Betsy Siggins with the Club Passim Lifetime Achievement Award, appearing guitarless for the evening's finale alongside more recent alums from the local music scene, not least Josh Ritter whom she had mentored only a few years before. "Rainbow Connection" probably would not have been her choice of song but she alone on that stage had cavorted with Kermit and Miss Piggy—way back in 1980, when her career was a mere twenty years old.

So what then of the Baez legacy? How will she be judged and remembered? Where will she fit in the pantheon of singer-songwriter musicians?

After 1960, any young woman who picked up a guitar was compared to her and judged against her. Rightly, in the sense that she influenced countless young singers, providing them with a ready-made repertoire—*The Joan Baez Songbook*, published in

1964, was a bestseller and remains in print to this day. Even her most talented direct contemporaries, notably Canadian singer-songwriter Bonnie Dobson who, like Baez, arrived in Greenwich Village having already established her credentials, and Judy Collins, who hailed from Denver and had started her career out west, inevitably suffered somewhat by comparison. When Jac Holzman of Elektra offered Collins a recording contract, it was with the words "We've found our Joan Baez." A double-edged sword, no doubt, though it never got in the way of their friendship. Collins had her own unique talent and style, but most who arrived in the Baez slipstream, and not just in America, had little to offer. Joni Mitchell occupies a pedestal as a great songwriter, probably the most influential among women songwriters, but as a singer and instrumentalist—as a *musician*—she can't hold a candle to Baez.

In a literal sense, Joan Baez was (and is) inimitable for the simple reason that her voice was so remarkable. For some folk purists it was too beautiful, too refined; it belonged in the conservatoire. Indeed, had the teenaged Joanie chosen to apply to music school rather than drama school, it's reasonable to assume she would not have been short of offers. Her excursions into the classical repertoire, most notably with Villa-Lobos's "Bachianas Brasileiras No. 5," which deserves wider exposure, reveal a consummate musician who, had she chosen formal study of the classical repertoire, would likely as not have won critical acclaim in that world also. Did she ever seriously consider such a path? Probably not, though she was clearly exposed to the great voices of the day and grew up loving them.

She has said she believed she was "too small" for the opera stage, and it's true that sopranos in the 1950s and 1960s were often voluptuous creatures, but she told me she preferred to keep "my feet in the dirt" of folk music, a reference not only to the music's roots but to the causes it served. It's interesting to note, however, her longtime role as an Honorary Advisor to the Jussi Björling Society. Björling is the Swedish tenor whose voice, with its "tears," moves her more than any other, as she said on a visit to his home in

Borlänge, now a museum. It's tantalizing to wonder what classical pieces she worked on with singing teacher Bob Bernard and whether anything exists in the vault which we may one day hear.

Janis Ian, for whom Baez was "always my first call for a song that I thought might work for her," says simply that she was "born with a great gift"—she just had to open her mouth and beautiful sounds came out. "When you're born with a great instrument like Joan's, initially you don't have to learn the work-arounds and phrasing tricks someone like me has to learn from the start." In the 1970s, there was a perceptible dip in the Baez voice, but lessons, practice, and self-discipline restored it.

The trained voice that emerged and carried her through the 1980s and 1990s was a far richer and more expressive instrument, age naturally deepening the voice, and technique liberating it. Which makes it all the more disappointing that she was able to make only a handful of recordings during that period and why *Speaking of Dreams* is both significant and a genuine treasure. Her voice was still in fine shape when she recorded *Ring Them Bells* in 1995 and it remained so well into her fifth decade of performing.

Technique improves stamina but, as with the rest of the body, the years take their toll: The vocal cord fibers thin and stiffen and the larynx cartilage hardens, with the result that the voice becomes less stable, the top notes less reliable. Baez agreed that it took time to accept the inevitable—but when, finally, she did, adjusting keys and tweaking melody lines, the resulting voice was warm and characterful, freighted with emotion—the Spanish would call it *duende*. The "achingly pure soprano" had been thrilling but the timbre of late Baez seemed ideally suited to the times, and to the songs chosen for her final studio album. On *Whistle Down the Wind*, Baez was the Wise Woman, singing from experience.

From the outset, classical music critics in America took her seriously as an artist, and fellow musicians held her in the highest regard. "The traditional ballads—she was made for that. Her voice is a miracle," singer-songwriter David Massengill told me after her final New York concert in spring 2019, "and it's *still* good. She would go out there and just *do* these things, musically, which were very brave. I never heard her hit a wrong note."

Her guitar playing has been taken for granted but it has always been rather sophisticated, a self-contained combination of rhythm and lead, Baez often picking out lines that either harmonized with her voice or were in counterpoint to it, while bass notes supported a song's harmonic architecture. For Massengill, it was always "exemplary, and it's still as clean and crisp as it was. She makes *such* clean chords, and she goes into the blues." Josh Ritter agrees: "She's a *fantastic* guitarist! I learned guitar from listening to Odetta, Joan and Mississippi John Hurt. Strong thumb-picking, intricate but it never gets in the way of the words, always in the service of the song. Beautifully played but without flash. Those three were so important to my guitar paying." Ritter contends that it's her skill as a guitarist in combination with her "absolutely glorious" voice that makes her "just such a great performer of songs."

Folk music and social activism have long been natural bedfellows, as Baez had seen with Pete Seeger, and keeping her feet "in the dirt" was more than just a metaphor—there was surely symbolism in her walking barefoot on the road from Selma to Montgomery, arm-in-arm with James Baldwin, intentional or otherwise. Twenty years later, she put in a shift at a Manhattan restaurant where Massengill—with whom she'd just performed at a twenty-five-year celebration of Gerde's Folk City—worked two nights a week to pay the bills. "She said, 'I'd like to see what it's like to wash dishes at a restaurant—do you mind if I come by?' She showed up on time and stayed nearly the whole shift. She was a good sport. Everybody had their picture taken with Joan in her kitchen whites." The staff came from the islands, from South America, from Thailand "and she had a song for everyone. She fit right in and was so unassuming."

Betsy Siggins, with whom she committed that first small act of civil disobedience as a BU freshman, reflected that Baez used her gift "wisely and wonderfully" and that "her activism and her standup-and-be-counted went right in parallel. There were so many things that were wrong with the country in those days [the 1960s] and she led. She led quietly and she led loudly. Her parents were Quakers, so she understood nonviolence and pacifism probably from the get-go."

Remembering a long-ago evening spent tweaking the noses of the John Birch Society at the Monterey Fairgrounds, following the 1963 Monterey Folk Festival, Siggins recalls how skillful Baez was, even then, in making her point. "Joan was very coy about how she set them up. We went over and she began asking questions—I don't think they recognized her. She started by asking what do you do, what do you stand for—and once she had their full attention she started opening up the door to peace and activism and inequality and all the things the John Birch Society probably didn't want to hear, and they got uncomfortable. Once she homed in, there was no mercy, but she was very aware of her own presence and aware of how words mattered. I always found that she knew what to say. She sounded like a person who was far more mature than her age, but it was this gift she had of looking for the pony in a roomful of shit. She had a *life*, she was on her way to becoming an important person." Fifteen years later, a television encounter with the tricksy conservative commentator William F. Buckley Jr. on his long-running public affairs show *The Firing Line* revealed a sophisticated debater—clad, appropriately for the occasion, in a silk dress and heels.

Siggins agrees that Baez had a calling. "I didn't see it as ambition, I saw it as her life's work. She had a path and she grew into that path as it opened up for her. As the path moved forward and she stayed on it, it became more evident that she had that gift and she was able to speak eloquently about injustice. She was able to take chances. That trip to Vietnam . . . She was very brave, and it's not to show off—it's to make a point. Her work is *still* cut out for her. It will take a different path. I think it will always include standing up for the injustices in the world. She's given countless, *countless* younger people the inspiration and courage to do better, to do more, to think harder, to be responsible, to be a part of the solution not a part of the problem. *She gave back.* You look at her history and you see thousands and thousands of people who, to one degree or another, were influenced by her, took solace from her. She was a role model for a generation of young girls."

Baez is often referred to as a "protest singer" but that is a reductive and demeaning term. She is someone who has used her unique gifts on the road to finding personal meaning, and who, nevertheless, has endeavored always to put these talents at the service of those less fortunate, whether in Birmingham or Buenos Aires, Hanoi or Sarajevo, in refugee camps in Thailand or the West Bank and Gaza. It took sangfroid and real guts to visit Latin America in the 1980s where, effectively banned from the stage and with threats to her life, Baez sang for students and other activists, and for the grieving Madres de Plaza de Mayo. "Joan's presence in Argentina was a great source of support and strength for the human rights cause," said Nobel laureate Adolfo Pérez Esquivel. "It gave us strength to continue struggling."

Alan Abrahams, her 1980s producer, mused: "A career spanning over sixty years? She has done everything, and as we all know she dedicated her life to others, her fame used to fight (nonviolently) for peace, civil rights, human rights, justice for us all. A deep care and devotion for our planet and its future. Her legacy? 'To whom much is given, much is expected'—she has exceeded all expectations. Joan once said in an article that 'one of the best things about working with Alan, he was never impressed with my legend.' I *was* impressed—with her as an artist, her work ethic and discipline, and as a beautiful, kind human being. I'm grateful for the gift of her true friendship."

David Massengill reflected: "She is one of those Picasso people. One in a couple of million people . . . She carried herself with a lot of grace and bravery and she has something to be really proud of, and for other people to take pride in . . . Joan will have the highest legacy you could possibly have. Not only was her singing incredible but her moral stance was impeccable."

For Janis Ian, Baez is "a force of nature. Who else could have introduced Bob Dylan to the world, and done it with grace, eloquence, and humor? What other singer has been consistently brave and consistently right? History will judge, but for my generation, there were Pete and Woody, followed by Baez, and Dylan. Those are the fulcrums in folk music. No one has come along to match any of them."

It has taken a long time for Dylan fans to acknowledge the key role Baez played in his early career, or even the fact that he cared about her. Baez was accused of using *him* and it wasn't until years later that Dylan would acknowledge that it was her voice, just as much as the fabled Guthrie, that drew him to New York in the first place: She sounded "like a siren off some Greek island," he said in an interview for his website with Bill Flanagan. "Just the sound of it could put you into a spell. She was an enchantress. You'd have to get yourself strapped to the mast like Odysseus and plug your ears so you wouldn't hear her. She'd make you forget who you were."

Joan Baez has cast both a deep spell and a long shadow. She will always stand at the crossroads of music and social activism, a woman who consistently put doing what was right ahead of doing what was popular. "For anybody interested in social justice, she is a great beacon," singer-songwriter Rhiannon Giddens has observed. "It's very inspiring as a female artist to see how she has done things on her own terms and become a byword for musical activism." There's no doubt that she will continue to raise her voice in support of the causes she holds dear, locally and globally, but as a singer Baez has taken her final bow. She deserves time to herself, at home amid the rustic tranquility of the Santa Cruz Mountains, where she has lived since the 1970s and where she can now devote herself to painting, but she will be missed.

My goal in *Joan Baez: The Last Leaf* has been both to celebrate and illuminate a remarkable figure whose like we will never see again. To show what shaped her and how in turn she helped shape us. And why she matters, because she does, very much, and she will continue to matter even though she has stepped down from the stage, and even when she finally crosses that Jordan river.

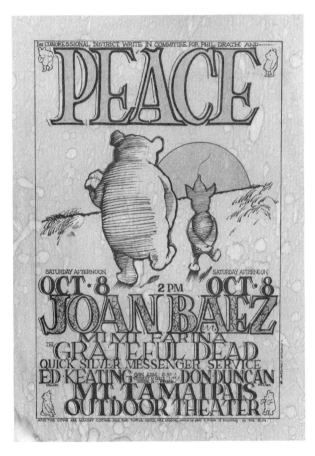

Stanley Mouse's poster for a concert at the Mount Tamalpais Mountain Theater, a benefit for the congressional campaign of antiwar candidate Phil Drath, October 8, 1966

DISCOGRAPHY, FILMOGRAPHY AND BIBLIOGRAPHY

The life and work of Joan Baez has been far less documented than that of the musician with whom she is so often linked. The purpose of *The Last Leaf* has been to draw together the various threads of her music and social activism and to demonstrate her centrality to our recent socio-cultural history. Encountering her music led me on a journey of discovery into the American hinterland, its highways and byways. Thus, my aim here has been to create a starting point for serious study and exploration of a remarkable career – and one that is far from over.

The Discography, Filmography and Bibliography that follow are necessarily selective.

The Discography gives original U.S. release dates only. Noted are the titles of bonus tracks that were added when the various catalogs (via Vanguard, A&M, Gold Castle, Virgin, Guardian/EMI, KOCH, Razor & Tie, Proper, Bobolink) began to be properly reissued starting in 2001, some 24 albums in all, featuring detailed new liner notes on each entry by music historian Arthur Levy.

International releases (from European tours and suchlike) are only included where there is no American equivalent (or when they contain songs unavailable elsewhere), with alternate tracks from country-specific albums listed where appropriate.

No attempt is made to list the innumerable "best-of" compilations of previously released material drawn from the Baez catalogs. Nor indeed to document the track changes that occurred on early pressings of her earliest albums: the purpose here is to identify the sequence of the settled content of the Baez catalog for those seeking to build and study the complete collection of her recordings.

DISCOGRAPHY

FOLKSINGERS 'ROUND HARVARD SQUARE (Veritas)

On the Banks of the Ohio (Joan Baez)
O What a Beautiful City (Joan Baez)
Sail Away Ladies (Joan Baez)
Black Is the Color (Joan Baez)
Lowlands (Joan Baez)
What You Gonna Call Your Pretty Little Baby (Joan Baez)
Kitty (Joan Baez with Bill Wood)
So Soon In the Morning (Joan Baez with Bill Wood)
Careless Love (Joan Baez with Bill Wood)
Le Cheval Dans La Baignoire (The Horse in the Bathtub) (Bill Wood)
John Henry (Bill Wood)
Travelin' Shoes (Bill Wood)
Bold Soldier (Bill Wood)
Walie (Ted Alevizos)
Rejected Lover (Ted Alevizos)
Astrapsen (The Sun Is Risen) (Ted Alevizos)
Lass From the Low Country (Ted Alevizos)
Don't Weep After Me (Joan Baez with Bill Wood, Ted Alevizos)

RECORDED: Steve Fassett's Recording Studio, Beacon Hill, Boston, May 1959
PRODUCER: Lemuel Marshall Wells.
RELEASED: January 1960

—

JOAN BAEZ (Vanguard)

Silver Dagger
East Virginia
Fare Thee Well (or 10,000 Miles)
House Of the Rising Sun
All My Trials
Wildwood Flower
Donna (Sholom Secunda, Aaron Zeitlin)
John Riley
Rake and Rambling Boy
Little Moses
Mary Hamilton (Child 173)
Henry Martin (Child 250)
El Preso Número Nuevo (Antonio Cantoral Garcia,
     Roberto Cantoral Garcia)

2001 REISSUE PREVIOUSLY UNRELEASED BONUS TRACKS:
Girl Of Constant Sorrow
I Know You Rider
John Riley (full-length master)

ALL SONGS TRADITIONAL AND ARRANGED BY JOAN BAEZ EXCEPT WHERE NOTED
RECORDED: The Manhattan Towers Hotel Ballroom, New York, July 1960
PRODUCER: Maynard Solomon
RELEASED: October 1960

—

JOAN BAEZ, VOL 2 (Vanguard)

Wagoner's Lad
The Trees They Do Grow High
The Lily Of the West
Silkie (Child 113)
Engine 143
Once I Knew a Pretty Girl
Lonesome Road
Banks Of the Ohio, with the Greenbriar Boys
Pal Of Mine, with the Greenbriar Boys
Barbara Allen (Child 84)
The Cherry Tree Carol (Child 54)
Old Blue
Plaisir d'Amour (Martini il Tedesco)

2001 REISSUE PREVIOUSLY UNRELEASED BONUS TRACKS:
I Once Loved a Boy
Poor Boy (aka Bow Down)
Longest Train I Ever Saw (aka Who's Gonna Shoe Your Pretty Little Foot?)

ALL SONGS TRADITIONAL AND ARRANGED BY JOAN BAEZ EXCEPT WHERE NOTED
RECORDED: The Manhattan Towers Hotel Ballroom, New York, 1961
PRODUCER: Maynard Solomon
RELEASED: September 1961

—

JOAN BAEZ IN CONCERT (Vanguard)

Babe I'm Gonna Leave You (Anne Breedon)
Geordie (Child 209)
Copper Kettle (Albert Frederick Beddoe)
Kumbaya
What Have They Done To the Rain (Malvina Reynolds)

Black Is the Color (arranged by John Jacob Niles)
Danger Waters (Jacob Browne, Arthur S. Alberts)
Gospel Ship (Herbert Buffum)
The House Carpenter (Child 243)
Pretty Boy Floyd (Woody Guthrie)
Lady Mary
Até Amanhã
Matty Groves (Child 81)

2002 REISSUE PREVIOUSLY UNRELEASED BONUS TRACKS:
Streets of Laredo
My Good Old Man
My Lord, What a Morning

ALL SONGS TRADITIONAL AND ARRANGED BY JOAN BAEZ EXCEPT WHERE NOTED
RECORDED: live on tour at various concerts, 1962
PRODUCER: Maynard Solomon
RELEASED: September 1962

–

JOAN BAEZ IN CONCERT, PART 2 (Vanguard)

Once I Had a Sweetheart
Jackaroe
Don't Think Twice, It's All Right (Bob Dylan)
We Shall Overcome (Guy Carawan, Arthur Hamilton, Zilphia Horton,
    Pete Seeger) (recorded at Miles College, Birmingham, Alabama)
Portland Town (Derroll Adams)
Queen Of Hearts
Manhã de Carnaval/Te Ador (Luiz Bonfá, Antônio Maria)
Long Black Veil (Marijohn Wilkin, Danny Dill)
Fennario
'Nu Bello Cardillo
With God On Our Side (Bob Dylan)
Three Fishers (John Pyke Hullah, Charles Kingsley)
Hush Little Baby
Battle Hymn of the Republic (Julia Ward Howe)

2002 REISSUE PREVIOUSLY UNRELEASED BONUS TRACKS:
Rambler Gambler
Railroad Bill
The Death Of Emmett Till (A.C. Bilbrew)
Tomorrow Is a Long Time (Bob Dylan)
When First Unto This Country A Stranger I Came

ALL SONGS TRADITIONAL AND ARRANGED BY JOAN BAEZ EXCEPT WHERE NOTED
RECORDED: live on tour at various concerts, 1962 & 1963
PRODUCER: Maynard Solomon
RELEASED: November 1963

—

JOAN BAEZ IN SAN FRANCISCO (Fantasy Records)

Island In the Sun (Harry Belafonte, Lord Burgess)
Water Boy
Annie Had a Baby (Henry Glover, Lois Mann)
Oh Freedom
Man Smart, Woman Smarter (Norman Span aka King Radio)
Scarlet Ribbons (Evelyn Danzig, Jack Segal)
Dark As a Dungeon (Merle Travis)
Told My Captain
Young Blood (Jerry Leiber, Mike Stoller, Doc Pomus)
I Gave My Love a Cherry
La Bamba
Every Night

ALL SONGS TRADITIONAL AND ARRANGED BY JOAN BAEZ EXCEPT WHERE NOTED
RECORDED: June 1958
PRODUCER: Dick Tognazzini for Storm Records
RELEASED: May 1964

—

JOAN BAEZ/5 (Vanguard)

There But For Fortune (Phil Ochs)
Stewball (Ralph Rinzler, Bob Yellin, John Herald)
It Ain't Me Babe (Bob Dylan)
The Death Of Queen Jane (Child 170)
Bachianas Brasileiras/5 with the cellos of the Utah State Symphony
     Orchestra conducted by Maurice Abravanel,
     David Soyer solo cello (Heitor Villa-Lobos)
Go 'Way From My Window (John Jacob Niles)
I Still Miss Someone (Roy Cash Jr., Johnny Cash)
When You Hear Them Cuckoos Hollerin' (guitar accompaniment by Gino
     Foreman)
Birmingham Sunday (Richard Fariña)
So We'll Go No More a-Roving (Lord Byron, Richard Dyer-Bennett)
O'Cangaceiro (Alfredo Ricardo do Nascimento)
The Unquiet Grave (Child 78)

2002 REISSUE PREVIOUSLY UNRELEASED BONUS TRACKS:
Tramp On the Street (Grady & Hazel Cole)
Long Black Veil (Marijohn Wilkin, Danny Dill)

RECORDED: 1964
PRODUCER: Maynard Solomon
RELEASED: October 1964

–

FAREWELL, ANGELINA (Vanguard)

Farewell, Angelina (Bob Dylan)
Daddy, You Been On My Mind (Bob Dylan)
The Wild Mountain Thyme (traditional)
Ranger's Command (Woody Guthrie)
Colours (Donovan Leitch)
Satisfied Mind (Joe Hayes, Jack Rhodes)
The River In the Pines (traditional)
Pauvre Rutebeuf (Léo Ferré, Rutebeuf)
Sagt Mir wo die Blumen Sind (Pete Seeger)
A Hard Rain's a-Gonna Fall (Bob Dylan)

2002 REISSUE PREVIOUSLY UNRELEASED BONUS TRACKS:
One Too Many Mornings (Bob Dylan)
Rock, Salt and Nails (Bruce Duncan 'U Utah' Phillips)
The Water is Wide (Child 204)

MUSICIANS: Bruce Langhorne, Ralph Rinzler, Richard Romoff, Russ Savakus
RECORDED: 1965
PRODUCER: Maynard Solomon
RELEASED: October 1965

–

NOËL (Vanguard)

O Come, O Come Emmanuel
Coventry Carol
Good King Wenceslas (instrumental)
The Little Drummer Boy (Katherine Kennicott Davis, Henry Onorati,
    Harry Simeone)
I Wonder As I Wander (John Jacob Niles)
Bring a Torch, Jeanette, Isabella (instrumental)
Down In Yon Forest
The Carol Of the Birds (dedicated to Pablo Casals)
Angels We Have Heard On High (instrumental)
Ave Maria (Franz Schubert)
Mary's Wandering
Deck the Halls (instrumental)

Away In a Manger
Adeste Fidelis (instrumental)
Cantique de Noël (Adolphe Adam)
What Child Is This
Silent Night (Franz Gruber)

2001 REISSUE PREVIOUSLY UNRELEASED BONUS TRACKS:
The First Noël
We Thee Kings (instrumental)
Virgin Mary
Good Christian Kings (instrumental)
Burgundian Carol
Away in a Manger (French version)

ALL SONGS TRADITIONAL EXCEPT WHERE NOTED
ARRANGED AND CONDUCTED by Peter Schickele
RECORDED: 1966
PRODUCER: Maynard Solomon
RELEASED: November 1966

—

JOAN (Vanguard)

Be Not Too Hard (Christopher Logue, Donovan Leitch)
Eleanor Rigby (John Lennon, Paul McCartney)
Turquoise (Donovan Leitch)
La Colombe (Jacques Brel, English translation Alasdair Clayre)
Dangling Conversation (Paul Simon)
The Lady Came from Baltimore (Tim Hardin)
North (Nina Duschek, Joan Baez)
Children Of Darkness (Richard Fariña)
The Greenwood Side (*aka* The Cruel Mother, Child 20)
If You Were a Carpenter (Tim Hardin)
Annabel Lee (Edgar Allan Poe, Don Dilworth)
Saigon Bride (Nina Duschek, Joan Baez)

2003 REISSUE PREVIOUSLY UNRELEASED BONUS TRACKS:
Oh, Had I a Golden Thread (Pete Seeger)
Autumn Leaves aka Les Feuilles Mortes (Joseph Kosma, Jacques Prévert)

ARRANGED AND CONDUCTED by Peter Schickele
RECORDED: Vanguard Studios, New York, April–June 1967
PRODUCER: Maynard Solomon
RELEASED: August 1967

—

JOAN BAEZ IN ITALY (non-U.S. Vanguard release)

Farewell, Angelina (Bob Dylan)
Oh Freedom (traditional)
Yesterday (John Lennon, Paul McCartney)
Blowin' In the Wind (Bob Dylan)
There But For Fortune (Phil Ochs)
Kumbaya (traditional)
Pilgrim Of Sorrow (A City Called Heaven) (traditional)
Saigon Bride (Nina Duschek, Joan Baez)
It's All Over Now, Baby Blue (Bob Dylan)
Where Have All the Flowers Gone? (Pete Seeger)
With God On Our Side (Bob Dylan)
We Want Our Freedom Now (traditional)
We Shall Overcome (Guy Carawan, Arthur Hamilton, Zilphia Horton,
    Pete Seeger)
Donna (Sholom Secunda, Aaron Zeitlin)
C'era Un Ragazzo Che Me Amava i Beatles e i Rolling Stones (Mauro
    Lusini, Franco Migliacci)

RECORDED: Milan and Vienna, on May 29 and June 2, 1967
RELEASED: 1967

—

LIVE IN JAPAN (non-U.S. Vanguard release)

Oh Freedom (traditional)
There But For Fortune (Phil Ochs)
Saigon Bride (Nina Duschek, Joan Baez)
House Of the Rising Sun (traditional)
Donna (Sholom Secunda, Aaron Zeitlin)
Blowin' In the Wind (Bob Dylan)
It Ain't Me Babe (Bob Dylan)
What Have They Done To the Rain? (Malvina Reynolds)
The Wild Mountain Thyme (traditional)
Pilgrim of Sorrow (A City Called Heaven) (traditional)
Farewell To This Today (S Kanedo)
We Shall Overcome (Guy Carawan, Arthur Hamilton, Zilphia Horton,
    Pete Seeger)

RECORDED: Kosei-Nenken Hall, Tokyo, February 1, 1967
RELEASED: 1967

—

BAPTISM: A JOURNEY THROUGH OUR TIME (Vanguard)

Old Welsh Song (Henry Treece)
I Saw the Vision Of the Armies (Walt Whitman)
Minister Of War (translated from the Chinese by Arthur Waley)
Song In the Blood (Jacques Prévert, translated by Lawrence Ferlinghetti)
Casida Of the Lament (Federico García Lorca, translated by Stephen
    Spender & J. L. Gili)
Of the Dark Past (James Joyce)
London (William Blake)
In Guernica (Norman Rosten)
Who Murdered the Minutes (Henry Treece)
Oh, Little Child (Henry Treece)
No Man Is an Island (John Donne)
Portrait Of the Artist As a Young Man (James Joyce)
All the Pretty Little Horses (Negro Lullaby)
Childhood III (Arthur Rimbaud, translated by Louise Varèse)
The Magic Wood (Henry Treece)
Poems from the Japanese (translated by Kenneth Rexroth)
Colours (Yevgeny Yevtushenko, translated by Robin Milner-Gulland &
    Peter Levi)
All in Green Went My Love Riding (e.e. cummings)
Gacela Of the Dark Death (Federico García Lorca, translated by Stephen
    Spender & J. L. Gili)
The Parable of the Old Man and The Young (Wilfred Owen)
Evil (Arthur Rimbaud, translated by Norman Cameron)
Epitaph For a Poet (Countee Cullen)
Old Welsh Song (Henry Treece)

2003 REISSUE PREVIOUSLY UNRELEASED BONUS TRACKS:
Mystic Numbers – 36
When the Shy Star Goes Forth In Heaven (James Joyce)
The Angel (William Blake)

MUSIC COMPOSED AND CONDUCTED by Peter Schickele
CONCEIVED AND COMPILED by Maynard Solomon
RECORDED: Vanguard Studios, New York
RELEASED: June 1968
–

ANY DAY NOW - SONGS OF BOB DYLAN (Vanguard)

Love Minus Zero, No Limit
North Country Blues
You Ain't Goin' Nowhere

Drifter's Escape
I Pity the Poor Immigrant
Tears Of Rage (Bob Dylan, Richard Manuel)
Sad-Eyed Lady of the Lowlands
Love Is Just a Four-Letter Word
I Dreamed I Saw St. Augustine
The Walls Of Redwing
Dear Landlord
One Too Many Mornings
I Shall Be Released
Boots Of Spanish Leather
Walkin' Down the Line
Restless Farewell

2002 REISSUE PREVIOUSLY UNRELEASED BONUS TRACKS:
Blowin' In the Wind
It Ain't Me Babe

ALL SONGS COMPOSED BY BOB DYLAN EXCEPT WHERE NOTED
MUSICIANS LED BY Grady Martin: Harold Bradley, David Briggs, Kenny
Buttrey, Fred Carter, Pete Drake, John Gimble, Junior Huskey, Tommy Jackson,
Jerry Kennedy, Grady Martin, Bill Purcell, Norbert Putnam, Jerry Reed, Hargus
Robbins, Hal Rugg, Buddy Spicher, Steve Stills. Pete Wade
RECORDED: Columbia Studio A, Nashville, October 1968
PRODUCER: Maynard Solomon; Associate Producer: Jack Lothrop
RELEASED: December 1968
—

DAVID'S ALBUM (Vanguard)
If I Knew (Pauline Marden, Nina Duschek)
Rock, Salt and Nails (Bruce Duncan 'U Utah' Phillips)
Glad Bluebird Of Happiness (Darryl Skrabak)
Green, Green Grass of Home (Curly Putnam)
Will the Circle Be Unbroken, with the Jordanaires (Ada R. Habershon,
    Charles H. Gabriel)
The Tramp On the Street (Grady & Hazel Cole)
Poor Wayfaring Stranger, with Mimi Fariña Melvin (traditional)
Just a Closer Walk With Thee (traditional)
Hickory Wind (Gram Parsons, Bob Bucannan)
My Home's Across the Blue Ridge Mountains (Thomas Ashley)

2005 REISSUE PREVIOUSLY UNRELEASED BONUS TRACKS:
How Can I Miss You (Dan Hicks)
The Last Thing On My Mind (Tom Paxton)

MUSICIANS LED BY Grady Martin: Harold Bradley, Kenny Buttrey, Fred Carter, Pete Drake, Junior Huskey, Tommy Jackson, Jerry Kennedy, Grady Martin, Bill Purcell, Norbert Putnam, Jerry Reed, Hal Rugg, Hargus Robbins, Buddy Spicher, Pete Wade
RECORDED: Columbia Studio A, Nashville, October 1968
PRODUCER: Maynard Solomon; Associate Producer: Jack Lothrop
RELEASED: May 1969

—

ONE DAY AT A TIME (Vanguard)

Sweet Sir Galahad (Joan Baez)
No Expectations (Mick Jagger, Keith Richards)
Long Black Veil (Marijohn Wilkin, Danny Dill)
Ghetto (Homer Banks, Bonnie Bramlett, Bettye Crutcher)
Carry It On (Pete Seeger, Gil Turner)
Take Me Back to The Sweet Sunny South, with Jeffrey Shurtleff
    (traditional)
Seven Bridges Road, with Jeffrey Shurtleff (Steve Young)
Jolie Blonde (traditional)
Joe Hill (Alfred Hayes, Earl Robinson)
A Song for David (Joan Baez)
(I Live) One Day At a Time, with Jeffrey Shurtleff (Willie Nelson)

2005 REISSUE PREVIOUSLY UNRELEASED BONUS TRACKS:
Mama Tried (Merle Haggard)
Sing Me Back Home (Merle Haggard)

MUSICIANS LED BY Grady Martin: Harold Bradley, David Briggs, Kenny Buttrey, Fred Carter, Pete Drake, Rich Festinger, Junior Huskey, Tommy Jackson, Jerry Kennedy, Grady Martin, Norbert Putnam, Jerry Reed, Hal Rugg, Hargus Robbins, Buddy Spicher, Henry Strezlecki, Pete Wade
RECORDED: Bradley's Barn, Mount Juliet, Tennessee, October 1969
PRODUCER: Maynard Solomon; Associate Producer: Jack Lothrop
RELEASED: January 1970

—

JOAN BAEZ I MILANO 1970 (non-U.S. Vanguard release)

Farewell, Angelina (Bob Dylan)
Love Is Just a Four-Letter Word (Bob Dylan)
Joe Hill (Alfred Hayes, Earl Robinson)
A Song for David (Joan Baez)
The Brand New Tennessee Waltz (Jesse Winchester)
Suzanne (Leonard Cohen)
C'era Un Ragazzo Che Me Amava i Beatles e i Rolling Stones (Mauro
    Lusini, Franco Migliacci)
The Hitchhiker's Song (Joan Baez)
Sweet Sir Galahad (Joan Baez)

North (Nina Duschek, Joan Baez)
Where Have All the Flowers Gone? (Pete Seeger)
Ghetto (Homer Banks, Bonnie Bramlett, Bettye Crutcher)
Kumbaya (traditional)

RECORDED: Arena Civica, Milan, Italy, July 24, 1970
RELEASED: 1971

—

BLESSED ARE . . . (Vanguard)

Blessed Are . . . (Joan Baez)
The Night They Drove Old Dixie Down (Jamie Robbie Robertson)
The Salt Of the Earth (Mick Jagger, Keith Richards)
Three Horses (Joan Baez)
The Brand New Tennessee Waltz (Jesse Winchester)
Last, Lonely and Wretched (Joan Baez)
Lincoln Freed Me Today (The Slave) (David Patton)
Outside the Nashville City Limits (Joan Baez)
San Francisco Mabel Joy (Mickey Newbury)
When Time Is Stolen (Joan Baez)
Heaven Help Us All (Ron Miller)
Angeline (Mickey Newbury)
Help Me Make It Through the Night (Kris Kristofferson)
Let It Be (John Lennon, Paul McCartney)
Put Your Hand In the Hand (Gene MacLellan)
Gabriel and Me (Joan Baez)
Milanese Waltz/Marie Flore (Joan Baez)
The Hitchhiker's Song (Joan Baez)
The 33rd Of August (Joan Baez)
Fifteen Months (Joan Baez)

2005 REISSUE PREVIOUSLY UNRELEASED BONUS TRACKS:
María Dolores (Fernando García Morcillo, Jacobo Morcillo)
Plane Wreck At Los Gatos (Deportee) (Woody Guthrie, Martin Hoffman)
Warm and Tender Love (Bobby Robinson, Clara A. Thompson)

ARRANGED BY Norbert Putnam and David Briggs
MUSICIANS LED BY Grady Martin: Norman Blake, David Briggs, Kenny
Buttrey, Charlie McCoy, Buddy Spicher, Pete Wade; with the Memphis Horns and
Nashville Strings; background vocals by the Holladay Singers and the Town and
Country Singers
RECORDED: Quadrafonic Sound Studios, Nashville
PRODUCER: Norbert Putnam; Co-producer: Jack Lothrop
RELEASED: August 1971

—

COME FROM THE SHADOWS (A&M)

Prison Trilogy (Billy Rose) (Joan Baez)
Rainbow Road (Donnie Fritts, Dan Penn)
Love Song To a Stranger (Joan Baez)
Myths (Joan Baez)
In the Quiet Morning (Mimi Fariña)
All the Weary Mothers Of the Earth (People's Union #1) (Joan Baez)
To Bobby (Joan Baez)
Song of Bangladesh (Joan Baez)
A Stranger In My Place (Kenny Rogers, Kin Vassy)
Tumbleweed (Douglas Van Arsdale)
The Partisan (Anna Marly, Hy Zaret)
Imagine (John Lennon)

MUSICIANS: Stuart Basore, David Briggs, Kenny Buttrey, Grady Martin, Charlie McCoy, Farrell Morris, Weldon Myrick, Norbert Putnam, Glen Spreen, Pete Wade, John 'Bucky' Wilkin
RECORDED: Quadrafonic Sound Studios, Nashville
PRODUCER: Joan Baez; Co-producer: Norbert Putnam.
RELEASED: May 1972

–

WHERE ARE YOU NOW, MY SON? (A&M)

SIDE 1:

Only Heaven Knows (Joan Baez)
Less Than the Song (Hoyt Axton)
A Young Gypsy (Joan Baez)
Mary Call (Mimi Fariña)
Rider, Pass By (Joan Baez)
Best Of Friends (Mimi Fariña)
Windrose (Joan Baez)

SIDE 2:

Where Are You Now, My Son? (Joan Baez)

MUSICIANS AND VOCALISTS: David Briggs, Jerry Carrigan, Mimi Fariña, Mike Leech, Grady Martin, Norbert Putnam, Pete Wade, Reggie Young
SIDE 1 RECORDED: Quadrafonic Sound Studios, Nashville, January 1973
PRODUCERS: Joan Baez and Norbert Putnam
SIDE 2 RECORDED: Hanoi, North Vietnam, December 18-27, 1972
PRODUCERS: Joan Baez and Henry Lewy
RELEASED: May 1973

–

GRACIAS A LA VIDA (A&M)

Gracias a la Vida– Here's To Life (Violetta Parra)
Llegó Con Tres Heridas – I Come With Three Wounds
   (Miguel Hernández, Joan Manuel Serrat)
La Llorona – The Weeping Woman (traditional)
El Preso Número Nuevo – Prisoner Number Nine
   (Antonio Cantoral Garcia, Roberto Cantoral Garcia)
Guantanamera (José Marti, Joséito Fernández, Pete Seeger)
Te Recuerdo Amanda – I Remember You Amanda (Victor Jara)
Dida, with Joni Mitchell (Joan Baez)
Cucurrucucu Paloma (Tomás Méndez)
Paso Rio – I Pass a River (traditional)
El Rossinyol – The Nightingale (traditional)
Las Madres Cansadas – All The Weary Mothers of the Earth (Joan Baez)
No Nos Moveran – We Shall Not Be Moved (traditional)
Esquinazo del Guerillero – Guerilla Warrior's Serenade
   (Rolando Alarcón, Fernando Alegria)

MUSICIANS: Rondalla Amerindia, Milt Holland, Jim Hughart, Lalo Lindgron, Edgar Lustgarten, Tom Scott, Tommy Tedesco, Mariachi Uclatlan; Vocalists: Sally Stevens, Jackie Ward Singers, Andra Willis
RECORDED: A&M Studios, Los Angeles, early 1974
PRODUCERS: Joan Baez and Henry Lewy
RELEASED: March 1974
–

DIAMONDS & RUST (A&M)

Diamonds & Rust (Joan Baez)
Fountain Of Sorrow (Jackson Browne)
Never Dreamed You'd Leave In Summer (Stevie Wonder)
Children and All That Jazz (Joan Baez)
Simple Twist Of Fate (Bob Dylan)
Blue Sky (Dickey Betts)
Jesse (Janis Ian)
Winds Of the Old Days (Joan Baez)
Dida, duet with Joni Mitchell (Joan Baez)
I Dream Of Jeannie (Stephen Foster)
Danny Boy (Fred Weatherly)

JOAN BAEZ: vocals, acoustic guitar, synthesizers; arrangements
ADDITIONAL MUSICIANS: Max Bennett, Larry Carlton, Malcolm Cecil, Isabel Daskoff, Jesse Ehrlick, Wilton Felder, Ronald Folsom, James Getzoff, Jim Gordon, John Guerin, Hampton Hawes, Jim Horn, William Hymanson, Raymond Kelly, Larry Knechtel, Robert Konrad, William Kirasch, Carla la Manga, Rick lo Tiempo, Ollie Mitchell, Buck Monari, Robert Osstrowsky, David Paich, Dean Parks, Reinie Press, Red Rhodes, Joe Sample, Tom Scott, Sid Sharp. Tibor Zelig

RECORDED: A&M Studios, Los Angeles; Wally Heider Studios, Los Angeles, January 1975
PRODUCERS: David Kershenbaum and Joan Baez
RELEASED: April 1975

—

FROM EVERY STAGE (A&M)

DISC 1 (ACOUSTIC):

Ain't Gonna Let Nobody Turn Me Around (traditional)

Blessed Are… (Joan Baez)

Suzanne (Leonard Cohen)

Love Song To a Stranger/Part II (Joan Baez)

I Shall Be Released (Bob Dylan)

Blowin' in the Wind (Bob Dylan)

Stewball (Ralph Rinzler, Bob Yellin, John Herald)

Natalia (Shusha Guppy, Roy Apps, G.T. Moore)

The Ballad Of Sacco & Vanzetti Part 2 (Joan Baez, Ennio Morricone)

Joe Hill (Alfred Hayes, Earl Robinson)

DISC 2 (ELECTRIC):

Love Is Just a Four-Letter Word (Bob Dylan)

Forever Young (Bob Dylan)

Diamonds & Rust (Joan Baez)

Boulder To Birmingham (Emmylou Harris, Bill Danoff)

Swing Low, Sweet Chariot (traditional)

Oh, Happy Day (Edwin Hawkins)

Please Come To Boston (Dave Loggins)

Lily, Rosemary And the Jack Of Hearts (Bob Dylan)

The Night They Drove Old Dixie Down (Jamie Robbie Robertson)

Amazing Grace (traditional)

RECORDED: Philadelphia Spectrum and Nassau Coliseum (July 1975); Hollywood Bowl, Sacramento Convention Center, Berkeley Greek Theatre, and Monterey Peninsula College (August 1975)
PRODUCER: David Kershenbaum
JOAN BAEZ: vocals and guitar
ADDITIONAL MUSICIANS: David Briggs, Larry Carlton, Dan Ferguson, Jim Gordon, James Jamerson
RELEASED: January 1976

—

GULF WINDS (A&M)

Sweeter for Me

Seabirds

Caruso

Still Waters At Night

Kingdom Of Childhood
O Brother!
Time Is Passing Us By
Stephanie's Room
Gulf Winds

ALL SONGS COMPOSED BY JOAN BAEZ
JOAN BAEZ: vocals, guitar, piano
ADDITIONAL MUSICIANS: Malcolm Cecil, Duck Dunn, Jesse Ehrlich,
Jim Gordon, Ray Kelly, Larry Knechtel, Dean Parks, Sid Sharp
RECORDED: Sound Labs, Los Angeles; Tonto, Santa Monica
PRODUCER: David Kershenbaum
RELEASED: November 1976

(In 2003, the five A&M albums – *Come From The Shadows, Where Are You Now, My
Son?, Gracias a la Vida, Diamonds & Rust, From Every Stage, Gulf Winds* – were newly
remastered and annotated, and reissued together as *Joan Baez: The Complete A&M
Recordings*, a four-CD box-set via the A&M/Chronicles series.)
–

BLOWIN' AWAY (Portrait/CBS)
Sailing (Gavin Sutherland)
Many a Mile to Freedom (Steve Winwood, Anna Capaldi)
Miracles (Joan Baez)
Yellow Coat (Steve Goodman)
Time Rag (Joan Baez)
A Heartfelt Line Or Two (Joan Baez)
I'm Blowin' Away (Eric Kaz)
Luba, the Baroness (Joan Baez)
Altar Boy and the Thief (Joan Baez)
Cry Me a River (Arthur Hamilton)

JOAN BAEZ: vocals, guitar
ADDITIONAL MUSICIANS AND VOCALISTS: Jeff Baxter, Mike Botts,
Malcolm Cecil, Duck Dunn, Wilton Felder, Jim Gordon, Larry Knechtel, David
Mansfield, Dean Parks, Elliott Randall, Joe Sample, Tom Scott, Rick Shlosser
RECORDED: Cherokee Studios, Los Angeles
PRODUCER: David Kershenbaum
RELEASED: June 1977
–

HONEST LULLABY (Portrait/CBS)
Let Your Love Flow (Larry E. Williams)
No Woman, No Cry (Bob Marley, Vincent Ford)
Light a Light (Janis Ian)
The Song At the End Of the Movie (Pierce Pettis)
Before the Deluge (Jackson Browne)
Honest Lullaby (Joan Baez)

Michael (Joan Baez)
For Sasha (Joan Baez)
For All We Know (Sam M. Lewis, J. Fred Coots)
Free At Last (Joan Baez, George Henry Jackson)

JOAN BAEZ: vocals, acoustic guitar
ADDITIONAL MUSICIANS AND VOCALISTS: Hill Abrahams, Ava Aldridge,
Barry Beckett, Larry Byrom, Pete Carr, James Crozier, Roger Hawkins, David
Hood, George Jackson, Jimmy Johnson, Lenny LeBlanc, Mac McNally, Charlie
McCoy, Cindy Richardson, George Soule, Eddie Struzick, Marie Tomlinson
RECORDED: Muscle Shoals Sound Studios
PRODUCER: Barry Beckett
RELEASED: July 1979

—

VERY EARLY JOAN (Vanguard live compilation)

Last Night I Had the Strangest Dream (Ed McCurdy)
Willie Moore (traditional)
She's a Trouble Maker (Jerry Ragovoy, V McCoy)
Tears In My Eyes (Pauline Marden)
Somebody Got Lost In a Storm
The Water Is Wide (traditional)
Man Of Constant Sorrow (traditional)
Freight Train (Elizabeth Cotten)
Lady Gay (traditional)
Johnny Cuckoo (traditional)
Lonesome Valley, with Pete Seeger (traditional)
The Riddle Song, with Pete Seeger (traditional)
Streets Of Laredo (traditional)
Railroad Bill (traditional)
My Good Old Man (traditional)
Little Darlin' (Maurice Williams)
In the Pines (traditional)
Pilgrim Of Sorrow (traditional)
Where Have All the Flowers Gone? (Pete Seeger)
Rambler Gambler (traditional)
Come All Ye Fair And Tender Maidens (traditional)
Hallowed Be Thy Name (traditional)
Twelve Gates To the City (traditional)
Silver Dagger (traditional)

**ALL SONGS TRADITIONAL AND ARRANGED BY JOAN BAEZ EXCEPT
WHERE NOTED
ALL PERFORMANCES PREVIOUSLY UNRELEASED**
RECORDED: live on tour at various concerts, 1961–1963
PRODUCER: Maynard Solomon
RELEASED: November 1982

—

LIVE EUROPE '83 CHILDREN OF THE EIGHTIES
(Ariola/Germany, Gamma/Canada non-U.S. release)

Farewell, Angelina (Bob Dylan)
Warriors Of the Sun (Joan Baez)
A Hard Rain's a-Gonna Fall (Bob Dylan)
Lady Di and I (Joan Baez)
*A Tous les Enfant (Boris Vian, Claude Vence)
*Prendre un Enfant (Yves Duteil)
(For The) Children of the Eighties (Joan Baez)
The Love Inside (Barry Gibb)
Me and Bobby McGee (Kris Kristofferson)
No Woman, No Cry (Bob Marley, Vincent Ford)
Imagine (John Lennon)
Jaria Hamuda (Ahmed Hamza)
Here's To You (Joan Baez, Ennio Morricone)
Land Of a Thousand Dances (Antoine Domino, Chris Kenner)

*ON THE GERMAN RELEASE, THESE SONGS ARE SUBSTITUTED WITH:
Wozu Sind Kriege Da (Udo Lindenberg)
Wenn Unsere Brüder Kommen (Konstantin Wecker)

JOAN BAEZ: Vocals and acoustic guitar
ADDITIONAL MUSICIANS: Charles Cohen, J. Jacques Generarle, Marc
Longchampt, Yves Sanat
RECORDED: live in concert at various locations in Europe, 1983
PRODUCER: Gerard Tempesti
RELEASED: 1983
–

RECENTLY (Gold Castle)

Brothers in Arms (Mark Knopfler)
Recently (Joan Baez)
Asimbonanga (Johnny Clegg)
The Moon Is a Harsh Mistress (Jimmy Webb)
James & the Gang (Joan Baez)
Let Us Break Bread Together/Freedom (traditional)
MLK (Paul David Hewson, David Howell Evans, Larry Mullen Jr,
    Adam Clayton)
Do Right Woman, Do Right Man (Dan Penn, Chips Moman)
Biko (Peter Gabriel)

2017 REISSUE PREVIOUSLY UNRELEASED BONUS TRACK:
Lebanon (David Palmer)

JOAN BAEZ: Vocals and acoustic guitar
ADDITIONAL MUSICIANS: Alex Acuna, Laythan Armor, Cabar Feidh Piper, Cesar Cancino, John Hobbs, Paul Jackson Jr, Abraham Laboriel, Caleb Quaye, John Robinson, Fred Tackett, Tony Wilkins; Strings arranged by Gene Page; Background vocalists: L.A. Choir directed by Donald Taylor, Ciaphus Semenya, Beau Williams
RECORDED: Capitol Studios, Los Angeles, 1987
PRODUCER: Alan Abrahams
RELEASED: June 1987
–

DIAMONDS & RUST IN THE BULLRING (Gold Castle)

SIDE 1 (IN ENGLISH):

Diamonds & Rust (Joan Baez)
Ain't Gonna Let Nobody Turn Me Around (traditional)
No Woman, No Cry (Bob Marley, Vincent Ford)
Famous Blue Raincoat (Leonard Cohen)
Swing Low, Sweet Chariot (traditional)
Let It Be (John Lennon, Paul McCartney)

SIDE 2 (IN SPANISH):

El Preso Numero Nuevo (Antonio Cantoral Garcia,
    Roberto Cantoral Garcia)
Llegó Con Tres Heridas (Miguel Hernández, Joan Manuel Serrat)
Txoria Txori (J. A. Artze, M. Laboa)
Ellas Danzan Solas (Sting, R Livi)
Gracias a la Vida, with Mercedes Sosa (Violetta Parra)
No Nos Moveran (traditional)

ADDITIONAL MUSICIANS: John Acosta, Begnat Amorena, Laythan Armor, Cesar Cancino, Jean Marie Eday, Jose Agustin Guereu, Costel Restea; Background vocalists: L.A. Mass Choir directed by Donald Taylor
RECORDED: Bilbao, Spain, 1988; Capitol Studios, Hollywood, 1989
PRODUCER: Alan Abrahams
RELEASED: November 1989
–

SPEAKING OF DREAMS (Gold Castle)

China (Joan Baez)
Warriors Of the Sun (Joan Baez)
Carrickfergus (Van Morrison, Patrick Moloney)
Hand To Mouth, with Gipsy Kings (George Michael)
Speaking of Dreams (Joan Baez)
El Salvador (Greg Copeland)
★Rambler Gambler/Whispering Bells, with Paul Simon, acoustic guitar,
    background vocals (traditional / Fred Lowry, Clarence Quick)
Fairfax County (David Massengill)

2017 REISSUE PREVIOUSLY UNRELEASED BONUS TRACKS:

A Mi Manera (My Way) with Gipsy Kings (Paul Anka, Gilles Thibault, Claude François, Jacques Revaux)

Goodnight Saigon (Billy Joel)

Warriors Of the Sun / She's Got a Ticket (Joan Baez / Tracy Chapman)

JOAN BAEZ: vocals and acoustic guitar
ADDITIONAL MUSICIANS: Laythan Armor, Jackson Browne, Larry Carlton, Tony Cedras, Shawna Culotta, Paulinho da Costa, Ardeshir Farah, Pavel Parkas, Charles Fearing, Dick Fegy, Francis Fuster, Gipsy Kings, Morris Goldberg, John Goux, John Hobbs, David Jackson, Bakhiti Kumalo, Abraham Laboriel, Isaac Mtshali, Ray Phiri, Nicolas Reyes, John Robinson, John Selolwane, Jorge Strunz, Neal Stubenhaus; Background vocalists: Roy Galloway, Luther & Oren Waters
RECORDED: Capitol Studios, Hollywood, 1989
PRODUCER: Alan Abrahams
*PRODUCERS: Paul Simon & Alan Abrahams
RELEASED: November 1989

(The 2017 release of *The Complete Gold Castle Masters* (via Bobolink/Razor & Tie) reissued the three albums recorded with producer Alan Abrahams as originally conceived. Thus, "Lebanon" by David Palmer, from the *Recently* sessions, now became that album's closing track. Likewise, "Goodnight Saigon," "Warriors Of the Sun," and "She's Got a Ticket" were restored to their intended place on *Speaking of Dreams*.)

—

PLAY ME BACKWARDS (Virgin)

Play Me Backwards (Joan Baez, Wally Wilson, Kenny Greenberg, Karen O'Connor)

Amsterdam (Janis Ian)

Isaac & Abraham (Joan Baez, Wally Wilson, Kenny Greenberg)

Stones in the Road (Mary Chapin Carpenter)

Steal Across the Border (Ron Davies)

I'm With You (Joan Baez, Wally Wilson, Kenny Greenberg, Pat Bunch)

Strange Rivers (John Stewart)

Through Your Hands (John Hiatt)

The Dream Song (Joan Baez, Ron Davies)

Edge of Glory (Joan Baez, Wally Wilson, Kenny Greenberg, Karen O'Connor)

2011 COLLECTORS EDITION REISSUE VIA BOBOLINK/PROPER CONTAINS A SECOND CD, THE PLAY ME BACKWARDS DEMOS, 10 PREVIOUSLY UNRELEASED TRACKS:

Medicine Wheel (unknown)

Rise From the Ruins (Mark Heard)

Trouble With the Truth (Gary Nicholson)

Much Better View Of the Moon (Pat Bunch, Wally Wilson, Kenny Greenberg)
Seven Curses (Bob Dylan)
In My Day (Joan Baez, Ashley Cleveland)
Dark Eyed Man (Ron Davies)
We Endure (Janis Ian)
The Last Day (John Hadley)
Lonely Moon (Mark Heard)

JOAN BAEZ: vocals, acoustic guitar
ADDITIONAL MUSICIANS: Richard Bennett, Chad Cromwell,
Jerry Douglas, Carl Gorodetzky, Kenny Greenberg, Mike Lawler, Bob Mason,
Edgar Meyer, Steve Nathan, Tom Roady, Pam Sixfin, James Stroud, Marcos Suzano,
Willie Weeks, Kristen Wilkenson, Wally Wilson, Glen Worf; Background vocals:
Greg Barnhill, Ashley Cleveland, Vicki Hampton, Jonell Mosser, Cyndi Richardson,
Chris Rodriguez
RECORDED: Treasure Isle Recorders and Woodland Sound, Nashville, 1992
PRODUCERS: Wally Wilson and Kenny Greenberg
RELEASED: October 1992
–

RARE, LIVE & CLASSIC (Vanguard compilation of previously released
and unreleased studio recordings and live performances, from 1958 to 1989)

DISC 1:

Scarlet Ribbons (Evelyn Danzig, Jack Segal)
Jimmy Brown (traditional)
Careless Love, with Bill Wood (traditional)
Auctioneer, with Bill Wood (Leroy Van Dyke, Buddy Black)
Black is the Color (traditional)
John Hardy (traditional)
We Are Crossing Jordan River, with Bob Gibson (traditional)
John Riley (traditional)
Silver Dagger (traditional)
House Of the Rising Sun (traditional)
Low Down Chariot, with Eric Von Schmidt (Alan Lomax, John Lomax)
Wagoner's Lad (traditional)
Last Night I Had the Strangest Dream (Ed McCurdy)
Geordie (traditional)
What Have They Done To the Rain (Malvina Reynolds)
Troubled And I Don't Know Why, with Bob Dylan (Bob Dylan)
With God On Our Side (Bob Dylan)
We Shall Overcome (Guy Carawan, Arthur Hamilton, Zilphia Horton,
    Pete Seeger)
Go 'Way From My Window (John Jacob Niles)
Mama, You Been On My Mind, with Bob Dylan (Bob Dylan)
There But For Fortune (Phil Ochs)

Colours, duet with Donovan (Donovan Leitch)
The River In the Pines (traditional)

DISC 2:

Pack Up Your Sorrows (Richard Fariña, Pauline Marden)
The Swallow Song (Richard Fariña)
Legend Of the Girl Child Linda, with Judy Collins, Mimi Fariña
   (Donovan Leitch)
Children Of Darkness (Richard Fariña)
Catch the Wind, with Mimi Fariña (Donovan Leitch)
I Am A Poor Wayfaring Stranger, with Mimi Fariña (traditional)
Sweet Sir Galahad (Joan Baez)
Donna Donna (Sholom Secunda, Aaron Zeitlin)
Long Black Veil (Marijohn Wilkin, Danny Dill)
Mama Tried, with Jeffrey Shurtleff (Merle Haggard)
Sing Me Back Home, with Jeffrey Shurtleff (Merle Haggard)
Joe Hill (Alfred Hayes, Earl Robinson)
The Night They Drove Old Dixie Down (Jamie Robbie Robertson)
Blessed Are (Joan Baez)
Hello In There, with Kris Kristofferson (John Prine)
Love Song To a Stranger (Joan Baez)
In the Quiet Morning (Mimi Fariña)
Angel Band, with Jeffrey Shurtleff (traditional)
Johnny, I Hardly Knew Yeh (traditional)
Gracias a la Vida (Violetta Parra)

DISC 3:

Diamonds & Rust (Joan Baez)
Children and All That Jazz (Joan Baez)
Blowin' In the Wind, with Bob Dylan (Bob Dylan)
Swing Low, Sweet Chariot (traditional)
Jesse (Janis Ian)
Honest Lullaby (Joan Baez)
Jackaroe, with Mickey Hart, Jerry Garcia (traditional)
Marriott USA, with Mickey Hart, Bob Weir & friends (Joan Baez)
Amazing Grace (traditional)
Forever Young (Bob Dylan)
Farewell, Angelina (Bob Dylan)
A Hard Rain's a-Gonna Fall (Bob Dylan)
Here's To You (Joan Baez, Ennio Morricone)
Blues Improv, with Odetta (Joan Baez, Odetta)
Ring Them Bells (Bob Dylan)
El Preso Numero Nuevo (Antonio Cantoral Garcia, Roberto Cantoral Garcia)
Speaking of Dreams (Joan Baez)

EXECUTIVE PRODUCERS: Joan Baez, Nancy Lutzow, Mark Spector;
Co-producer: Manny Greenhill
RELEASED: September 1993

—

RING THEM BELLS (Guardian)

The Lily of the West (traditional)
Sweet Sir Galahad (Joan Baez)
And the Band Played Waltzing Matilda (Eric Bogle)
Willie Moore, with Kate and Anna McGarrigle (traditional)
Swallow Song, with Mimi Fariña (Richard Fariña)
Don't Make Promises (Tim Hardin)
Jesse, with Janis Ian (Janis Ian)
Ring Them Bells, with Mary Black (Bob Dylan)
Welcome Me (Amy Ray)
Suzanne (Leonard Cohen)
You're Aging Well, with Dar Williams (Dar Williams)
Pajarillo Barranqueño, with Tish Hinojosa (Alfonso
    Esparza Oteo)
Don't Think Twice, It's All Right, with Indigo Girls (Bob Dylan)
Diamonds & Rust, with Mary Chapin Carpenter (Joan Baez)
The Night They Drove Old Dixie Down (Jamie Robbie Robertson)

The *Collectors Edition* (via Proper/UK, 2007; and Razor & Tie-Bobolink/U.S.,
2009) contains six previously unreleased tracks from the live recordings at the
Bottom Line. The resulting 21-song double-CD package was re-sequenced to reflect
better the spirit of the original 1995 shows. *Ring Them Bells* is thought to be the last
recorded appearance by Mimi Fariña, who died six years later on July 18, 2001.

DISC ONE:

The Lily of the West (traditional)
*Love Song to a Stranger (Joan Baez)
Sweet Sir Galahad (Joan Baez)
And the Band Played Waltzing Matilda (Eric Bogle)
Willie Moore, trio with Kate and Anna McGarrigle (traditional)
Swallow Song, duet with Mimi Fariña (Richard Fariña)
Don't Make Promises (Tim Hardin)
Jesse, duet with Janis Ian (Janis Ian)
Ring Them Bells, duet with Mary Black (Bob Dylan)
*Welcome Me (Amy Ray)

DISC TWO:

*Geordie (traditional)
*You Ain't Goin' Nowhere (Bob Dylan)

Suzanne (Leonard Cohen)
You're Aging Well, with Dar Williams (Dar Williams)
Pajarillo Barranqueño, with Tish Hinojosa (Alfonso Esparza Oteo)
★Gracias a la Vida, with Tish Hinojosa (Violetta Parra)
The Water is Wide, with Indigo Girls (traditional)
Don't Think Twice It's All Right, with Indigo Girls (Bob Dylan)
★Stones in the Road, with Mary Chapin Carpenter (Mary Chapin Carpenter)
Diamonds & Rust, with Mary Chapin Carpenter (Joan Baez)
The Night They Drove Old Dixie Down (Jamie Robbie Robertson)

*INDICATES PREVIOUSLY UNRELEASED
JOAN BAEZ: vocals and acoustic guitar
ADDITIONAL MUSICIANS AND VOCALISTS: Pat Crowley, Paul Pesco,
Fernando Saunders, Carol Steele
RECORDED: Live at the Bottom Line, New York, April 10–11, and
April 16–17, 1995
PRODUCERS: Mark Spector and Mitch Maketansky
RELEASED: September 1995

—

LIVE AT NEWPORT (Vanguard compilation)

Farewell, Angelina (Bob Dylan)
Long Black Veil (Marijohn Wilkin, Danny Dill)
The Wild Mountain Thyme (Francis McPeake)
Come All Ye Fair and Tender Maidens (traditional)
Lonesome Valley, with Mary Travers (traditional)
Hush Little Baby, with Peter Yarrow (traditional)
Te Ador / Te Manha (traditional) *
All My Trials (traditional)
It's All Over Now, Baby Blue (Bob Dylan)
The Unquiet Grave (traditional)
Oh Freedom (traditional) *
Satisfied Mind, with the Lilly Brothers (traditional)
Fennario (traditional)
Don't Think Twice, It's All Right (Bob Dylan)
Johnny Cuckoo (Bessie Jones)
It Ain't Me Babe, with Bob Dylan (Bob Dylan)
With God On Our Side, with Bob Dylan (Bob Dylan) ★

ALL LIVE PERFORMANCE TRACKS PREVIOUSLY UNRELEASED
EXCEPT WHERE INDICATED *
RECORDED: Newport Folk Festivals, 1963, '64, '65 (track dates not identified)
EXECUTIVE PRODUCERS: Mark Spector and Nancy Lutzow
RELEASED: November 1996

—

GONE FROM DANGER (Guardian)

No Mermaid (Sinéad Lohan)
Reunion Hill (Richard Shindell)
Crack in the Mirror (Betty Elders)
February (Dar Williams)
Fishing (Richard Shindell)
If I Wrote You (Dar Williams)
Lily (Joan Baez, Sharon Rice, Wally Wilson and Kenny Greenberg)
Who Do You Think I Am? (Sinéad Lohan)
Mercy Bound (Mark Addison)
Money for Floods (Richard Shindell)

ADDITIONAL MUSICIANS: Richard Bennett, Dennis Bernside, Steve Conn, Chad Cromwell, Eric Darken, Dan Dugmore, Kenny Greenberg, Jim Hoke, Tim Lauer, Greg Morrow, Steve Nathan, Michael Rhodes, Matt Rollings, Joe Spivey, Willie Weeks, Ellie Wilson, Sam Wilson, Wally Wilson; Background vocals: Jim Collins, Marabeth Jordan, Allison Moorer, Sharon Rice, Dar Williams, Curtis Young
RECORDED: MCA Music Studios, Nashville, winter 1997
PRODUCERS: Wally Wilson and Kenny Greenberg; Executive Producer Mark Spector
RELEASED: September 1997

The 2009 *Collectors Edition* (via Razor & Tie/Bobolink/U.S. and Proper/UK) contains a second CD with 11 songs from Joan's NPR *Mountain Stage* performance on August 11, 1987. Eight of the songs appeared on *Gone From Danger.* Four of their songwriters joined Joan for the *Mountain Stage* performances:

If I Wrote You (Dar Williams)
No Mermaid, with Sinéad Lohan (Sinéad Lohan)
Reunion Hill, with Richard Shindell (Richard Shindell)
Crack in the Mirror, with Betty Elders (Betty Elders)
*Long Bed from Kenya, with Betty Elders (Betty Elders)
February, with Dar Williams (Dar Williams)
*You're Aging Well, with Dar Williams (Dar Williams)
Fishing, with Richard Shindell and Dar Williams (Richard Shindell)
Money for Floods, with Richard Shindell (Richard Shindell)
Who Do You Think I Am? with Sinéad Lohan (Sinéad Lohan)
*To Ramona, with Sinéad Lohan (Bob Dylan)

ALL COMPOSITIONS ORIGINALLY HEARD ON *GONE FROM DANGER* EXCEPT *
JOAN BAEZ: vocals and acoustic guitar
ADDITIONAL *MOUNTAIN STAGE* MUSICIANS AND VOCALISTS: Gene Elders, Kenny Greenberg, Mark Peterson, Carole Steele

—

DARK CHORDS ON A BIG GUITAR (KOCH)

Sleeper (Greg Brown)
In My Time Of Need (Ryan Adams)
Rosemary Moore (Caitlin Cary)
Caleb Meyer (Gillian Welch, David Rawlings)
Motherland (Natalie Merchant)
Wings (Josh Ritter)
Rexroth's Daughter (Greg Brown)
Elvis Presley Blues (Gillian Welch, David Rawlings)
King's Highway (Joe Henry)
Christmas in Washington (Steve Earle)

JOAN BAEZ: vocals, acoustic guitar, percussion
ADDITIONAL MUSICIANS: Byron Isaacs, George Javori, Duke McVinnie,
Doug Pettibone; Background vocals: Rani Arbo, Gale Ann Dorsey
RECORDED: Allaire Studios, Shokan, New York
PRODUCER: Mark Spector
RELEASED: September 2003

—

BOWERY SONGS (KOCH)

Finlandia (Jean Sibelius)
Rexroth's Daughter (Greg Brown)
Deportee (Plane Wreck at Los Gatos) (Woody Guthrie, Martin Hoffman)
Joe Hill (Alfred Hayes, Earl Robinson)
Christmas in Washington (Steve Earle)
Farewell, Angelina (Bob Dylan)
Motherland (Natalie Merchant)
Carrickfergus (traditional)
Jackaroe (traditional)
Seven Curses (Bob Dylan)
Dink's Song (traditional)
Silver Dagger (traditional)
It's All Over Now, Baby Blue (Bob Dylan)
Jerusalem (Steve Earle)

JOAN BAEZ: vocals and acoustic guitar
ADDITIONAL MUSICIANS AND VOCALISTS: Erik Della Penna, George
Javori, Duke McVinnie, Graham Maby
RECORDED: The Bowery Ballroom, New York, November 6, 2004
PRODUCER: Mark Spector
RELEASED: 2005

—

DAY AFTER TOMORROW (Razor & Tie)

God Is God (Steve Earle)
Rose of Sharon (Eliza Gilkyson)
Scarlet Tide (Elvis Costello, T Bone Burnett)
Day After Tomorrow (Tom Waits, Katherine Brennan)
Henry Russell's Last Words (Diana Jones)
I Am a Wanderer (Steve Earle)
Mary (Patti Griffin)
Requiem (Eliza Gilkyson)
The Lower Road (Thea Gilmore)
Jericho Road (Steve Earle)

JOAN BAEZ: vocals, acoustic guitar
ADDITIONAL MUSICIANS AND VOCALISTS: Steve Earle, Thea Gilmore,
Ray Kennedy, Siobhan Kennedy, Viktor Krauss, Kenny Malone, Tim O'Brien,
Darrell Scott
RECORDED: Sound Emporium, and Room and Board, Nashville, December 2007
– March 2008
PRODUCER: Steve Earle
RELEASED: September 2008
–

75TH BIRTHDAY CELEBRATION (Razor & Tie/Bobolink)

DISC 1:

God Is God (Steve Earle)
There But For Fortune (Phil Ochs)
Freight Train, duet with David Bromberg (Elizabeth Cotten)
Blackbird, duet with David Crosby (John Lennon, Paul McCartney)
She Moved Through The Fair, with Damien Rice (traditional)
Catch The Wind, with Mary Chapin Carpenter (Donovan Leitch)
Hard Times Come Again No More, with Emmylou Harris (Stephen Foster)
Deportee (Plane Wreck at Los Gatos), with Emmylou Harris and
    Jackson Browne (Woody Guthrie, Martin Hoffman)
Seven Curses (Bob Dylan)
Swing Low, Sweet Chariot (traditional)
Oh Freedom / Ain't Gonna Let Nobody Turn Me Around,
    with Mavis Staples (traditional)

DISC 2:

The Water Is Wide, with Mary Chapin Carpenter and Indigo Girls
    (traditional)
Don't Think Twice, It's All Right, with Indigo Girls (Bob Dylan)
House of the Rising Sun, with David Bromberg and Richard Thompson
    (traditional)

She Never Could Resist A Winding Road, with Richard Thompson
   (Richard Thompson)
Before The Deluge, with Jackson Browne (Jackson Browne)
Diamonds & Rust, with Judy Collins (Joan Baez)
Gracias a la Vida, with Nano Stern (Violetta Parra)
The Boxer, with Paul Simon (Paul Simon)
The Night They Drove Old Dixie Down (Jamie Robbie Robertson)
Forever Young (Bob Dylan)

**RELEASED IN THREE CONFIGURATIONS: A 21-TRACK DOUBLE-CD;
A 21-TRACK DVD; AND THE DELUXE DOUBLE-CD + DVD PACKAGE.**
JOAN BAEZ: vocals and acoustic guitar
Additional musicians and vocalist: Gabriel Harris, Dirk Powell, Grace Stumberg
RECORDED: The Beacon Theater, New York, January 27, 2016
PRODUCER: David Horn, Bill Kabel, Michael Owgang, Frank Filipetti
RELEASED: June 10, 2016
–

WHISTLE DOWN THE WIND (Razor & Tie/Bobolink)

Whistle Down the Wind (Tom Waits)
Be of Good Heart (Josh Ritter)
Another World (Anohni)
Civil War (Joe Henry)
The Things That We Are Made Of (Mary Chapin Carpenter)
The President Sang Amazing Grace (Zoe Mulford)
Last Leaf (Tom Waits, Kathleen Brennan)
Silver Blade (Josh Ritter)
The Great Correction (Eliza Gilykson)
I Wish The Wars Were All Over (Tim Eriksen)

JOAN BAEZ: vocals and acoustic guitar
ADDITIONAL MUSICIANS: Jay Bellerose, Tyler Chester, Mark Goldenberg,
Gabriel Harris, Janeen Rae Heller, Greg Leisz, David Piltch, John Smith,
Patrick Warren
RECORDED: United Recording in Hollywood, February 19-20, May 1-5,
and September 25-27, 2017
PRODUCER: Joe Henry
RELEASED: March 2, 2018

RARITIES, CURIOS, AND COLLECTIBLES

Many festival recordings feature performances by Joan Baez, often versions of songs available elsewhere. Most of the Newport Folk Festivals tracks are collected on the *Live at Newport* compilation of 1996, though the original albums, featuring a roster of key contemporaries, are a worthwhile addition for the serious collector: *Evening Concerts at Newport, Vol 1 and Vol 2*, which includes "Pilgrim of Sorrow," and "We Shall Overcome"; *Newport Broadside*. Essential for the Baez completist, is *Folk Festival at Newport, Vol 2*, from 1959, which features the legendary performance with Bob Gibson that launched her career – "Virgin Mary Had One Son" and "We Are Crossing Jordan River." All are Vanguard releases.

Of great socio-historical significance is *We Shall Overcome: Documentary of the March on Washington*, released by Folkways. It features highlights of the day, August 28, 1963, including Baez ("We Shall Overcome"), Bob Dylan, Odetta, Marian Anderson, and Dr Martin Luther King's celebrated "I have a dream speech."

In 1967, Baez was one of the participants on *Save the Children: Songs from the Hearts of Women*, an album produced by the Women's Strike for Peace Coalition. "Legend of the Girl-Child Linda," which she sang with Mimi Fariña and Judy Collins, appears on *Rare, Live & Classic*, but a duet with Judy Collins, "Oh, Had I a Golden Thread," has never been otherwise released. It is easily findable on YouTube. Collins and Ethel Raim coordinated the project.

On *Memories: Richard and Mimi Fariña* (Vanguard, 1968), the album she helped her sister assemble after Richard's death in 1966, Baez sings "A Swallow Song" (Richard Fariña) and "All the World Has Gone By" (Joan Baez, with Richard Fariña and Kim Chappell).

Baez was one of the biggest names at Woodstock but, even on the fiftieth anniversary ten-CD set, she is represented only by a handful of songs. However, as part of that epochal celebration the full hour-long set was released digitally. Baez is accompanied by Jeffrey Shurtleff and Richard Festinger, the trio calling themselves The Struggle Mountain Resistance Band. Part of the set is included in the documentary *Carry It On* (*see below*). A studio version of "Warm and Tender Love" appears as a bonus track on the 2005 re-release of *Blessed Are . . .*

There were two all-star concerts in memory of Woody Guthrie, one on the east coast and one on the west, at which Baez performed. She is represented by "Hobo's Lullaby" on *A Tribute to Woody Guthrie: Highlights from Concerts at Carnegie Hall, 1968 and Hollywood Bowl, 1970* (Warner Bros, 1972). In 2017, the fiftieth anniversary of Guthrie's death, Bear Family Records released a lavish box-set comprising three CDs and two books, making the complete Hollywood Bowl concert available for the first time. In addition to "Hobo's Lullaby," Baez's set comprises "So Long, It's Been Good To Know Yuh" (with Pete Seeger), Hard Travelin'," "Pastures of Plenty," "I've Got to Know" (with Arlo Guthrie), "This Train is Bound for Glory" and "Deportee," as well as the finale of "This Land is Your Land."

Credited as "The Lady," Baez makes an appearance on Kris Kristofferson's 1971 album *The Silver-Tongued Devil and I* (Monument). They sing "The Taker."

Baez produced Jeffrey Shurtleff's solo album *State Farm* (A&M, 1972) and sings backing vocals on three songs: "Como Tu," "Hello in There" and "Angel Band," the latter appearing on *Rare, Live & Classic.* Shurtleff also sings Baez's "Prison Trilogy."

The festivals at Big Sur yielded two records, *Celebration at Big Sur*, recorded in 1970 (A&M), and, from 1971, *One Hand Clapping* (A&M, 1972) which captures Baez duetting with Kris Kristofferson on "Hello in There."

Baez made one of her first New York City appearances with Earl Scruggs, and on *The Earl Scruggs Revue Anniversary Special* (CBS, 1975) she duets with Johnny Cash on "Gospel Ship," and is joined by Leonard Cohen and Buffy Sainte-Marie on "Passing Through" (when she sings a verse in Dylan's voice). She is also part of the "Royal Majesty" singalong. (Tracks from David Hoffman's 1972 documentary, *see below*, are found on compilations.)

There are two albums from the annual Bread & Roses Festival, 1977 and 1979, both on Fantasy Records. The latter includes a duet with Mimi Fariña on "Bread and Roses."

In 1979 Baez joined The Amazing Rhythm Aces for "Homestead in My Heart" on *The Amazing Rhythm Aces* (Columbia).

In 1980, without a record label but with her star still shining brightly in Europe, Baez released four live albums recorded at concerts in France (Colmar), Spain (Barcelona and Alicante), and what was then West Germany (Wurzburg and Loreley): *European Tour, Tournée Européene, Europa Tournée* and *Tour Europa.* Each featured a half-dozen Baez classics plus a new original "Cambodia," inspired by the Boat People campaign. Other songs not available elsewhere – "Jari Yahamouda," "Soyuz Druzyei,"

"Le Deserteur, and "Kinder (Sind So Kleine Hande)" – are distributed across the albums.

In 2001, Baez contributed a track to *Clinch Mountain Sweethearts* (Rebel Records), a celebration of bluegrass by Ralph Stanley and Friends. She sings "Weeping Willow," a song from the 1920s popularized by the Carter Family.

In 2002, Baez toured with folk duo Tracy Grammer and Dave Carter. She described his writing as "a kind of genius" and, following his sudden death, recorded the song Carter had written specially as a duet for Baez and Grammar: "Til We Have Faces," a perfect miniature. It appears on *Remembering Dave Carter*, an unreleased tribute album, along with a second duet "The Mountain."

On *Born to the Breed: A Tribute to Judy Collins* (Wildflower, 2008), Baez offers her own interpretation of "Since You've Asked," Collins' first song (1967). And on *Paradise* (2010), Baez duets with Collins on "Diamonds & Rust," which they had recently performed live at Newport 2009.

Luv is the Foundation (Epiphyte, 2009) finds Baez collaborating (on lead and back-up vocals) with reggae pioneer Rocker-T: "The Way Life Should Be," "Luv is the Foundation" (dance remix), "Dub is the Foundation" (dubstep remix), "Brother and Sisterly Love" (downtempo remix), and "Binghipella."

Baez and Gabriel Harris played a key role in the career of Marianne Aya Omac, a busker they encountered in France, bringing her to the States to record. Both of them feature on "Duele," a rumba-flamenco number on *Solo* (Disques Nuits d'Afrique, 2011).

Having played a three-song set for protesters at Occupy Wall Street, Baez joined forces with Steve Earle and James McMurtry for a version of "We Can't Make It Here" on the fundraising four-CD set *Occupy This Album: 99 Songs for the 99 Percent* (Music for Occupy, 2012).

Baez joined A Fragile Tomorrow to record a version of Richard and Mimi Fariña's song "One Way Ticket" – twins Sean and Dominic Kelly and their brother Brendan, who founded the band, are cousins of Richard. The Indigo Girls also played on the track, which appears on *Make Me Over* (MPress, 2015).

Of all Joan Baez's collaborations, the duets with Bob Dylan naturally exert a particular fascination and Dylan's Bootleg release project means a good deal of material which has long circulated *un*officially is now available officially. The entire New York Philharmonic Halloween concert can be found on *The Bootleg Series, Vol 6: Bob Dylan Live 1964* (Sony, 2004) and it features the duets "Mama, You Been On My Mind," "With God on Our Side" and "It Ain't Me Babe," plus a Baez solo of "Silver Dagger," Dylan adding harmonica. The Rolling Thunder releases do not feature Baez solos but duets and ensembles can be found on *The Bootleg Series, Vol 5: Bob Dylan Live 1975* (Sony, 2002) and *Bob Dylan – The Rolling Thunder Revue: The 1975 Live Recordings* (Sony, 2019).

Finally, for those wishing to explore further the music that was in the air as Joan Baez and her *confrères* were embarking on their careers amid the burgeoning folk revival, the following albums may be of interest:

THE FOLK BOX (Elektra, 2014)
Like Vanguard, Elektra Records played a pivotal role in the 1960s music scene, founder Jac Holzman signing Phil Ochs, Tom Paxton, and Judy Collins, "our Joan Baez," as he put it. This four-LP set was released in 1964 (in cooperation with Folkways) and reissued in 2014, compiled and annotated by Robert Shelton of *The New York Times*. The lavish booklet includes Shelton's contextual essay, plus notes and lyrics to each song, and drawings by Moses Asch.

THE BEST OF BROADSIDE 1962-1988
(Smithsonian Folkways Recordings, 2000)
A lovingly annotated five-CD set of songs featured in *Broadside*, the influential mimeographed magazine founded by Sis Cunningham and Gordon Friesen, who said: "A whole generation of song-writers, some of whom have become household names in the America of the 1960s, made their first appearances in *Broadside*…" They included Janis Ian, Buffy Sainte-Marie, Tom Paxton, Phil Ochs, Richard Fariña and Bob Dylan. The 89 songs collected here are arranged by topic, many of them recorded during the magazine's regular hootenannies, or for occasional *Broadside* albums.

WASHINGTON SQUARE MEMOIRS: THE GREAT URBAN FOLK BOOM 1950-1970 (Rhino, 2001)
A three-CD celebration of "the Mecca of coolness and guitars: Washington Square", as Ted Myers, who compiled and produced this collection, puts it. Washington Square Park is both the geographic and spiritual heart of Greenwich Village, and in those heady days the heart of the New York folk revival. Three essays, lots of photos and 72 tracks make this set a valuable summing-up of the time and the place. Featuring Woody Guthrie and Pete Seeger, without whom, plus Joan Baez, Bob Dylan, Bonnie Dobson, Richie Havens, Dave van Ronk, Odetta and many others.

FILM SOUNDTRACKS

SACCO & VANZETTI (1971)

Docudrama written by Giuliano Montaldo based on real-life events surrounding the 1920 trial and execution of Nicola Sacco and Bartolomeo Vanzetti. The score was written by Ennio Morricone and Baez wrote the lyrics to "The Ballad of Sacco & Vanzetti," which is in three parts. Part 1 incorporates "The New Colussus," the 1883 sonnet by Emma Lazarus which is inscribed on a bronze plaque on the Statue of Liberty. "Here's To You," sung at the end of the movie, became something of an anthem across Europe, Baez's lyrics quoting from Vanzetti's 1927 statement to a journalist who visited him in prison. It has been used in other films, including *Germany in Autumn*, and is familiar to the video game generation from the *Metal Gear Solid* series, and it has been used in other films, and in video games. Baez sings on the film soundtrack, which won the Nastro d'Argento for Best Original Score from the Italian National Syndicate of Film Journalists.

JOE HILL (1971)

A drama based on the life of Joseph Hillstrom who emigrated from Sweden to the US and, as Joe Hill, became a celebrated union organizer and songwriter. Baez sings "The Ballad of Joe Hill" on the film's soundtrack. She did not of course write the song - Alfred Hayes wrote the poem in the 1920s and Earl Robinson set it to music a decade later - but Baez's version has become more widely known even than that by Paul Robeson. It is included here for that reason.

SILENT RUNNING (1972)

Post-apocalyptic science fiction movie set after the end of all botanical life on earth. The score is by Peter Schickele, and Baez sings two songs: "Rejoice in the Sun" and the title. The lyrics are by Diana Lampert.

TO KILL A PRIEST (1988)

A political drama based on the life Father Jerzy Popieluszko, whose outspoken support of Poland's Solidarity movement led to his death. The score is by Georges Delerue. Baez is featured singing "The Crimes of Cain," for which she wrote the lyrics. The song is rich in symbolism: "the solidarity of hearts;" the Black Madonna of Częstochowa, a venerated icon that survived the Soviet occupation; and of course the title itself, an allusion to the Old Testament story of Cain and Abel, one brother killing another.

SELECT FILMOGRAPHY

Since the outset of her career, Joan Baez has featured in countless documentaries – about civil rights, free speech, nonviolence, Vietnam and of course about music. Many of them can now be found on DVD or as downloads, sometimes as old videos.

She has also made innumerable television appearances – standalone interviews, and discussion and news programs, as well as chat shows. There were some unlikely-seeming guest spots for someone apparently so serious – on *The Smothers Brothers Comedy Hour*, a daring satirical show that ran into trouble with NBC executives, for instance, or *Playboy After Dark*, a variety show into which Hugh Hefner smuggled socially conscious content. The aim was always to put her message across and, if possible, evade the censors. Many of these come and go on YouTube, mostly as short fragments, occasionally as complete episodes.

Some notable full-length interviews (often for public television) survive intact, many capturing Baez at crucial moments in the late-twentieth century American psychodrama. By the 1970s, her confidence as a speaker, and her eloquence, are rather remarkable. Discussing Vietnam, human rights, and nonviolence, she gives the combative arch-conservative William F Buckley a run for his money on *Firing Line* (1979). With Roger Ailes (1994), a fan of her voice but not her politics, she has a wide-ranging and sparky dialogue. Other in-depth interviews to be found online include *Day at Night* (1974) with James Day, and *Face to Face* (1998) with Jeremy Isaacs. Shorter but no less worthwhile interviews with Bob Costas (1993), Christiane Amanpour (2018), Jeffrey Brown (2019) and Dan Rather (2019) are easy to find.

There are similar interviews on international television, mostly voiced or subtitled, but Baez is occasionally to be found speaking in French or Spanish.

Many Joan Baez performances have been captured for TV, specials from around the world, from the mid-1960s through to 2019, as well as live concert footage: the BBC TV concerts from 1965, Christmas Eve on the steps of Notre-Dame Cathedral, Bratislava just a few months before the Velvet Revolution, and a novel performance aboard the MS *Nieuw Amsterdam* for the annual *Nation* cruise in 2012 – there is an accompanying interview, her interlocutor ill-prepared.

The following list, arranged chronologically by release date, is by no means exhaustive. It features three key documentaries about Joan Baez herself: *Carry It On, There But For Fortune: Joan Baez in Latin America,* and, most notably, *How Sweet the Sound*. Others explore the lives and work of fellow musicians whose paths she crossed, and their shared milieu, helping to give context to Baez's life and work. There is also some remarkable and stylistically wide-ranging concert footage.

Almost all exist as DVDs and downloads, though some can be hard to find.

THE BIG TNT SHOW (Larry Peerce, 1966)
Recorded before a live audience at the Moulin Rouge in Los Angeles, performers including Donovan, The Byrds, The Ronettes and Ray Charles. Baez looks uncomfortable and sings "500 Miles," "There But For Fortune" and, with Phil Spector at the piano, "You've Lost That Loving Feeling."

DON'T LOOK BACK (D A Pennebaker, 1967)
Painful but crucial: Bob Dylan's 1965 British tour, from touchdown to the "farewell kiss." Reissued with bonus material.

FESTIVAL (Murray Lerner, 1967)
Thrilling documentary chronicling the Newport Folk Festivals 1963-66. Interviews, conversation and evocative performances by Baez, Dylan, the Fariñas and many more.

WOODY GUTHRIE ALL-STAR TRIBUTE (Jim Brown, 1970)
Footage from the Hollywood Bowl, Baez featured prominently throughout, with Pete Seeger, Odetta, Arlo Guthrie and others.

WOODSTOCK (Michael Wadleigh, 1970)
An audio version of Baez's pre-dawn set can now be downloaded in full (*see above*). In the original documentary release she was represented by "Joe Hill" and "Swing Low, Sweet Chariot." The 2009 cut added "One Day At a Time," another, in 2014, "Oh, Happy Day" and "I Shall Be Released."

CARRY IT ON (James Coyne, 1970)
A remarkable film featuring Joan Baez and David Harris as they toured American campuses following their wedding – a honeymoon like no other. The film includes concert footage, speeches, and a behind-the-scenes glimpse of the couple's life on the Los Altos commune as Harris awaited arrest for draft resistance. All the songs featured on the soundtrack album, including those from Woodstock, can be found elsewhere.

CELEBRATION AT BIG SUR
(Baird Bryant and Johanna Demetrakas, 1971)
Big Sur was for many years an annual festival, held in the grounds of the Esalen Institute on the spectacular Big Sur coast. Baez was the lynchpin of the event and features prominently throughout.

**EARL SCRUGGS: THE BLUEGRASS LEGEND –
FAMILY AND FRIENDS** (David Hoffman, 1972)
Documentary about the banjo player featuring a down-home session filmed
at Baez's Los Altos home, baby on her knee and dog at her feet. With Scruggs
and his son Randy and others, she performs "My Home's Across the Blue
Ridge Mountains," "Love is Just a Four-Letter Word," "It Ain't Me, Babe,"
"I Dreamed I Saw St Augustine" and "If I Were a Carpenter."

SING THANKSGIVING (David Hoffman, Harry Wiland, T C Garcia, 1974)
Joan Baez, Mimi Fariña, B B King and The Voices of East Harlem, recorded
live at Sing Sing Prison on Thanksgiving 1972. The documentary includes a
Baez original, sung over the credits, and a duet with Fariña on "Mi Corazon."

BANJOMAN: A TRIBUTE TO AMERICAN MUSIC
(Richard G Abramson and Michael C Varhol, 1975)
Baez contributes three songs to this concert movie with the Earl Scruggs
Revue. All appear on a soundtrack album.

HARD RAIN (1976)
Filmed in the rain at Fort Collins, Colorado, the penultimate show of the
second Rolling Thunder tour. A turbaned Baez boogies around, singing
backing vocals and duetting with Dylan on "Blowin' in the Wind,"
"Railroad Boy," "Deportee," and "I Pity the Poor Immigrant." The duets
are not on the album.

RENALDO AND CLARA (Bob Dylan, 1978)
There are some spine-tingling moments in this sprawling four-hour home
movie – and not just the music, Baez, and Dylan head-to-head in near-
identical clothing, singing together for the first time in a decade. Off-stage,
the scenes between them in Mama's Dream Away Lodge have acquired
mythic status. David Blue, from his place at the pinball machine, offers
fascinating insights into the 1960s Greenwich Village folk scene.

**THERE BUT FOR FORTUNE: JOAN BAEZ IN LATIN
AMERICA** (Julio Molina and John Chapman,1981)
A chronicle of Baez's 1981 tour, concerts providing the cover for a first-hand
investigation of the continent's human rights abuses during its darkest hours.
"Something is amiss," she concludes, with characteristic understatement, as
she herself faced threats.

MERTON (Paul Wilkes, 1984)
Film biography of Thomas Merton, the Trappist monk Baez and Ira Sandperl
visited at Gethsemani, Kentucky, about which she wrote a song. Baez is
interviewed and "Blessed Are . . ." features on the soundtrack.

LIVE AID (Vincent Scarza and Kenneth Shapiro,1985)
Baez was allowed only the opening slot in Philadelphia. Introduced by Jack Nicholson, she sings "Amazing Grace" and a snatch of "We Are the World," though she hadn't been invited to sing on the record.

THREE WORLDS, THREE VOICES, ONE VISION
(Doris Rischmüller, 1988)
Joan Baez, Mercedes Sosa, and Konstantin Wecker in concert in the Roman amphitheater in Xanten, Germany.

JOAN BAEZ IN CONCERT (Jim Yukich, 1990)
Filmed at the Ventura Theatre, Ventura, California, in December 1989. Jackson Browne joins Baez for "El Salvador" and "Before the Deluge."

MESSAGE TO LOVE: THE ISLE OF WIGHT FESTIVAL
(Murray Lerner, 1997)
Mired in legal problems, this film of the 1970 festival was released long after the event. Baez is featured singing "Let It Be."

NO DIRECTION HOME: BOB DYLAN (Martin Scorsese, 2005)
Mesmerizing documentary of Dylan's Greenwich Village years, 1961-65. Baez talks and sings from her California kitchen.

THE OTHER SIDE OF THE MIRROR: BOB DYLAN LIVE AT THE NEWPORT FOLK FESTIVAL 1963-65 (Murray Lerner, 2007)
Essentially a chronicle of Dylan's going electric, but it of course includes the celebrated Baez-Dylan duets, and the Newport '63 finale.

SLACKER UPRISING (Michael Moore, 2007)
Documentary of the 2004 US presidential election. Joan Baez is interviewed briefly and sings "Finlandia"

PETE SEEGER: THE POWER OF SONG (Jim Brown, 2007)
Award-winning documentary of Seeger, one of the architects of the folk revival, and the musician and activist whose life and music inspired the teenage Baez.

92Y: JOAN BAEZ IN CONVERSATION WITH ANTHONY DECURTIS (92Y, 2008)
In-depth interview with music, Baez back at the scene of her first New York City concert in 1960.

HOW SWEET THE SOUND (Mary Wharton, 2009)
A two-hour American Masters documentary featuring many with whom
Baez has worked over the course of her long career, including Bob Dylan.
Due attention is paid to her social activism. The backbone of the film is
the interview with Baez, who reflects on her life with the aid of family
photos and home movie footage, which includes a remarkable 1958
performance of "Barbara Allen" from Club 47. The DVD is packaged with
an accompanying CD featuring 14 songs.

**THE CLEARWATER CONCERT: PETE SEEGER'S
90TH BIRTHDAY CELEBRATION FROM MADISON
SQUARE GARDEN** (David Horn, 2009)
Joan Baez, along with Bruce Springsteen, Emmylou Harris, Steve Earle,
and many others in a beautifully staged birthday celebration. Baez solos on
"Where Have All the Flowers Gone?," leads on "Jacob's Ladder," and joins
in several ensembles.

**IN PERFORMANCE AT THE WHITE HOUSE:
A CELEBRATION OF MUSIC FROM THE CIVIL
RIGHTS MOVEMENT** (PBS)
The Obamas' at-home, with The Freedom Singers, John Mellencamp and
Bob Dylan among those appearing with Baez, "a New York-born daughter
of immigrants," as the President introduces her. She sings "We Shall
Overcome" and talks briefly about MLK's anxiety over Vietnam.

PHIL OCHS: THERE BUT FOR FORTUNE (Kenneth Bowser, 2010)
A biography of Phil Ochs, a tragic figure who provided Baez with one of
her most enduring songs. A fascinating look at the topical song and anti-war
movements. Baez is interviewed and shown playing with Ochs at his War is
Over concert.

HARRY BELAFONTE: SING YOUR SONG (Susanne Rostock, 2011)
Belafonte is known by everyone as a singer. Less well known is the
extent of his involvement with the civil rights movement – his New York
apartment was King's home-from-home when he was in the city.

**FOR THE LOVE OF THE MUSIC: THE CLUB 47
FOLK REVIVAL** (Todd Kwait and Rob Stegman, 2012)
The history of the legendary Club 47, where Joan Baez and many others
began their careers. Specially commissioned interviews and archive footage
shine a light on the folk revival generally and the importance of the
Boston/Cambridge scene.

ANOTHER DAY ANOTHER TIME: CELEBRATING THE MUSIC OF LLEWYN DAVIS (Christopher Wilcha, 2013)
Inspired by the Coen Brothers' movie set in Greenwich Village in 1961, a concert filmed at New York's Town Hall featuring Joan Baez, Rhiannon Giddens, The Milk Carton Kids, Marcus Mumford, Patti Smith, The Punch Brothers, Gillian Welch, and Jack White, as well as Oscar Isaac, the film's star. Superb musicianship – the double-CD soundtrack is well annotated and atmospheric. Baez sings a solo version of "House of the Rising Sun" and contributes to ensemble numbers with Elvis Costello, Colin Meloy, Mumford, Welch and others.

JOAN BAEZ: REBEL ICON
(Nusrat Durrani, Eric Mahoney and Ben Herson, 2015)
Short but informative feature in which Baez discusses the central tenets of nonviolent resistance which have shaped her life.

ROLLING THUNDER REVUE: A BOB DYLAN STORY
(Martin Scorsese, 2019)
Restored and previously unseen footage from the 1975 Rolling Thunder tour. Baez, "The Balladeer", is not accorded a solo spot, but the duets with Dylan are magical and the backstage scenes, not least where they discuss love and marriage, offer yet another look at their endlessly complicated relationship.

★ ★ ★

Joan Baez is part of the warp and the weft of American social history, from the 1960s on. While her music can stand alone and be appreciated like any other musical corpus, it is nevertheless an intrinsic part of the weave of late twentieth and early twenty-first century society and culture, and her life needs to be understood in that context. The following documentaries provide the reader curious to know more with a broader context.
A documentary, *The Boys Who Said NO! Draft Resistance and the Vietnam War*, directed by Judith Ehrlich, is poised for release.

KING: A FILMED RECORD... MONTGOMERY TO MEMPHIS
(Sidney Lumet, 1970)
Preserved in the National Film Registry at the Library of Congress, a biography of Martin Luther King and his creation and leadership of the nonviolent campaign for civil rights and social and economic justice.

THE MEMORY OF JUSTICE (Marcel Ophüls, 1976)
Inspired by Telford Taylor's book *Nuremberg and Vietnam: An American Tragedy*, an exploration of wartime atrocities and judgment. Baez is among the interviewees.

BERKELEY IN THE SIXTIES (Mark Kitchell, 1990)
An award-winning documentary about the roots of the Free Speech
movement and the development of the counterculture. Archival footage
and interviews.

TREE SIT: THE ART OF RESISTANCE
(James Ficklin and Penelope Andrews, 2001)
Focusing on the destruction of ancient forest ecosystems and Julia Butterfly
Hill's protest, which was joined by Baez and Bonnie Raitt.

FIERCE LIGHT: WHEN SPIRIT MEETS ACTION
(Velcrow Ripper, 2008)
Much-praised Canadian documentary exploring spiritual activism fueled
by the belief that another world is possible. Participants include Baez, Thich
Nhat Hanh, Desmond Tutu, and John Lewis.

WILLIAM KUNSTLER: DISTURBING THE UNIVERSE (Emily
Kunstler and Sarah Kunstler, 2009)
Kunstler, who famously refused to sign Baez's Open Letter, was a firebrand
leftist lawyer who spoke on behalf of King and Malcolm X, negotiated for
inmates at Attica State Prison, and defended the Chicago Eight. A valuable
1960s primer.

FREEDOM RIDERS (Stanley Nelson, 2010)
Watch and weep – at the bravery and selflessness of those who participated
in the interstate protests to desegregate buses, trains, and terminals. Based on
Freedom Riders: 1961 and the Struggle for Racial Justice by Raymond Arsenault.

THE MARCH (John Akomfrah, 2013)
Powerful, in-depth documentary of the August 1963 March on Washington,
with several contributions from Baez alongside archive footage. (In Britain it
was titled *Martin Luther King and the March on Washington*.)

KING IN THE WILDERNESS (Peter Kunhardt, 2018)
Award-winning documentary about Martin Luther King's last years, as the
rise of Black Power threatened his core beliefs and Vietnam forced him to
make tough choices. The full interview with Baez is easily available online
(Kunhardt Film Foundation).

SELECT BIBLIOGRAPHY

BY AND ABOUT JOAN BAEZ

Baez, Joan, *Daybreak,* New York, Dial Press, 1968

Baez, Joan, *Playboy Interview,* Playboy Press, Chicago, 1971

Baez, Joan, *And a Voice to Sing With: A Memoir,* New York, Summit Books, 1987

Baez, Joan, And a Voice to Sing With: A Memoir, with a new introduction by Anthony DeCurtis, New York, Simon & Schuster, 2009

Baez Sr., Joan, *Inside Santa Rita: Prison Memoir of a War Protester,* Santa Barbara, John Daniel & Company, 1994,

Baez, Joan Bridge, *One Bowl of Porridge: Memoirs of Somalia,* Palo Alto, The Wordshop, 1985

Baez, Albert V and Baez Sr., Joan, *A Year in Baghdad,* Santa Barbara, John Daniel & Company, 1988

Fuss, Charles J, *Joan Baez: A Bio Bibliography,* Westport, Greenwood Press, 1996,

Garza, Hedda, *Joan Baez,* in Hispanics of Achievement, Philadelphia, Chelsea House, 1991

Hajdu, David, *Positively 4th Street: The Lives and Times of Joan Baez, Bob Dylan, Mimi Baez Fariña and Richard Fariña,* New York, Farrar, Straus & Giroux, 2001

Harris, David, *Goliath,* with an introduction by Joan Baez Harris, New York, Avon, 1970

Harris, David, & Harris, Joan Baez, *Coming Out,* New York, Pocket Books, 1971

Heller, Jeffrey, *Joan Baez: Singer With a Cause,* Chicago, Children's Press, 1991

Jäger, Marcus, *Joan Baez and the Issue of Vietnam: Art and Activism versus Conventionality,* Stuttgart, Ibidem, 2003

Jäger, Marcus, *Popular is Not Enough: The Political Voice of Joan Baez – A Case Study in the Biographical Method,* Stuttgart, Ibidem, 2010

Ligney, Nicole, & Grundmann, Pierre, *Joan Baez,* Paris, Bréa Editions, 1981

Romero, Maritza, *Joan Baez: Folksinger for Peace,* in Great Hispanics of Our Time, New York, Rosen Publishing Group, 1997

Swanekamp, Joan, *Diamonds & Rust: A Bibliography and Discography on Joan Baez,* Pierian Press, 1980

MUSIC - BIOGRAPHIES AND BACKGROUND READING

Belafonte, Harry, with Shnayerson, Michael, *My Song: A Memoir,* New York, Knopf, 2011

Cantwell, Robert, *When We Were Good: The Folk Revival,* Cambridge, Harvard University Press, 1996

Collins, Judy, *Sweet Judy Blue Eyes: My Life in Music,* New York, Crown, 2011

Cohen, Ronald D, *Rainbow Quest: The Folk Music Revival & American Society, 1940-1970,* Amherst and Boston, University of Massachusetts Press, 2002

Denisoff, R Serge, *Great Day Coming: Folk Music and the American Left,* Chicago, University of Illinois Press, 1971

Denselow, Robin, *When the Music's Over: The Story of Political Pop,* London, Faber, 1989

DeTurk David A & Poulin Jr, A, *The American Folk Scene: Dimensions of the Folksong Revival,* New York, Dell, 1964

Dunaway, David King, *How Can I Keep from Singing: Pete Seeger*, London, Harrap, 1985

Dunaway, David King, & Beer, Molly, *Singing Out: An Oral History of America's Folk Music Revivals*, New York, Oxford University Press, 2010

Dylan, Bob, *Chronicles Volume One*, New York, Simon & Schuster, 2004

Eliot, Marc, *Phil Ochs: Death of a Rebel*, London, Omnibus Press,1990

Eisen, Jonathan (editor), *The Age of Rock*, New York, Vintage, 1969

Fong-Torres, Ben (editor), *The Rolling Stone Rock 'n' Roll Reader*, New York, Bantam, 1974

Fong-Torres, Ben (editor), *What's That Sound?* New York, Anchor, 1976

Fornatale, Pete, *Back to the Garden: The Story of Woodstock and How It Changed a Generation*, New York, Touchstone, 2009

Gibson, Bob, & Bender, Carole, *Bob Gibson: I Come For to Sing*, Naperville, Kingston Korner, 1999

Ian, Janis, *Society's Child*, New York, Tarcher, 2008

Lankford Jr., Ronald D, *Folk Music USA: The Changing Voice of Protest*, New York, Schirmer, 2005

Lynskey, Dorian, *33 Revolutions Per Minute: A History of Protest Songs*, London, Faber, 2010

McNally, Dennis, *On Highway 61: Music, Race and the Evolution of Cultural Freedom*, Berkeley, Counterpoint, 2014

Marqusee, Mike, *Chimes of Freedom: The Politics of Bob Dylan's Art,* New York, New Press, 2003

Massimo, Rick, *I Got a Song: A History of the Newport Folk Festival*, Middletown, Wesleyan University Press, 2017

Maymudes, Victor, with Maymudes, Jacob, *Another Side of Bob Dylan*, New York, St Martin's Press, 2014

Petrus, Stephen, & Cohen, Ronald D, *Folk City: New York and the American Folk Music Revival*, New York, Oxford University Press, 2015

Ritchie, Fiona, & Orr, Doug, *Wayfaring Strangers: The Musical Voyage from Scotland and Ulster to Appalachia*, Chapel Hill, University of North Carolina Press, 2014

Rodnitzky, Jerome L, *Minstrels of the Dawn: The Folk Protest Singer as a Cultural Hero*, Chicago, Nelson-Hall, 1976

Ryback, Timothy W, *Rock Around the Block: A History of Rock Music in Eastern Europe and the Soviet Union,* New York, Oxford University Press, 1990

Schumacher, Michael, *There But for Fortune: The Life of Phil Ochs*, New York, Hyperion, 1996

Schnabel, Tom, *Stolen Moments: Conversations with Contemporary Musicians*, Los Angeles, Acrobat, 1988

Shelton, Robert, *No Direction Home: The Life and Music of Bob Dylan*, Milwaukee, Backbeat, 2011

Simmonds, Sylvie, *I'm Your Man: The Life of Leonard Cohen*, London, Cape, 2012

Sloman, Larry, *On the Road with Bob Dylan*, New York, Bantam, 1978

Unterberger, Richie, *Turn! Turn! Turn! The Sixties Folk-Rock Revolution*, Milwaukee, Backbeat, 2002

Van Ronk, Dave, with Wald, Elijah, *The Mayor of MacDougal Street: A Memoir*, New York, Da Capo, 2005

Vulliamy, Ed, *When Words Fail: A Life With Music, War and Peace,* London, Granta, 2018

Wald, Elijah, *Dylan Goes Electric!*, New York, HarperCollins, 2015

Wein, George, with Chinen, Nate, *Myself Among Others: A Life in Music*, New York, Da Capo, 2003

Weissman, Dick, *Which Side Are You On? An Inside History of the Folk Music Revival in America*, New York, Continuum, 2006

Weissman, Dick, *Talkin' Bout a Revolution: Music and Social Change in America*, Milwaukee, Backbeat, 2010

Wilentz, Sean, *Bob Dylan in America*, London, Bodley Head, 2010

Yaffe, David, *Reckless Daughter: A Portrait of Joni Mitchell*, New York, Sarah Crichton Books/Farrar, Straus & Giroux, 2017

Zack, Ian, *Odetta: A Life in Music and Protest*, Boston, Beacon Press, 2020

GENERAL BACKGROUND

Anderson, Terry H, *The Movement and the Sixties: Protest in America from Greenboro to Wounded Knee*, New York, Oxford University Press, 1995

Anderson, Walt (editor), *The Age of Protest*, Pacific Palisades, Goodyear, 1969

Berrigan, Daniel, *The Dark Night of Resistance*, New York, Doubleday, 1971

Berrigan, Daniel, *To Dwell in Peace: An Autobiography*, San Francisco, Harper& Row, 1987

Berrigan, Daniel, Secrets: *A Memoir of Vietnam and the Pentagon Papers*, New York, Viking Press, 2002

Branch, Taylor, *Parting the Waters: America in the King Years 1954-63*, New York, Simon & Schuster, 1988

Branch, Taylor, *Pillar of Fire: America in the King Years 1963-65,* New York, Simon & Schuster, 1998

Branch, Taylor, *At Canaan's Edge: America in the King Years, 1965-1968*, New York, Simon & Schuster, 2006

Brick, Howard, *Age of Contradiction: American Thought & Culture in the 1960s,* Ithaca, Cornell University Press, 1998

DeGroot, Gerard, *60s Unplugged: A Kaleidoscopic History of a Disorderly Decade*, London, Macmillan, 2008

Dickstein, Morris, *Gates of Eden: American Culture in the 1960s*, New York, Basic Books, 1977

Didion, Joan, *Slouching Towards Bethlehem*, Harmondsworth, Penguin, 1974

Doyle, Michael, *Radical Chapters: Pacifist Bookseller Roy Kepler and the Paperback Revolution*, Syracuse, Syracuse University Press, 2012

Ferber, Michael K, with Lynd, Staughton, *The Resistance*, Boston, Beacon, 1971

Finder, Henry (editor), *The New Yorker Book of The 60s: Story of a Decade*, London, Heinemann, 2016

Finn, James, *Protest: Pacifism and Politics*, New York, Vintage, 1968

Gaillard, Frye, *A Hard Rain: America in the 1960s – Our Decade of Hope, Possibility and Innocence Lost*, Montgomery, New South Books, 2018

Gandhi, Mohandas, & Duncan, Alastair (ed), *Selected Writings*, New York, Dover, 2005

Gandhi, Mohandas K, *Autobiography: The Story of My Experiments with Truth*, New York, Dover, 1983

Gitlin, Todd, *The Sixties: Years of Hope, Days of Rage*, New York, Bantam, 1987

Goldberg, Danny, *In Search of the Lost Chord: 1967 and the Hippie Idea*, New York, Akashic, 2017

Grant, Bruce, *The Boat People*, Harmondsworth, Penguin, 1979

Hall, Simon, *Peace and Freedom: The Civil Rights and Antiwar Movements in the 1960s*, Philadelphia, University of Pennsylvania Press, 2005

Harris, David, *I Shoulda Been Home Yesterday*, New York, Delacorte, 1976

Harris, David, *Dreams Die Hard: Three Men's Journey Through the Sixties,* New York, St Martin's Press, 1982

Harris, David, *Our War: What We Did in Vietnam and What It Did To Us*, New York, Random House, 1996

Hudson, Robert, *The Monk's Record Player: Thomas Merton, Bob Dylan, and the Perilous Summer of 1966,* Grand Rapids, Erdmans, 2018

James, David E, *Power Misses: Essays Across (Un)Popular Culture*, London, Verso, 1996

Jones, William P, *The March on Washington: Jobs, Freedom, and the Forgotten History of Civil Rights*, New York, Norton, 2013

Kennan Warnecke, Grace, *Daughter of the Cold War*, Pittsburgh, University of Pittsburgh Press, 2018

Long, Michael G, *We the Resistance: Documenting a History of Nonviolent Protest in the United States*, San Francisco, City Lights, 2019

Loughery, John, & Randolph, Blythe, *Dorothy Day: Dissenting Voice of the American Century*, New York, Simon & Schuster, 2020

Marwick, Arthur, *The Sixties*, Oxford, Oxford University Press, 1998

Mehnert, Klaus, *Twilight of the Young: The Radical Movements of the 1960s and Their Legacy*, New York, Holt, Rinehart & Winston, 1976

Merton, Thomas, *Dancing in the Water of Life: Seeking Peace in the Hermitage*, New York, HarperOne, 1997

Merton, Thomas, *Turning Toward the World: The Pivotal Years*, New York, HarperOne, 1997

Merton, Thomas, *The Other Side of the Mountain: The End of the Journey*, New York, HarperOne, 1999

Merton, Thomas, *The Seven Story Mountain*, London, SPCK, 1990

Sheehan, Neil, et al, *The Pentagon Papers: The Secret History of the Vietnam War*, New York, Racehorse Publishing, 2017

Weiner, Rex, & Stillman, Deanne, *Woodstock Census: The Nationwide Survey of the Sixties Generation*, New York, Viking, 1979

Younge, Gary, *The Speech: The Story Behind Martin Luther King's Dream*, London, Guardian Books, 2013

SONGBOOKS

The Joan Baez Songbook, New York, Ryerson Music Publishers, 1964

Noel: The Joan Baez Christmas Songbook, New York, Ryerson Music Publishers, 1967

Joan Baez: Diamonds & Rust, Hollywood, Almo Publications, 1975

Joan Baez: From Every Stage, Hollywood, Almo Publications, 1976

Joan Baez: Gulf Winds, Hollywood, Almo Publications, 1977

Joan Baez: Blowin' Away, Hollywood, Almo Publications, 1977

Joan Baez: And Then I Wrote... New York, The Big 3 Music Corporation, 1979

INDEX

ACKNOWLEDGMENTS

Across a half-century, many people have—wittingly and unwittingly—contributed to this book, not least my parents, generally indulgent of my interest in Joan Baez and her musical and socio-political milieu that deepened into an obsession. At times they heard too much of her—but when I left home they continued to play a Baez compilation as if to conjure up my presence. Oddly, my sister has no recollection of buying the record that so caught my eleven-year-old ears. Along with countless friends, my family would all experience Baez concerts, and Maureen's presence at her final concert, in Madrid, represented the completion of a circle.

Robert Shelton, *The New York Times* critic whom I met in Britain in 1979 and who had reported on the American folk revival and knew many of the musicians, brought to life a time and a place which then existed only in my imagination. He always felt that some day I would write about Baez. His published writings, and his papers, were a great resource when the time came.

Thanks also to: producer Alan Abrahams, for his recollections of working with Baez on her late 1980s albums; to Ros Asher, consummate musician and inspiring teacher and friend, for thoughts on vocal technique and the passing years; to Marc Aubort, recording engineer, for recollections of the early Vanguard years; Regalada Costello, for memories of "Father B" and "Mother B", as Baez's grandparents were known; the late Robert Cox and Aaron Rubinstein at UMass Amherst Libraries for uncommon help with photo research; Mitch Greenhill, son of Baez's first manager, for photographs and for sharing his own manuscript; Hilary Hale, for helping me trace the Baez and Bridge family ancestry; Janis Ian, who provided Baez with some singular songs and who contributed to the Bottom Line sessions I was privileged to attend—for thoughtful responses to my questions; Arthur Levy, music historian, for advice, friendship and memorabilia; Judy Longman, whose keen editor's eye got me through a last-minute impasse; singer-songwriters David Massengill and Josh Ritter, for recollections and reflections of working with Baez, and assessments of her legacy; Martina Müller for the photograph of Baez's final concert in Madrid; Donna Seager Liberatore and the Seager Gray Gallery, for use of Baez's self-portrait; and Betsy Siggins, for her friendship and hospitality, and for photographs and memories of her friend that stretch back over sixty years.

That I came to know Greenwich Village so well is thanks to the Paul family, who bought "that crummy hotel over Washington Square" in 1973 and, as Baez remarked to me, "dolled it up", turning it into my wonderful New York home-from-home, the Washington Square Hotel. It led to my creating a festival, The Village Trip, through which I have made many enriching friendships all of which, in their way, contributed to this book. And to the fabulous team behind Boston's Folk Americana Roots Hall of Fame who welcomed me behind the scenes of their important new endeavour.

Lastly, thanks to David Inglesfield, an eagle-eyed editor, and designer Becky Clarke; Jo Rippon, Rob Nichols and Team Palazzo; and to my agent, Ros Edwards.

And of course to Joan Baez, for a lifetime of inspirational music and social activism who I have been privileged to interview across forty years. The offer of a self-portrait, "Black is the Color", featured on the back jacket, was an unexpected gift.

PICTURE CREDITS

Back cover image: "Black is the Color" by Joan Baez.
Painting courtesy of Joan Baez and Seager Gray Gallery, inspired by a photograph from © Jim Marshall Photography

"Black is the Color" is from Mischief Makers 2, the second exhibition of art by Joan Baez.
Joan Baez is represented by the Seager/Gray Gallery
Contemporary Fine Art, 108 Throckmorton Avenue,
Mill Valley, CA 94941
www.seagergray.com

Charles Frizzell/UMass Amherst Libraries 2, i top; Elizabeth Thomson 16, 26, 38, 44, 54, 61, 65, v bottom, viii top left & right; Earl Crabb and Rick Shubb 32; David Gahr/Getty Images i bottom; Chicago History Museum ii top; Rowland Scherman/UMass Amherst Libraries ii bottom, iii top; AP/Shutterstock iv top; Mitch Greenhill 58, iv bottom left; Stanford Libraries iii bottom, iv bottom right; Icon and Image/Getty Images v top; Esaias Baitel/AFP via Getty Images vi top; Michael Stravato/AP/ Shutterstock vi middle; Sean Gallup/Getty Images vi bottom; Eric Baradat/ AFP via Getty Images vii top; Ron Pownall/Getty Images vii bottom; Martina Müller viii bottom

Harvey Goldsmith presents
JOAN BAEZ in Concert plus support
Funds from this concert will be donated to
OPERATION NAMIBIA and CAAT

EVENING 8-0 p.m.
Monday, Dec. 19th, 197

STALLS £3·75

BLOCK
25   SEAT
            H

NO TICKET EXCHANGED
NO RE-ADMISSION

...RATION this concert plus support
...ERATION NAMIBIA and CAAT
EVENING 8-0 p.m.
Wednesday, Dec. 21st, 1977
CIRCLE
£3·25
BLOCK
3   SEAT
           S54
NO TICKET EXCHANGED NOR MONEY REFUNDED
NO RE-ADMISSION

STALLS   ROW   O   SEAT
STALLS
ASGARD PROMOTIONS PRESENT
JOAN BAEZ
PLUS SPECIAL GUESTS
CARLING APOLLO HAMMERS
QUEEN CAROLINE STRE
SUN 01-FEB-04 19:3
£ 27.50
SC 3.25
30.75   15220

Mark Howes
present
An Evening With Joan Baez
No support

Sun, 4 Mar 2007
Flat Floor
D 17
Account :10130043

BARBICAN HALL
Mark Howes by Arrangement With Asgard Presents
An Evening With JOAN BAEZ
No Support

Wednesday 08 Mar 2006
£30.00 STA
Level −1 DOOR 2   STALLS D32
booking ref: 4635852

CMP & Mark Howes present
JOAN BAEZ
plus support
Day After Tomorrow
Thu, 02 October 2008
At 7:30 PM

Account No 21742178

Doors open at 6:45 PM

Door
Arena
Row
Seat

RO
ALB
HA

Standard
£37.50
4838616 we 2 08CMJB01

Marshall Arts
ARTISTES
BAEZ
GUEST
DATE   NAME/SIGNATURE
20/6   HAMM

Mark Ti...
Joan Baez
Fare Thee Well Tour
No Support & No Interval
Mon, 28 May 2018
At 7:30 PM
Doors open at 6:45 PM

Royal Albert Hall
Door 9
      0

TEATRO REAL
200 AÑOS

JOAN BAEZ

Precio: 117,00 eur.
Gastos de servicio: 3,00 eur.
Total: 120,00 eur.

DNI/NIE: 529029897
elizabethmthomson@googlemail.com
LIZ THOMSON

Universal Music Festival 2019 Prohibido filmar y fotos
Primeras filas adicionales de Patio - reservas invitados

Fecha: 28/07/2019   Hora: 21:30

Acceso:
Entrada Plaza Oriente
Zona:
Butaca de Platea
Planta: Fila: Butaca:
0   1   16

TR 9999999 18ZZJ0 AC1 001 016

EVENING
Wednesday
CIRCLE
£3·25
BLOCK
SEAT

SHEPHERDS BUSH
EMPIRE
ASGARD Presents
JOAN BAEZ
IN CONCERT
PLUS SUPPORT
Wednesday 25th October 1995
Showtime 7:30pm
Tickets £16.50 in advance - Doors 7:00pm
ROW : H SEAT : 16
DOWNSTAIRS
RESERVED SEATING
NO SMOKING
00181

ODEON   HAMMERSMITH Tel. 01-748-4081
        Manager: Philip Leivers
ADVANCE BOOKING TICKET
CONCERT As advised at the time
DATE } of purchase. (See re-
TIME } verse). Please see full
PRICE   seating plan on display
STALLS
BLOCK
24 | K22
NO TICKET EXCHANGED NOR MONEY REFUNDED
This portion to be retained   No re-admission

ON HAMMERSMITH Tel. 01-748-40
        Manager: Phillip Leivers
Goldsmith presents
EZ in Concert plus support
...m this concert will be donated to the
...ON NAMIBIA and CAAT
...ING 8-0 p.m.
...day, Dec. 19th, 1977
...ALLS
5
BLOCK   SEAT
25   H 5
...NOR MONEY RE